Affirmative Dynamic Psychotherapy with Gay Men

Affirmative Dynamic Psychotherapy with Gay Men

Edited by
Carlton Cornett, LCSW

JASON ARONSON INC.
Northvale, New Jersey
London

Permission of the following authors and publishers to reprint the papers listed below is gratefully acknowledged.

Richard Isay: "On the Analytic Therapy of Homosexual Men," in *Psychoanalytic Study of the Child*, vol. 40, pp. 235–254. Copyright © 1985 by Yale University Press, and "The Homosexual Analyst: Clinical Considerations," in *Psychoanalytic Study of the Child*, vol. 46, pp. 199–216. Copyright © 1991 by Yale University Press.

William Herron, Thomas Kinter, Irwin Sollinger, and Julius Trubowitz: "Psychoanalytic Psychotherapy for Homosexual Clients: New Concepts," in *Journal of Homosexuality*, vol. 7, pp. 177–192. Copyright © 1982 by Haworth Press.

Alan Malyon: "Psychotherapeutic Implications of Internalized Homophobia in Gay Men," in *Journal of Homosexuality*, vol. 7, pp. 59–69. Copyright © 1982 by Haworth Press. Grateful acknowledgment is also made to Mr. Allen Chivens, executor of Dr. Malyon's estate, for permission to include Dr. Malyon's paper.

Charles Silverstein, "The Borderline Personality and Gay People," in *Journal of Homosexuality*, vol. 15, pp. 185–212. Copyright © 1988 by Haworth Press.

This book was set in 11 point Goudy by Lind Graphics of Upper Saddle River, New Jersey, and printed and bound by Haddon Craftsmen of Scranton, Pennsylvania.

Library of Congress Cataloging-in-Publication Data

Affirmative dynamic psychotherapy with gay men / edited by Carlton
   Cornett.
      p. cm.
   Includes bibliographical references and index.
   ISBN 1-56821-001-9 (hard cover)
   1. Gay men—Mental health. 2. Psychodynamic psychotherapy.
   3. Psychotherapist and patient. I. Cornett, Carlton.
   [DNLM: 1. Homosexuality—psychology. 2. Psychoanalytic therapy—
   methods. 3. Men—psychology. WM 460.6 A256 1993]
   RC451.4.G39A34 1993
   616.85'834'0081—dc20
   DNLM/DLC
   for Library of Congress   93-12886

Manufactured in the United States of America. Jason Aronson Inc. offers books and cassettes. For information and catalog write to Jason Aronson Inc., 230 Livingston Street, Northvale, New Jersey 07647.

For DeWayne:

With love and appreciation for the constant,
quiet, and loving sanity he imparts to those
of us around him.

Contents

Preface

My interest in a book on affirmative dynamic psychotherapy with gay men began when I was in graduate school ten years ago with the recognition that there was no such work available. The roots of this interest, however, stretch back to my adolescence. Like most of my friends in that developmental period, I had a profound interest in sex, but very little knowledge about what it was that was so captivating. I also knew something else, though; I knew I was somehow different from my male friends. I knew that my interest was not really in girls, but beyond that there was only a vague haze. I had heard words like *homo*, *fairy*, and *faggot*, and even had them applied to me, but I had no real understanding of homosexuality apart from it being something that was shameful.

Then my friends and I discovered Reuben's (1971) *Everything You Always Wanted to Know About Sex, But Were Afraid to Ask*. We sought answers to the mysteries that prevented our minds from keeping pace with our hormonally driven bodies. On reading the pages that described homosexuality, I made an important and painful discovery. He was describing me. His pejorative descriptions of homosexuals and the "sex" acts in which they engaged, totally devoid of any description of affection or love (indeed, in most cases reading like a moral commentary on sadism), I unfortunately accepted at face value. My shame intensified.

I ran from that shame, attempting to escape it by denying my sexuality throughout my adolescence. Finally, though, it was impossible to escape who I was, and I began to try to understand what it meant (and still means) to be gay. This was also the period, during undergraduate and graduate school, in which I discovered Freud.

The elegance and explanatory power of Freud's theories were captivating. His ideas, revolutionary in their day, were still of immense help in understanding the motivations underlying the external appearances of the world. Psychoanalytic theory became one of my passions.

I soon came to realize, however, that much of the disparagement that found its way to gay men, whether political, social, or even religious, began with psychoanalytic theory. I also learned through my own therapy and the therapies and analyses of colleagues that psychoanalytic practitioners, ostensibly aiming for neutrality, were anything but neutral toward gay men. Although these practitioners were more refined in their approach, the cumulative effect of working with them was often the same as the experience of reading Reuben's book.

OVERVIEW

The authors in this volume point out in a variety of ways that psychoanalytic theory has not traditionally been affirming of gay men as healthy and functional. Rather, it has tended to view gay men as inherently pathological because of their sexual orientation. For that reason, psychoanalytic technique has most often focused on changing the homosexual to a heterosexual. There is a paucity of literature examining the applications of psychoanalytic theory to the affirmative dynamic psychotherapy of gay men. Over the past ten years, there have been a number of fine attempts to integrate an affirmative view of homosexuality with psychoanalytic theory (Leavy 1986, Lewes 1989). However, these integrative works have not produced a large number of corresponding works concerning the application of theory to psychotherapeutic technique. That is the focus of this volume.

The contributing authors of this volume offer discussions of the technique of affirmative dynamic psychotherapy with gay men. The emphasis throughout is on the processes, skills, and perspectives involved in doing affirmative psychotherapy with gay men. Although each author approaches this task from a different vantage point, all begin with the basic premise that homosexuality is itself a healthy sexual variation equivalent in functionality to heterosexuality.

The authors of these chapters represent all of the mental health professions—social work, psychiatry, psychology, and psychoanalysis. The traditions of each of these professions offer slightly different perspectives on the authors' task. Those differences in perspective are well represented in these chapters; however, all of the authors also share a commitment to the idea that psychodynamic psychotherapy represents the best that we can offer to our patients.

Noteworthy, too, is the fact that all the authors in this volume address the role society plays in the genesis and maintenance of the psychosocial difficulties that bring gay men to psychotherapy. Psychodynamic psychotherapy has often been criticized as a system that emphasizes the importance of fantasy at the expense of history (Miller 1981). In the chapters that follow there is a consistent emphasis placed on the roles that homophobia and intolerance (including manifestations of these in the psychotherapist's office) play in creating and continually renewing shame, guilt, and other distressing symptomatology in the gay man.

Unfortunately, psychoanalysis has been a primary player in this societal drama. In Chapter 1, William Herron, Thomas Kinter, Irwin Sollinger, and Julius Trubowitz review the traditional psychoanalytic position that homosexuality is an inherently pathological sexual orientation. They propose this to be a countertransferentially based perspective that interferes in the therapist's ability to understand the gay patient. They note that all forms of sexual behavior may express a myriad of developmental deficits and conflicts and view homosexuality as no different from heterosexuality in this regard. They take a fairly traditional view of dynamic psychotherapy in their belief that it serves primarily as a means of discovering and resolving intrapsychic conflicts. Through clinical vignettes they demonstrate that dynamic psychotherapy can be affirming of homosexuality. However, to do so it must be returned to its roots as an endeavor to understand the whole person as a complex product of development, whatever his sexual orientation.

Chapter 2, by Richard Isay, follows this theme by elaborating the consequences for homosexual patients who are involved in a psychotherapy not characterized by neutrality (i.e., which Isay defines as a positive regard for the patient and a sense of curiosity about his story). He reviews the development of the philosophy that homosexuals should be changed to heterosexuals. He argues that the primary technique involved in attempts to change sexual orientation is manipulation of the transference through the analyst/therapist's discouragement of homosexual behavior and encouragement of heterosexual behavior. This approach to the patient, however, is also confirmation of the societal antihomosexual bias that homosexual patients have internalized. The transference manipulation of orientation-changing psychotherapy, which Isay agrees is motivated by countertransference, becomes complementary to the patient's transference. Through case examples, Isay describes the rage, depression, anxiety, and confusion that accompany second analytic treatments when sexual orientation change was the goal of the first. Like the authors of Chapter 1, Isay proposes that psychoanalytic treatment can be of benefit to gay men if analysts and psychotherapists are willing to give up their reductionistic views of "good" and "bad," "healthy" and "sick," and return to a stance of positive regard for their patients, which would mandate a truly open and exploratory perspective.

Chapter 3, which focuses on the applications of self psychology to the understanding of gay men, expands Isay's idea of positive regard. Like the authors of the first two chapters, I believe that a key dynamic that brings a gay man to a psychotherapist's office is the internalization of the rejection and devaluation he has experienced in the heterosexual culture. This internalization, which results in shame, can find expression in a number of symptoms, but is most often seen in overt self-contempt and self-loathing. Rather than focusing on psychotherapy as a neutral or interpretive enterprise, I propose that the most important element of psychotherapy lies in its capacity to affirm the patient. This approach is illustrated through the psychotherapy of a young gay man.

Chapter 4, by the late Alan Malyon, describes a phasic model of dynamic psychotherapy directed toward the resolution of internalized homophobia. Although Malyon's model argues against a reductionistic view of the difficulties that bring gay men to psychotherapy, it sees the effects of socialized antihomosexual bias as pervasive and at the root of many symptomatic difficulties. Most importantly, this internalized bias prevents successful adolescent development in the gay man who often experiences delayed resolution of the developmental tasks of adolescence. There are similarities and differences between Malyon's model and that presented in Chapter 3. The most notable of the differences lies in the differing values that are afforded the role of interpretation of unconscious conflicts and defenses. Malyon's is a four-phase model that utilizes concepts from cognitive and social learning theories, as well as from Erikson's psychosocial model. Like mine in Chapter 3 and Silverstein's in Chapter 6, Malyon's model includes an existential component. This existential emphasis is valuable, although often neglected, in psychotherapy with gay men.

There is an important dynamic that can interfere in any attempt at resolution of shame or internalized homophobia. Chapter 5 looks at a form of resistance that often appears in clinical work with gay men. As it has traditionally been viewed, resistance concerns a subtly adversarial relationship between a patient who is afraid of personal change and a therapist attempting to facilitate such change. Self psychology has argued that resistance is a means by which the patient protects himself from injuries to his self-esteem and/or self-cohesion. The view offered in this chapter is that resistance appearing with gay men concerns both of these elements and is organized around a fear of hope. This fear of hope is a further expression of the rejection and devaluation that gay men have internalized. They are frightened of allowing themselves to hope that they may be due more in life than denigration, because hope offers both the potential for change (and identity disjunction) and the potential for further disappointment and injury. This resistance may be addressed both interpretively and through the stance the therapist assumes vis-à-vis the patient. A case study is offered in which this form of resistance plays a major role.

In Chapter 6, Charles Silverstein, through a discussion of the Borderline Personality Disorder (BPD) and its relevance for gay people, offers an alternative to the view that guilt and shame are the most important dynamics in the symptomatology that brings gay men to psychotherapy. He argues that object relations theory, with its emphasis on family interactions, explains some aspects of this complex phenomenon. Silverstein, however, also sees cultural changes occurring over the last thirty years as a compelling explanation for BPD. He notes that the liberalization of American culture has forced more choices upon the individual with less guidance and structure from the larger society. Groups, like gay men, that are removed from the standards and models of the heterosexual culture are particularly prone to overwhelming confusion. For Silverstein, confusion and associated depression are more prominent for gay men than are shame and guilt. For those gay men whose families did not prepare them to deal with conflict and ambiguity there is an increased likelihood that their adaptation will take the form of BPD. Silverstein presents a detailed case study of a gay male patient to illustrate his conceptualization.

Chapter 7, by Ross Hudson and myself, describes the process of dynamic psychotherapy with gay men infected with the human immunodeficiency virus (HIV). This view of the process is compatible with, and perhaps a variation on, Malyon's earlier model and is predicated on a perspective that affords equal weight to both the internal and external as determinants in the patient's adaptation to HIV. The therapist's initial response to the patient's revelation of his diagnosis sets the tone for the remainder of the therapy. If the therapist responds empathically, the patient moves into a phase that involves the resolution of guilt about his having contracted HIV and often about his homosexuality. Mourning is an important part of adapting to HIV infection, and guilt must be resolved before effective mourning can occur. With the resolution of his mourning, the patient can develop aspects of his identity, including his identity as a spiritual being, that were blocked by guilt and grief. The therapist must approach psychotherapy with HIV-infected gay men with a good deal of flexibility because the often austere frame of traditional dynamic psychotherapy is not fully applicable to them. In addition, there are a number of countertransference dangers inherent in psychotherapy with this population. All of these areas are illustrated through clinical vignettes and a case study of the course of one man's thirteen-month psychotherapy.

Richard Isay describes issues related to being an openly gay analyst and psychotherapist in Chapter 8. He maintains, as do previous authors, that disclosure of the therapist's homosexuality may be beneficial to the progress of a gay patient's treatment. He notes that gay patients often assume that their therapists or analysts are heterosexual because of their internalization of society's bias that homosexuals are "sick." The therapist's revelation of his homosexuality confronts this shame and can also confront a patient's denial of his own homoerotic longings. The failure of the therapist to acknowledge his homosexuality, especially when asked directly by a gay patient, may communicate his own shame and reinforce shame in the patient. Although not using the language of self psychology, Isay describes the twinship functions that such therapist disclosures may serve. Isay also looks at the issue of transference development following such disclosures and proposes, as does Nash in Chapter 9, that the patient will develop a transference relationship with the therapist that expresses his developmental yearnings and conflicts, despite knowledge of the therapist's sexual orientation. Finally, he discusses countertransference concerns for gay therapists working with gay patients. These include using gay patients to compensate for professional isolation and responding destructively to homophobic transferences. He also describes the countertransference difficulties that can arise for gay psychotherapists treating gay men living with HIV, adding to the discussion offered in Chapter 7.

In the final chapter, James Nash reminds us that heterosexual analysts and psychotherapists can also be affirming of homosexuality. He describes the development of two men, one homosexual, the other heterosexual. Both men developed in environments that were intolerant of difference. Both men learned to fear and hate homosexuals, among other groups. However, the social upheaval of the 1960s and 1970s forced the heterosexual man to question a number of his fears and hatreds. Ultimately, this man became a psychoanalyst. By the time he met the homosexual man, as a patient, he had discarded the loathing that our culture holds for homosexuality, including that embedded in his beloved psychoanalysis. Nash then describes a psychoanalysis that focused on helping the homosexual patient discard his self-loathing. Through the presentation of this analysis, Nash offers thoughts about why some gay men choose a gay therapist while others choose a heterosexual therapist. He sees some determinants of this choice as involving the patient's status in the coming out process, and, for those still entrenched in their own homophobia, the transferential hope of finding the perfect heterosexual therapist to emulate. Finally, he describes dynamics that are common themes in the process of a heterosexual analyst treating a gay patient, including sexualization and secrecy.

A FINAL NOTE

A note of explanation is in order about terms. Gay and homosexual are used interchangeably throughout the text, as are patient and client, and are a reflection of the particular author's preference. The word gay has political and social connotations that go beyond the scope of psychotherapy and this book. However, I often use gay to refer to the awareness and acceptance by one of his homosexual orientation. In this context it is meant to reflect the manner in which patients often identify themselves (i.e., as "gay" rather than "homosexual"). This book also presupposes that there are fundamentally similar processes in dynamically oriented psychotherapy and psychoanalysis that have mutual applicability in understanding gay men. For that reason, there is no clear distinction made in the order of the chapters, or in the intent of the presentation, to differentiate the effectiveness of the two clinical endeavors.

Discussions of affirmative dynamic technique in the treatment of gay men are rare. Perhaps the chapters in this volume will encourage further sharing of thoughts about this topic and will expand the horizons of our creativity in serving gay men. The ultimate beneficiaries of that sharing will be our patients, the men who trust us with the most precious and intimate in their lives. Valuing that trust, however, we too will benefit as we refine our skills to offer the best of our craft.

Carlton Cornett, LCSW
Nashville, Tennessee

REFERENCES

Leavy, S. (1986). Male homosexuality reconsidered. *International Journal of Psychoanalytic Psychotherapy* 11:155–174.

Lewes, K. (1988). *The Psychoanalytic Theory of Male Homosexuality.* New York: Simon and Schuster.

Miller, A. (1981). *The Drama of the Gifted Child.* New York: Basic Books.

Reuben, D. (1971). *Everything You Always Wanted to Know about Sex, But Were Afraid to Ask, Explained by David R. Reuben.* New York: Bantam.

Acknowledgments

Editing this volume has been an enriching experience. All of the contributors to this work have lifted their voices, sometimes at great personal and professional cost, to challenge psychodynamic thinking to expand. They have done this out of a fundamental respect for the spirit of liberation that formed the nucleus of Freud's fledging psychoanalysis. For those who granted permission to reprint their previously published papers and for those who took time from their busy schedules to write original chapters, I am appreciative of the interest in making this book successful.

A special note of thanks is due to Richard Isay, who has been a leader in challenging the core heterosexual assumptions of American psychoanalysis. His interest in this volume has made the task of pulling it together all the more rewarding.

I did not get an opportunity to talk with the late Alan Malyon; however, in coordinating the inclusion of his chapter I talked with a number of people who were close to him. Without fail they spoke of him and his work with respect and affection. It is an honor to have a part of his legacy in this book.

Jason Aronson and the staff of Jason Aronson Inc. have been patient and helpful. It is to the credit of Dr. Aronson that he is willing to publish works that keep debate alive on controversial topics in psychotherapy.

My thanks to Ross Hudson, who has been my friend, co-therapist, colleague, and companion in many personal and professional struggles over the past ten years.

Thanks also to Volney Gay, Ph.D., who taught me much about self psychology and who also encouraged me to grow in directions that were not necessarily his. There have been a number of other colleagues over the years who have also contributed to my work. These include Sandra Willman, Ed.D.; Lewis Lipsius, M.D.; Allison Grant, M.D.; Richard Davy, Ph.D.; Jeffrey Binder, Ph.D.; and William P. Henry, Ph.D. My heartfelt thanks to all.

There is one man without whom this project would not have come to pass. My lover, DeWayne Fulton, has been an incredibly loving, supportive, and patient man throughout this endeavor. He not only helped with technical aspects of this project (compensating for my computer illiteracy) but buoyed me when my spirits flagged. He enriched this project as he enriches all other aspects of my life.

Appreciation is due also to my friend Dan Wood, who assisted with preparation of the manuscript, and to Howard Roback, Ph.D., who read and offered suggestions on portions of the manuscript. Appreciation is also due to the staff of the Vanderbilt Independence Development Center for their support, patience, and the professional affirmation that working with them brings.

Finally, my thanks to my patients for trusting me to undertake the complex and wondrous journey of psychotherapy with them. I often find myself wishing for a way to express my appreciation for a professional life that is simultaneously rewarding, humbling, and sublime. It is a great joy to tangibly do so.

Contributors

Carlton Cornett, LCSW
Director, Independence Development Center
Vanderbilt University Medical Center
Private Practice
Nashville, Tennessee

William G. Herron, Ph.D.
Professor of Psychology
St. John's University
Jamaica, New York

Ross Hudson, LCSW
Senior Clinician, Independence Development Center
Vanderbilt University Medical Center
Private Practice
Nashville, Tennessee
(In the early stages of this volume, Mr. Hudson was
Director of Client Services at Nashville CARES)

Richard A. Isay, M.D.
Clinical Professor of Psychiatry
Cornell Medical College
Faculty, Columbia Center for Psychoanalytic Training
   and Research
New York, New York

Thomas Kinter, Ph.D.
Private Practice
Poughkeepsie, New York

Alan K. Malyon, Ph.D.
Until his death in 1988, Dr. Malyon was in
Private Practice in Los Angeles, California

James L. Nash, M.D.
Associate Professor of Psychiatry and
Director, Division of Psychodynamic Psychiatry
Vanderbilt University
Member, American Psychoanalytic Association
Nashville, Tennessee

Charles Silverstein, Ph.D.
Private Practice
Supervisor, The Institute for Human Identity
New York, New York

Irwin Sollinger, Ph.D.
Private Practice
Westport, Connecticut

Julius Trubowitz, Ed.D.
Assistant Professor of Educational Psychology
Queens College, City University of New York
New York, New York

1

Psychoanalytic Psychotherapy for Homosexual Clients: New Concepts

WILLIAM G. HERRON, PH.D.
THOMAS KINTER, PH.D.
IRWIN SOLLINGER, PH.D.
JULIUS TRUBOWITZ, ED.D.

In the past, psychoanalysis has had a reputation for "helping" homosexual men and women by attempting to change their sexual orientation to heterosexuality. Such attempts were based on a theoretical conception of homosexuality as inevitably pathological and therefore in need of change. Many recent developments in psychoanalytic theory and practice, however, cast doubt on the assumption of pathology and question the accompanying goal of sexual reorientation.

The authors view psychoanalysis as a treatment method capable of alleviating numerous problems in living and, in particular, improving a person's sexual functioning. This, of course, can include homosexuality. It is our purpose to show that psychoanalysis is indeed useful to homosexual clients.

First we will consider psychoanalytic theory in terms of what it means to us and what it has generally meant in regard to the treatment of homosexual patients. Next we will evaluate the evidence for the pathology of homosexuality per se. Then we will describe our own conceptual framework for treatment and conclude with illustrations from clinical cases in which psychoanalytic psychotherapy appeared to help the clients understand and express their sexual preferences, which were predominantly homosexual.

THEORETICAL ORIENTATION

Although all schools or systems of psychotherapy cannot be defined precisely, they do have approximate meanings that are generally understood in the psychotherapeutic field. Within this framework, our orientation is psychoanalytic. This raises a number of issues for us when we are working with someone who presents herself or himself as "homosexual."

The first task is to ascertain what homosexuality means to the patient. Does the patient want to change his or her sexual orientation, or does the patient consider it incidental to other problems, such as anxiety and depression? The patient's professed goal may be to become heterosexual, or to feel less guilty about homosexuality, or to leave the sexual orientation as is and focus on other issues experienced as disturbing.

After having found an answer, as far as is possible at this point in the therapeutic process, we then tell patients that our role is to help them explore their lives: past, present, and future. In so doing they will have the potential for developing new understanding of their behavior. We explain that much of their behavior is and has been uncon-

sciously determined, and that through a combination of constitutional predispositions and learning, the development of their
personalities over time has produced their current life-styles. Patients
must be willing to explore their total life development. In the process,
they may realize that their goals for therapy are not the same as when
they began, or that they cannot fully achieve their original goal. Our
basic message is that through the psychoanalytic process patients can
discover unconscious material available for insight and behavioral
change.

The analytic process can be used to work toward a number of
possible changes. One possibility is the change in sexual orientation to
heterosexuality, but the evidence indicates that this is very unlikely to
occur. Although a few psychoanalysts report success in this regard
(Bieber et al. 1962, Socarides 1978), their work gives no proof of
absolute or eternal absence of all homosexual interests, desires, and
thoughts in their "changed" patients. Gonsiorek (1977), who has
reviewed most of the psychoanalytic contributions to the treatment of
homosexuality, points out the limited data base used in generalizations about the power of psychoanalysis to cure homosexuality.
Nevertheless, Socarides (1979) asserts that a cure is indeed possible in
some instances. Freund (1974) postulates a universal potential for
sexual orientation with either sex, though one sex is usually preferred.
Changing a person's sexual behavior from homosexual to heterosexual might be accomplished by working with a potential already
present, but this would not really change the person's preference.
Although it may appear that psychoanalysis can change a person's
sexual orientation, in truth this is a limited accomplishment that
happens only occasionally and even then is of questionable duration.

Nonetheless, there continues to be a strong trend among psychoanalysts to attempt to "cure" homosexual men and women of their
homosexuality. Socarides (1974) exemplifies this position, for although he recognizes the variability in homosexuality, he also views
all homosexualities as pathological per se. His belief has considerable
historical precedent: religion has often denounced homosexuality as
sinful, the law has proscribed it as criminal, and the mental health

establishment has insisted it is a mental illness. Freud (1905) regarded homosexuality as a form of arrested development, and much of psychoanalytic thought has continued in that vein, construing homosexuality as a perversion, a form of ego-syntonic pathology definitely requiring treatment.

We agree that homosexuality, like many other forms of sexual expression, can serve as part of a pattern of disturbance in the patient's personality structure. We disagree with the idea that the homosexual orientation is automatically equivalent to psychopathology. In fact, the more usual treatment goal for our homosexual patients is the integration of their sexual orientation into a viable life-style. We use the analytic process to facilitate self-understanding free of value judgments on a particular sexual orientation. This view is in accord with the positive side of our culture's ambivalence toward homosexuality. Society is beginning to give credence to the possibility that exclusive homosexuality is one of a number of potentially effective sexual life-styles, others being asexuality, bisexuality, and exclusive heterosexuality. None of these is seen as being necessarily pathological. This view was reinforced in 1974 by the exclusion of homosexuality from the list of psychiatric disorders in the *Diagnostic and Statistical Manual* of the American Psychiatric Association (APA).

The position of the majority of psychoanalysts, however, remains at variance with the APA decision. Kwawer (1980), having traced the evolution of psychoanalytic thinking regarding homosexuality from Freud to the present, concludes that there has been a shift from a focus on a disturbance in the oedipal period, with guilt and castration anxiety as key factors, to a concern with preoedipal factors, such as difficulties in separation-individuation and wishes to merge with a maternal object. Despite this change, the reigning psychoanalytic attitude continues to be that homosexuality is a developmental disturbance to be resolved by conversion to heterosexuality. Hopefully, the increased knowledge of human development will provide greater understanding of the emergence of sexual identities and serve to rebut the notion that homosexuality is pathological.

Until recently, the possibility of offering useful psychotherapeutic services to people who may wish to recognize, explore, and accept a homosexual orientation came mainly from a model other than psychoanalysis (Coleman 1978). (There were some exceptions, of course. Thompson [1947] mentioned the possibility of homosexuality as an adaptive solution to certain interpersonal problems. Ovesey, Gaylin, and Hendin [1963] suggested additional motivations for homosexuality, such as power and dependency. Mitchell [1978] recommended exploring the psychodynamics of homosexuality but did not necessarily link them to a belief that homosexuality is an illness.) Lately, however, the prospect of psychoanalysis being used to acquire a successful homosexual identity has been suggested by Hencken and O'Dowd (1977). The potential includes the expansion of psychoanalytic developmental theory to accommodate recent social and biological findings; the use of psychoanalytic interpretations to understand meaning-systems; and the employment of psychoanalytic concepts to investigate the interrelationships among gender, sex roles, sexual orientation, personal identity, and sexuality. We have described in detail one example of using a psychoanalytic approach to facilitate sexual- and self-expression in a homosexual client (Herron et al. 1980). Lachman (1975) had already moved a bit in the direction of our thinking. In questioning the concept of genital primacy, and noticing how limited for some homosexual persons is the relationship between their sexuality and other aspects of living, he appeared not to ascribe standard psychoanalytic notions to homosexuality.

We view psychoanalysis as a developmental psychology with therapeutic applications that enable the patient to learn to make life choices based upon self-understanding. We believe sexual orientation to be a learned decision, one based on constitutional and experiential occurrences. It is often formed with a limited awareness on the part of the individual as to the manner and cause. The psychoanalytic method can help any person to discover the development, purpose, and consequences of any and all sexual orientations.

The psychoanalytic approach emphasizes the meaning of behavior within the context of the person's life development. The therapist's personal value judgments about the pathology or nonpathology of sexual orientations are not inherent to the psychoanalytic method and neither are the value judgments of the patient. Indeed, the psychoanalytic focus on unconscious motivations can enable homosexual clients to make more informed, less dutiful choices about therapeutic goals.

SEXUALITY AND PATHOLOGY

A person can manifest nonsexual conflicts through his or her sexual expression. This is the belief, for example, of psychoanalysts who consider homosexuality to be motivated by anxiety and to involve a variety of preoedipal and oedipal disturbances, such as the inability to distinguish adequately between the self and others, confused gender identity, and disturbances of thinking and perception. Such a description suggests that, on criteria of mental health, the average homosexual man or woman ought to "look sicker" than his or her heterosexual counterpart, but the existing research does not support this contention.

The most comprehensive and balanced review of the literature to date is by Gonsiorek (1977), who has shown the complexities involved in research on homosexuality, as well as the conclusions that can be drawn from existing research. Gonsiorek points up the fallacies in the persistent belief that anything but heterosexuality is a sign of psychic disturbance and in the practice of interpreting all individual differences between heterosexual and homosexual persons as indications of pathology. Major studies comparing the two sexual orientations do not support the idea that homosexual men and women are significantly maladjusted (Bell and Weinberg 1978, Saghir and Robbins 1973). The most general finding of differences is in the direction of homosexual individuals showing more intrapsychic stress. This is to be expected, however, considering the negative reaction of society to homosexuality. Although it is possible to discover some differences between heterosexual and homosexual people apart from their sexual orientations, Gonsiorek concludes: "It does not seem that homosexuals differ from heterosexuals in most important and measurable ways" (1977, p. 37).

Socarides (1974) is apparently unimpressed with this conclusion. He admits that some homosexual persons appear to function well, but he maintains that this is superficial, that the sexual deviation (namely, homosexuality) has momentarily neutralized conflicting intrapsychic forces. The sexual behavior allays anxiety and makes the individual look as if he or she were functioning adequately, yet the conflict remains and will continue as long as the individual does not adopt the appropriate human sexual pattern, heterosexuality.

A useful feature of Socarides' work is his concern with patient motivations, a concern shared by behaviorists in their dispute over offering orientation change programs to homosexual patients (Davison 1977). We concur that the motivations of homosexual clients require special scrutiny in order to learn what they really want from the therapy. We believe the psychoanalytic method provides a viable way to identify and attain the therapeutic goal, but the therapist must avoid outguessing the patient. Views such as Socarides' and Davison's show a lack of respect for the client's ability to form a sound judgment. Davison is the more ambivalent of the two, yet he states: "Even if we could effect certain changes, there is still the more important question of whether we should. I believe we should not" (1977, p. 203). We disagree, and once we ascertain that the client's sexual orientation has really been established, we do what we can to help the client enjoy his sexual orientation.

In its concern with homosexuality as an emotional illness, psychoanalysis often focuses on the dynamics of the homosexual behavior. (We ourselves take a broader view of personal and social functioning as part of a complete developmental approach.) Exemplifying the narrower, more traditional approach, Socarides (1978) describes five major forms of homosexuality, three of which are supposedly derived directly from unconscious conflicts.

The first, the preoedipal form, is the result of fixation in the developmental phases between birth and 3 years of age. It arises from anxiety, which tends to persist, and involves disturbances of gender identity and sexual identity. The homosexual behavior is obligatory and ego-syntonic. By identifying with a partner of the same sex, a man achieves masculinity and lessens castration fear. A similar reduction of this fear is found in the female who has a resonance identification with a female partner.

The oedipal form also involves castration fears, as well as a failure to resolve the Oedipus complex. The male assumes the role of the female (mother) with other men (the father); the situation is reversed for a female. The homosexuality is ego-syntonic, with guilt arising from conflicts of ego and superego whenever the person engages in homosexual acts, dreams, or fantasies.

The other three forms mentioned by Socarides are schizo-homosexuality, which is the coexistence of schizophrenia and homo-sexuality; situational homosexuality, which results from inaccessi-bility to heterosexuality; and variational homosexuality. Socarides also mentions latent homosexuality, meaning the preoedipal or oe-dipal psychic structure, but without overt sexual activity with a partner of the same sex. Finally, there is sublimated homosexuality, which denotes behaviors designed to avoid homosexual conflict, and what Ovesey (1976) calls pseudohomosexuality, namely, heterosexual persons' anxieties about being homosexual.

These taxa can be useful in describing developmental patterns and discerning key areas of conflict, but we have not found them unique to homosexual clients; nor have we always found the postu-lated correlations between a dynamic, such as castration fear, and homosexuality. Ross (1970) has pointed out that the sexual func-tioning of an individual may or may not reflect the sexual adequacy of other psychological functions. Lachman (1975) described four patients whose personality organization included a homosexual orientation. In each case, different dynamic formulations appeared as to the origin and role of the sexual orientation. This in turn suggested variations in treatment, which included goals such as "adaptive homosexuality" and exclusive heterosexuality. Lachman remarks that to consider homosexuality either as psychopathology or as only a sexual orienta-tion is simplistic. Instead, he suggests viewing homosexuality as a configuration of drives, defenses, and adaptive processes. Although his treatment goals comprehend therapy with patients who choose sexual orientations other than exclusive heterosexuality, in Lachman's article these other orientations appear to be second best, rather than truly equal alternatives. On the other hand, Lachman's emphasis on the personality configuration of the patient and his caution against automatically equating sexual orientation with the levels of interpersonal relations and ego development do represent an important shift from the usual psychoanalytic conceptions of homosexuality. Bell (1974) suggested that in doing therapy with homosexual clients it is more useful not to view them as troubled primarily by sexual concerns, but rather to see them as individuals who have a variety of interpersonal and intrapsychic styles with varying antecedents and consequences. May (1977) affirms this position for anybody, regardless of his or her sexual orientation.

Our aim, then, is to understand the patient by using psychoanalysis as a developmental framework, and, by employing psychoanalytically oriented methods, to increase the patient's insight into her or his own choices in order that she or he may act from greater self-knowledge.

We believe that there are reasons for all behaviors, including sexual behaviors, and we explore these possible reasons with the patient through verbalizing associations, fantasies, and dreams. In a number of instances, an apparently "symptomatic" behavior (e.g., homosexuality) will develop considerable autonomy from its origins. Behavior that started and even persisted for reasons that could be considered pathological, such as homosexuality born of a fear of the opposite sex, may now exist and ultimately continue for reasons that could not be labeled pathological. For example, the fear may disappear but the homosexuality may continue because it is enjoyable in itself.

CONCEPTUAL FRAMEWORK FOR TREATMENT

Psychoanalytic therapy is concerned with the entire life cycle, from birth through all developmental phases: infancy, early childhood, preadolescence, adolescence, early adulthood, middle age, and old age. Depending on the age of the client, some of these phases will be past, some present, and some—such as death—in the future. In accordance with our psychodynamic orientation, we are very concerned with the past, particularly the preoedipal (0–3 years) and the oedipal (4–7 years) periods. These stages appear especially important in forming the adult personality, influencing sexual orientation as well as the images, of the self and of others, that are related to any person's sexual preferences and sexual behavior.

For the therapy to be of value, the patient must participate fully in the analytic process and tolerate the anxiety engendered in the procedures of self-disclosure and self-discovery. The emphasis of therapy will be on phases most related to the issues of major concern to the patient, but the entire life cycle is appropriate material for exploration. Although we believe that humans are inherently sexual beings, we do not believe that sexual orientation is an automatic indicator of a person's ability to function successfully in life. In particular, it is erroneous to assume that the presence of heterosexuality establishes the presence of good interpersonal relationships, or the absence of symptoms. Conversely, the absence of symptoms and the ability to relate to others do not indicate the presence of heterosexuality.

Our conceptual schema within the psychoanalytic tradition is a mixture of ego psychology (Blanck and Blanck 1974, 1979) and object relations theory (Horner 1979). We start with the idea that the individual has undergone a continuity of development that includes a pattern of progressions and regressions, the major thrust being progressive. The infant begins as a psychophysiological organism and proceeds through the various developmental phases. These involve processes designed to build upon and complement each other and to eventuate in a mature, capable person.

The first of these phases, often called narcissistic or autistic, has an amorphous quality of total, but simplistic, responsivity. At about 6 months of age, this gives way to some patterned organization of responding, seen particularly in an attachment to a mother-person.

This period, frequently named symbiosis, probably involves fusion of mental images of the mother and child. Symbiosis serves as a bridge to the development of various aspects of a sense of independence and self-identity.

Symbiosis is followed by the separation-individuation stage, with its four substages. In the first of these, hatching or differentiation, the child sees itself as separate from the mother, who at the same time operates as a frame of reference for the child. The second stage is practicing, when, through locomotion, perception, and learning, the child experiences separateness, particularly from its mother. This is followed by rapprochement, when the child in its continuing striving for autonomy moves from a certain independence to the security of dependence and support. Finally there is the development of a relatively constant view of others, a beginning sense of identity, and a generally positive perception of significant others in the environment. This tends to be accomplished by the third year of life and results in an autonomous identity complete with sexual feelings and preferences.

At ages 5 and 6 there develop more intense sexual feelings toward the parent figures. Identification with parents and the taking on of various parental characteristics continue through other stages, such as adolescence-stages of greater autonomy and major social and sexual identifications of the self and others—stages that lead more directly to the individual's adult identity.

Sexual orientation evolves from the discovery of sexual sensations and pleasures and from the growth of autonomy, which includes a sense of the self as a sexual being and the desire to put one's sexual interest into action. The etiology of the homosexual orientation is a constitutional predisposition to an erotic preference for a body shape, female or male, activated by environmental factors. Although this does not eliminate the potential for other-sex interactions, a single sexual orientation is reinforced and becomes dominant.

In doing therapy with an individual who considers his or her sexual orientation to be homosexual, we are interested in the various components of his or her sexual identity. These include biological sex, gender identity, social sex-role, and sexual orientation (Shively and

De Cecco 1977). The biological sex, usually assigned at birth and confirmable by such criteria as genitalia and hormonal secretions, is something about which most patients are quite certain. Gender identity, or the conviction that one is female or male, should correspond to biological identification, but that is not always the case. Gender identity is formed in the course of the preoedipal stage and is usually established by 3 years of age. The relation of confused gender identity to homosexuality needs to be explored further. Our homosexual clients have spoken of transient confusion; constant gender identity confusion, on the other hand, appears to be infrequent. In general, homosexual males have a basic sense of maleness, homosexual females a basic identity of femaleness.

Social sex-role confusion is more common among homosexual clients, who feel conflicted over conforming to the culturally approved, rather stereotyped behaviors marking a person as feminine or masculine in this society. Social sex-roles appear in the oedipal period (ages 4 to 7) and are heavily influenced by adult models, particularly parents. These roles—often categorized in terms of physical attributes, mannerisms, speech, interests, and personality traits (Shively and De Cecco 1977)—are not inherent to biological sex or to gender identity. Nevertheless, most people do conform to the role expected for members of their sex. To openly disregard the social sex-roles is to risk being labeled as deviant and can bring the person into conflict with society.

The final component of sexual identity is sexual orientation. Considering that American society actively promotes heterosexuality, it is intriguing to ask how and why anyone would choose homosexuality. In attempting to answer the question, one recognizes that homosexuality is not a homogeneous categorization. Nor is there a single reason to explain the orientation of all homosexual men and women. Cass (1979) presents a theory of homosexual identity formation over six stages: identity confusion, identity comparison, identity tolerance, identity acceptance, identity pride, and identity synthesis. Hencken and O'Dowd's (1977) developmental approach to homosexual identity formation includes awareness, behavioral acceptance, and public identification. In both cases the authors concentrate on the experience and its meanings but suggest no probable genesis of the homosexual identity. Psychoanalysis is rather specific about why people become heterosexual, but it too offers little to explain the homosexual identity other than theories of "developmental disturbance," an inaccurate simplification. Cooper (1974) reviews genetic theories, hormonal theories, social explanations, and psychological theories for the development of homosexuality. He considers none completely acceptable and instead offers "a holistic psychoanalytic approach . . . . that homosexuality is acquired by various learning processes in individuals probably sensitized by hormonal and early life experiences" (1974, p. 1).

Our own view is that the sexual orientation of an individual is determined by many agencies, though primarily by psychological factors occurring relatively early in life. If the biological aspects of sexual desire are normal, the key factors will be the person's self-images and self-representations, and the interactions of these with images and representations of other people, especially parents. In the course of physical and psychic development, sexual orientation becomes endowed with a personalized meaning. An imagined model of sexual satisfaction is formed out of fantasized identifications, and at some point this is pursued into action. Later behavior refines and reinforces the sexual orientation deemed most pleasurable.

CLINICAL MATERIAL

The cases of a number of patients whom we have seen in psychoanalytic therapy during the last ten years serve to illustrate various derivations and uses of homosexuality. All of these people were experiencing problems they regarded as connected to their homosexuality, although not all saw their sexual orientation as the major source of concern. None would be considered in the category "Close-Coupled" as described by Bell and Weinberg (1978). Four of the people were married.

The first of the married patients, a man, traced the origins of his homosexuality to early childhood indoctrination by his older brother. Certain of the patient's characteristics, such as speech and mannerisms, were noticeably feminine and caused many people to assume that the patient was homosexual. He protested about this, yet tended to flaunt these characteristics whenever possible. His wife apparently knew nothing about his homosexuality, which must have required massive denial on her part. Their sexual relations were infrequent, and the patient considered them unsatisfactory. He viewed heterosexuality as a service to his partner and fretted about his adequacy to perform this duty. In homosexual relations, he played a "passive" role and consequently felt served, considering it the most pleasurable kind of sexual experience. The patient felt very guilty about his homosexuality, however, and was constantly vowing to give it up. He identified most strongly with his mother and appeared to feel he was restoring symbiosis through homosexual acts, since then he was being served as was his mother. Both his father and his older brother (whom his father favored) derided the patient and impugned his masculinity. He felt he was searching for the "ultimate cock," which would prove better than, or at least equivalent to, the penises of his father and brother. He liked to talk about his homosexual thoughts, feelings, and activity. He stressed the superiority of the gay world yet kept announcing his desire and intention to forswear it. He had focused on his homosexuality with two previous therapists. One, a woman, had worked on getting him to stop it, while the other, a man, had stressed acceptance. He left both therapists after two years, which may symbolize his peak of person-relatedness, namely, prior to object-constancy. Thus, he may have been unable to relate consistently because of increasing anxiety as to possible loss of personal identity.

Subsequently, when in therapy with one of us, he appeared to be heavily invested in the symbiotic period, his professed ambivalence about sexuality being primarily a defense against dealing with still more basic issues. He was extremely anxious, intermittently depressed with suicidal ideation, and filled with rage toward the world. He lacked basic trust or a sense of personal identity, and ranged in self-esteem from abasement to grandiosity. The therapist indicated to him that, in his opinion, the patient's concern about homosexuality was the least of his problems. The therapist helped him through a severe depressive episode. There were also a few sessions with the wife, who seemed to be immature, demanding, and so narcissistic as to be oblivious to the true nature of their sexual relationship. The only things she found disturbing were some of his symptoms, particularly flashes of anger directed at her. It was possible for the patient to establish some equilibrium of job and family functioning, which led to greater self-esteem and independence. Unfortunately repeating his flight from relationships, after approximately two years the patient again stopped treatment, although the therapy was incomplete from the therapist's point of view. The patient considered himself primarily homosexual at that time, but the therapist described his sexual orientation as "confused." It is probable that if he returns to therapy more could be done for him, but he needs to stay with a therapist and permit a therapeutic alliance to form that would allow a complete investigation of his life.

Another married patient, also male, approached the issue of his homosexuality differently. He told his wife about his homosexual desires, but for years he did not act upon them. He too had an older brother. A younger brother also had homosexual feelings but never acted on them. When the patient was a child, the home atmosphere was always one of conflict; the parents divorced when he was in high school. Both parents were demanding and critical. His mother showed some warmth, however, favoring the patient over both his brothers. The patient's homosexuality appeared to derive from longing to be with and to create a happy family: with his wife as a devoted mother caring for him, and with the patient himself as the strong, protective father. He saw a homosexual partner as the reincarnation of the deprived child he had been but who now would both fulfill and be fulfilled. Once he actually had a male lover, the patient experienced more turmoil with his wife than as a result of self-guilt. His wife also entered therapy. Gradually it became apparent that the patient had strongly bisexual interests. This alleviated his wife's fear that he was "really homosexual" and might want to leave her. Both of his sexual relationships, with his wife and with his lover, now appear to be quite permanent, but neither partner likes the concept of being part of a fantasy family for the patient. His rather narcissistic orientation interferes with his comprehension of how his wife and lover feel about him and how they feel about his behavior toward them. This narcissism, rather than the homosexuality, has become the focal problem of his therapy.

Another man unearthed his homosexual interests during the course of therapy but is primarily interested in autoerotic sex. He rarely has intercourse with his wife and as an adult has had no sexual experience with anyone else. The idea of a homosexual experience appeals to him, however. He had a domineering mother and sister, with a passive, ineffectual father. The patient had adolescent homosexual experiences, which he recalls favorably, but he really seems very afraid of any sexual experience, particularly if he might have to initiate it. The immaturity of his sexuality in general is an issue that combines with his general passivity and fear of people. His interest in homosexuality seems to be a wistful solution to the more basic fear of people, as well as repressed anger over an emotionally deprived childhood. In homosexuality he would unite with the desired parent.

Another patient was a woman who had been married but separated from her husband after about five years. She lived with a number of women after the separation. She describes this as a "safer" solution for herself than trying to live with a man. She had suffered considerable rejection by her father and became very angry and assertive, but quite successful in many aspects of her life. Indeed, she became a psychotherapist. She has a deep, ambivalent attachment to her mother, who was very domineering. The patient repeats this pattern with her female lovers, whom she dominates. She has occasional satisfactory sexual experiences with men. She lives with a woman but says the sex is not as good as with a man. She does not appear to experience guilt about the homosexuality and never presented it as a major issue in therapy. What concerned her more was her anger, depression, lack of impulse control, and occasional hallucinatory and delusional experiences. As the issues of the relationships with her parents and with several siblings were worked through in therapy, the depression lifted, her mood was optimistic, and therapy was concluded. Her sexual orientation is primarily homosexual and appears to be working well as a life-style.

Among the homosexual people we have seen who have never been married, there is a woman who entered therapy with the belief that her problem was her lesbianism. She had suffered a series of losses, including her mother's death during her adolescence; emotional distance from her father, who had been passively seductive at one time; and, at the time of starting therapy, rejection by a woman to whom she had admitted being sexually attracted. The patient viewed lesbianism as a disturbed life-style yet feared sexual intercourse with men—although she had experienced it and, at times, had enjoyed it. Her homosexual quest appeared to be directed toward regaining at least the image of her lost mother. She currently lives with a woman and finds this a comfortable situation, though she does not consider it permanent. It is her ideal to have a husband and children. The deprivation in her childhood, particularly the cold, austere home atmosphere and the death of her mother, seems to have prompted a search for another family, specifically for a mother. She has that now; sexual demands from her partner are kept at a minimum. At present much of her therapy is concerned with her distrust of herself and of others, and with the possibility of increasing her sensuality and sexuality. She retains some sexual interest in men but prefers women, although all her sexual activity, including masturbation, is quite limited, inhibited, and guilt-laden.

Two patients are priests, both of whom moved, when in elementary school, into an all-male environment where sexuality was discouraged and the only outlets were with the self or with a person of the same sex. Both of these men have domineering mothers. The elder of the two has an outwardly angry father, while the other's father is more passive and frightened. The elder priest is more committed to homosexuality and has no interest in women. His main problems center around excessive oral gratifications, such as alcohol and drugs, as well as a very poor self-image, which he feels can be enhanced only by a sexual encounter with an attractive man. The younger priest feels excessive guilt about his sexual desires. He contemplates leaving the priesthood as a solution because he equates not being a priest with somehow becoming heterosexual. A major obstacle to this plan, however, is that his only sexual experiences have been homosexual. He is sexually inexperienced with women and, in addition, he is afraid of them. Through therapy he has begun to realize that leaving the priesthood would actually allow him to pursue a homosexual life-style more freely, which is both appealing and frightening. Both men feel a conflict between their role as clergy and their sexuality, since as priests they are supposed to be celibate. Role conflicts have consequently played a large part in their therapies, as has the relationship of their role to their self-image.

CONCLUDING COMMENTS

This chapter contains considerable psychoanalytic terminology, which in itself has a reputation for emphasizing pathology and for being a secret language. Hopefully none of that will prevent readers from understanding that psychoanalytic theory, research, and practice can be very helpful to homosexual men and women.

Homosexuality was present in some form in all the patients we described; some were bisexual, and others were exclusively homosexual. All had concerns related to their homosexuality, such as guilt and social disapproval. Yet their sexual orientation as such was not what was pathological. In these patients we identified a variety of possible origins and uses of homosexuality—some protective, some enjoyable, some disturbing. We also discovered a variety of problems, with apparent origins and expressions in different developmental phases. Our aim is to consider the total personality organization of the patient, not just his or her sexual orientation, and to focus on the desired development of that organization.

In none of the cases cited did we prompt homosexual patients to convert to heterosexuality. Increasingly we find that people come to us with the hope of learning to enjoy their sexuality, whatever their orientation. They have a relatively good idea of what they would like to do, but they are having trouble doing it. We believe psychoanalytic psychotherapy is quite capable of facilitating sexual enjoyment. Through a nonjudgmental working alliance using explanations and interpretations in the context of a developmental psychology, we can help the patient achieve greater self-fulfillment regardless of his or her sexual orientation.

In viewing the choice of sexual orientation as an open possibility, we are departing from the customary psychoanalytic (and societal) view of identity development, of which a key characteristic is a sexual desire for members of the opposite sex. But we do not see our approach as nonpsychoanalytic. We do see it as a reformulation of the characteristics of a healthy feminine and masculine identity. The developing body of work on androgyny (Kaplan and Bean 1976) requires reconsideration of previous conceptions of sex roles and the characteristics of gender identity. Although our own formulations are tentative and limited to a particular area at the moment, more general revisions of psychoanalytic thinking are occurring (Gedo 1979, Klein 1976). These support a focus on the intentions and inner states that lead to varied behaviors. In our opinion, they involve a less restrictive view of what it means to be healthy in psychoanalytic terms.

Finally, Kwawer (1980) has suggested that how an analyst views homosexuality (that is, as pathology per se, or not) can be a statement of countertransference and can have an effect on interpretations made in the analytic situation. Under the guise of appropriate treatment flowing from accepted theory about homosexuality, the analyst may be operating more from her or his inner needs than the needs of the patient. Analysts should ask themselves about their opinion of homosexuality as such, for only if they view it as a sickness will they try to cure it by aiming for a change in sexual orientation. Our belief that all sexual behavior can serve a variety of purposes includes the conviction that homosexuality can be a healthy sexual orientation.

We realize such an approach is open to debate, but we regard this debate as appealing and helpful. For too long in psychoanalytic circles the estimate of homosexuality had been fixed. We base our own on the evidence, research and clinical. After years of personal analysis for all of us, we do not believe our position is founded on a desire to justify particular sexual orientations. In fact, we think that kind of counter-transference is likely to operate more in those who insist all homosexuality is pathological. For ourselves, we like to think that we are returning to the exploratory character of psychoanalysis that was so evident in its founder.

REFERENCES

American Psychiatric Association. (1980). *Diagnostic and Statistical Manual of Mental Disorders*. Washington, DC: American Psychiatric Press.

Bell, A. (1974). Homosexualities: their range and character. In *Nebraska Symposium On Motivation*, 1973, ed. J. Cole and R. Dienstbier. Lincoln, NE: University of Nebraska Press.

Bell, A., and Weinberg, M. (1978). *Homosexualities: A Study of Diversity Among Men and Women*. New York: Simon and Schuster.

Bieber, I., Dain, H., Dince, P., et al. (1962). *Homosexuality: A Psychoanalytic Study*. New York: Basic Books.

Blanck, G., and Blanck, R. (1974). *Ego Psychology: Theory and Practice*. New York: Columbia University Press.

———. (1979). *Ego Psychology II: Psychoanalytic Developmental Psychology*. New York: Columbia University Press.

Cass, V. (1979). Homosexual identity formation: a theoretical model. *Journal of Homosexuality* 4:219–235.

Coleman, E. (1978). Toward a new model of treatment of homosexuality: a review. *Journal of Homosexuality* 3:345–359.

Cooper, A. (1974). Aetiology of homosexuality. In *Understanding Homosexuality: Its Biological and Psychological Bases*, ed. J. Loraine. New York: American Elsevier.

Davison, G. (1977). Homosexuality and the ethics of behavioral intervention: paper 1–homosexuality, the ethical challenge. *Journal of Homosexuality* 2:195–204.

Freud, S. (1905). Three essays on the theory of sexuality. *Standard Edition* 7:125–145.

Freund, K. (1974). Male homosexuality: an analysis of the pattern. In *Understanding Homosexuality: Its Biological and Psychological Bases*, ed. J. Loraine, pp. 25–81. New York: American Elsevier.

Gedo, J. (1979). *Beyond Interpretation*. New York: International Universities Press.

Gonsiorek, J. (1977). Psychological adjustment and homosexuality. *JSAS Catalog of Selected Documents in Psychology* 7:45.

Hencken, J., and O'Dowd, W. (1977). Coming out as an aspect of identity formation. *Gay Academic Union Journal: Gai Saber* 1:18–22.

Herron, W., Kinter, T., Sollinger, I., and Trubowitz, J. (1980). New psychoanalytic perspectives on the treatment of a homosexual male. *Journal of Homosexuality* 5:393–403.

Horner, A. (1979). *Object Relations and the Developing Ego in Therapy*. New York: Jason Aronson.

Kaplan, A., and Bean, J., eds. (1976). *Beyond Sex-Role Stereotypes: Readings Toward a Psychology of Androgyny*. Boston: Little, Brown.

Klein, G. (1976). *Psychoanalytic Theory*. New York: International Universities Press.

Kwawer, J. (1980). Transference and countertransference in homosexuality: changing psychoanalytic views. *American Journal of Psychotherapy* 34:72–80.

Lachman, F. (1975). Homosexuality: some diagnostic perspectives and dynamic considerations. *American Journal of Psychotherapy* 29:254–260.

May, E. (1977). Discussion of: "Recent Trends and New Developments in the Treatment of Homosexuality" by J. Hinrichsen and M. Katahn. *Psychotherapy: Theory, Research and Practice* 14:18–20.

Mitchell, S. (1978). Psychodynamic homosexuality and the question of pathology. *Psychiatry* 41:254–260.

Ovesey, L. (1976). Pseudohomosexuality. *Medical Aspects of Human Sexuality* 10:147.

Ovesey, L., Gaylin, W., and Hendin, H. (1963). Psychotherapy of male homosexuality. *Archives of General Psychiatry* 9:19–24.

Ross, N. (1970). The primacy of genitality in the light of ego psychology: introductory remarks. *Journal of the American Psychoanalytic
Association* 18:267–275.

Saghir, M., and Robins, E. (1973). *Male and Female Homosexuality: A
Comprehensive Investigation*. Baltimore: Williams & Wilkins.

Shively, M., and De Cecco, J. (1977). Components of sexual identity.
Journal of Homosexuality 3:41–48.

Socarides, C. (1974). The sexual deviations and the diagnostic manual. *American Journal Of Psychotherapy* 32:414–426.

_____ (1978). *Homosexuality*. New York: Jason Aronson.

_____ (1979). Some problems encountered in the psychoanalytic
treatment of overt male homosexuality. *American Journal of
Psychotherapy* 33:506–520.

Thompson, C. (1947). Changing concepts of homosexuality in psychoanalysis. *Psychiatry* 10:183–188.

2

On the Analytic Therapy of Homosexual Men

RICHARD A. ISAY, M.D.

PSYCHOANALYTIC TRADITION
AND HOMOSEXUALITY

Most psychoanalysts assume that homosexuality reflects an unfavorable unconscious solution to developmental conflicts, and that, consequently, the entire personality of the homosexual shows various disturbances. The number and kind of pathological deficits attributed to homosexuals are very large, and I have selected only a few for illustrative purposes. Bergler (1956) wrote of six traits: masochistic provocation and injustice collecting, defensive malice, flippancy, hypernarcissism, refusal to acknowledge accepted standards in nonsexual matters, and general unreliability. "The most interesting feature of this sextet of traits," he writes, "is its universality. Regardless of the level of intelligence, culture, background, or education, all homosexuals possess it" (p. 49). Homosexuals have been said to suffer from a large variety of ego defects (Panel 1954), including "primitive features of the ego" (p. 344) similar to those found in schizophrenia (Panel 1960,

p. 556) and sociopathy.[1] Glover (1932) suggested that homosexuality and other perversions "help to patch over flaws in the development of reality-sense" (p. 230). Socarides (1968) wrote that approximately half of the patients who engage in homosexual practices have a "concomitant schizophrenia, paranoia, are latent or pseudoneurotic schizophrenics or are in the throes of a manic-depressive reaction. The other half, when neurotic, may be of the obsessional or, occasionally, of the phobic type" (p. 90). Most of the patients he labeled as schizophrenic would probably be classified in his later formulation (1978) as belonging to the class of Preoedipal Type #2, "Suffering from a transitional condition lying somewhere between the neuroses and psychoses" (p. 58).

Not all analysts subscribe to generalizations about the pathology of either homosexuals as a group or our homosexual patients. For example, Weiss remarked that many homosexuals he had known as patients and friends "did not reveal unrealistic, immature traits or neurotic symptoms, whereas many heterosexuals do reveal such traits" (Panel 1960, p. 560). Rangell is quoted as stating: "One may end up as a borderline homosexual, or a well-integrated homosexual, or a borderline or narcissistic heterosexual or a well-functioning heterosexual" (Panel 1977, p. 197). In a review, Person (1983) said, "It is particularly useful to be finished with some of the more pernicious stereotypes about homosexuality, and with the idea that homosexuality . . . must reflect a primitive level of ego integration" (p. 314). And, of course, Freud, in his well-known "Letter to an American Mother," wrote on April 9, 1935: "Homosexuality is assuredly no advantage, but it is nothing to be ashamed of, no vice, no degradation,

---

[1]In the first *Diagnostic and Statistical Manual* (*DSM-I*) of the American Psychiatric Association, homosexuality was listed in the category "sociopathic personality disturbance." It was listed under "personality disorders and certain other nonpsychotic mental disorders" in *DSM-II*. The decision of the Board of Trustees of the American Psychiatric Association in 1973 and a subsequent vote of the membership removed homosexuality per se from *DSM-III* as a mental disorder.

it cannot be classified as an illness; we consider it to be a variation of sexual function produced by a certain arrest of sexual development."

Because psychoanalysts generally regard homosexuality as a pathological and a psychologically uneconomical solution to early conflict, they tend to believe that, whenever possible, it is in the best interest of the patient to change his sexual orientation or sexual behavior. Presumably a homosexual man will then be able to live a happier life not only because he will be in less conflict with society, but because warring intrapsychic structures will be brought into greater harmony. He will be less inclined to act out "unacceptable impulses" as they become increasingly tolerated by a strengthened ego and successfully sublimated.

Freud was not sanguine about the possibility of changing a homosexual to a heterosexual or about its helpfulness. In the "Letter" quoted above, he continued:

> By asking me if I can help, you mean, I suppose, if I can abolish homosexuality and make normal heterosexuality take its place. The answer is, in a general way, we cannot promise to achieve it. In a certain number of cases we succeed in developing the blighted germs of heterosexual tendencies which are present in every homosexual, in the majority of cases it is no more possible. . . . What analysis can do for your son runs in a different line. If he is unhappy, torn by conflicts, inhibited in his social life, analysis may bring him harmony, peace of mind, full efficiency, whether he remains a homosexual or gets changed.

Why have analysts generally maintained the view of homosexuality as pathology, not only in contrast to what Freud wrote, but in the face of the evidence accumulated by nonanalytic studies? I shall briefly review these other approaches in order to give an idea of the nature of evidence and opinion that analysts have disregarded. The statistics cited by Kinsey and colleagues (1948) would appear to support a nonpathological view of homosexuality by force of the large numbers of homosexuals in the population at large: 4 percent of the adult white male population are exclusively homosexual throughout their lives after adolescence, and about 8 percent have been exclusively homosexual for at least three years between 16 and 55. In the postpubertal male population 37 percent have had at least one overt homosexual experience to the point of orgasm between the beginning of adolescence and old age, and this number rises to 50 percent if one includes only men who do not marry before age 35 (p. 650f.).[2]

Ford and Beach (1951), in their cross-cultural investigations and studies of subhuman primates, support the concept that homosexuality is not a disease. Their data show that

> . . . a biological tendency for inversion of sexual behavior is inherent in most if not all mammals including the human species. . . . Some homosexual behavior occurs in a great many human societies. It tends to be more common in adolescence than in adulthood and appears to be practiced more frequently by men than women. This is also true of the other animal species—and particularly so in the infra-human primates. . . . Even in societies which severely restrict homosexual tendencies—some individuals do exhibit homosexual behavior. . . . Within the societies which, unlike our own, provide socially acceptable homosexual roles, a number of individuals, predominantly men, choose to exhibit some measure of homosexual behavior. [p. 143]

Another source of data comes from psychology. The best known study is Evelyn Hooker's (1957), which was designed to determine the usefulness of projective psychological tests in diagnosing overt homosexual behavior and to assess whether or not there are distinguishable personality characteristics in exclusively homosexual men. Summa-

---

[2]Although there are methodological and sampling problems in this study, a number of European surveys report a comparably high incidence of homosexuality and homosexual experiences. Marmor writes, "The psychiatrically intriguing question is how so substantial a number of men and women become preferentially motivated towards such behavior in spite of the powerful cultural taboos against it" (see Freedman et al. 1975, p. 1512).

rizing the results, she wrote, "The three judges agreed on two-thirds of the group as being average to superior in adjustment. According to the judges, some [homosexuals] may not be characterized by any demonstrable pathology" (Marmor 1965, p. 89). A number of other investigators, using both projective and objective standardized tests, have also been unable to differentiate homosexual from heterosexual subjects and suggest that there is no greater pathology among homosexuals than heterosexuals (see the review by Riess 1980).

The well-publicized *Wolfenden Report*, which supported England's decriminalization of homosexual acts between consenting adults in private, also was strongly critical of the view that homosexuality was a disease. This report emphasized that no theories explaining the "perversion" were specific to it or conclusive of it, since the etiological factors were found in other states. Karl Menninger, in an introduction to the American edition (Great Britain Committee on Homosexual Offenses and Prostitution 1963, p. 7), wrote in repudiation of that part of the report that refers to the nonpathological state of homosexuality: "homosexuality . . . constitutes evidence of immature sexuality and either arrested psychological development or regression. Whatever it be called by the public, there is no question in the minds of psychiatrists regarding the abnormality of such behavior" (quoted in Bayer 1981, p. 39).

Finally, the fight against the American Psychiatric Association's December 1973 decision to delete homosexuality as a mental disorder from *DSM-III* was to a large extent led by psychoanalysts and other dynamically oriented therapists who felt that such action would keep homosexuals from seeking and receiving "help." Individual analysts as well as organized psychoanalysis, although not alone among mental health professionals and organizations, subsequently protested the decision and continue to do so (see Bayer 1981, pp. 121f., 155–178).

HOMOSEXUALITY AND ANALYTIC TECHNIQUE

The view of homosexuality as a disease has led many analysts to feel that it is in the best interest of their homosexual patients to help them

to become heterosexual. Our literature is replete with recommenda-
tions in support of modifications of analytic technique that are
deemed appropriate to the treatment of homosexual patients. Kolb
and Johnson (1955) state that analytic neutrality may at times be
misconstrued as permission for the patient to act out homosexual
behavior, that the therapist should not encourage the patient's "self-
destruction" and under some circumstances should terminate treatment if such behavior persists (p. 513). Serota expressed the belief that

> the analyst who undertakes the treatment of a homosexual must have
> already consciously or unconsciously arrived at certain diagnostic
> conclusions regarding the existence of an intrapsychic conflict re-
> garding homosexuality, a conviction that a heterosexual solution is
> possible, that the patient will attempt it at some point. [Panel 1960, p.
> 566]

Socarides (1968) is not alone in advocating under certain conditions
the use of nonanalytic techniques such as suggesting to a homosexual
patient that he seek out women or discussing with a patient how to
engage in heterosexual sex (see Wiedeman 1974, p. 676). Others would
agree that a "flexible" analytic approach is indicated, such as encouraging the homosexual patient's turn to heterosexuality where phobic
avoidance of women is involved (e.g., Bieber et al. 1962, Ovesey 1965,
Rado 1949). In his literature review, Wiedeman (1974) noted that "a
purely analytic approach consisting only of interpretations, without
any other elements of support, clarification, and confrontation with
reality, hardly exists" (p. 676).

I am defining as homosexual a person who has a predominant
erotic attraction, for a long period of time, for others of the same sex.
There are some heterosexuals who, for developmental reasons (ado-
lescents), opportunistic motives (some delinquents), or situational
reasons (prison inmates), or as a defense against anxiety, may engage
in homosexual behavior for varying periods of time and not be
homosexual (Isay 1986). Most homosexuals do engage in sexual activity, but one need not do so to be homosexual. There are individuals

who may be homosexual and are unaware of it because of the repression or suppression of their fantasies.

I am emphasizing in this definition that it is the erotic attraction as expressed in fantasy that defines the homosexual and not his behavior, since some homosexuals, like some heterosexuals, may be inhibited by social constraints from expressing their sexuality. I am taking into account that there is a preponderance, but not necessarily an exclusivity, of homoerotic fantasy. I am emphasizing the tenacity and longevity of the sexual orientation in adults, since the fantasy is usually recollected as being present from the latency years or early adolescence (Friedman and Stern 1980, p. 431). This does not preclude its presence in childhood—in fact, many gay men do recollect strong homosexual fantasies and impulses from childhood—any more than the repression of childhood sexuality in heterosexuals precludes its presence in childhood. Considering a man to be homosexual because of the predominant erotic fantasy for others of the same sex, rather than only because he necessarily expresses his sexuality in behavior, has implications for the assessment, understanding, and treatment of homosexual patients.

In my practice, I have seen a number of homosexual men who have returned for further help after interrupting or completing treatment with other analysts, whose goal, either explicitly stated or implicitly guiding the treatment, had been to help the patients change their sexual orientation. My clinical material suggests that such efforts may cause symptomatic depression by contributing to an already diminished and injured self-esteem, and in some cases they may produce severe social problems in later life. My conclusion from listening to these patients is that the analysts' internalized social values interfere with the proper conduct of an analysis by causing the analysts to be unable to convey an appropriate positive regard for their patients or to maintain therapeutic neutrality. I shall illustrate this conclusion with two brief clinical examples.

A. was referred for further treatment after he had left his previous psychotherapist, an experienced analyst with a fine reputation. A. was 20 and a college junior when I started to see him. He complained of severe dysphoria; an inability to form any kind of satisfying, lasting relationship; a lackluster college performance; and having no goals in his life. He also complained about being gay. His parents wished he were straight. His mother badly wanted grandchildren, and he wanted to be able to please her. He had friendships with girls and on one occasion he had had intercourse; but his sexual fantasies from age 9 or 10 had been almost exclusively about other boys. He felt a complete lack of sexual interest in girls, although he enjoyed their friendship. He wanted most of all to be able to fall in love and have a boyfriend because he felt so lonely, but anytime someone liked him, he began to find the boy unattractive and lost interest. His previous three-times-weekly analytically oriented therapy came to a halt because of A.'s continued feeling of his therapist's disapproval. Although he was never told explicitly not to be homosexual, whenever he cruised a bookstore or had sex, the therapist discouraged this behavior. Whenever he went out with another boy, his therapist wondered why he did not devote similar energy to a girl he had previously met and seemed to like. The therapist's interventions appeared to increase this patient's need for brief sexual encounters as A. grew to feel that these comments and interpretations were basically motivated by the therapist's disapproval of his homosexuality and the way he was expressing it. A.'s feeling that his therapist disapproved of his behavior and did not like him was analyzed as projection. He felt increasingly depressed, defeated, and self-critical.

This patient's description of his previous therapeutic experience appeared to be more than distortions due to past or current transference phenomena. His narrative had a ring of truth and reality to it. Furthermore, the manner in which he presented his dissatisfaction with his sexuality evoked in me an initial impression that he could and should alter this long-established sexual orientation. It became clear after several weeks, however, that A.'s wish to please his ambivalently viewed mother and his introjection of hostile social values inimical to his sexual feelings were motivating his request for change. It also became clear that these factors had produced a ready transference to which his previous therapist had responded, not by attempting to understand the conflicts underlying the wish, but by complying with it. I shall return later to the analyst's exploitation of transference in the service of attempting to change the patient's sexuality.

At some point in every intensive therapy, every gay patient expresses unhappiness and dissatisfaction with his homosexuality. With A., the despair over his homosexuality was an expression of transference, but it was also a displacement of anxiety that interfered with his ability to form close, meaningful relationships, to have gratifying sexual activity with other men, and to have a satisfying career. His unconscious or preconscious wish was that if the socially disadvantaged homosexuality were cured, then his anxiety would disappear. In aligning himself with that wish, the previous therapist joined the patient in magical thinking and was eventually perceived as being unempathic and ignorant. In colluding with that manifestation of transference expressed as "I hate being gay," the therapist became a further expression and extension of the incorporated values of a society perceived as being critical and hostile. A.'s correct perception of his therapist's values caused A. to interrupt treatment, but his identification with this trusted person's biased views of homosexuality further injured him. By challenging this important aspect of A.'s identity, the analyst unconsciously encouraged the self-denigration that contributed to his self-degrading and spiteful sexual behavior and depression.

Listening to this young man in what I believe to have been a manner that was both accepting of him and neutral in the sense of being nonjudgmental and curious established an atmosphere in which conflict, transference, defense, and resistance could be safely related and untangled. The early expressed wish to be heterosexual largely disappeared from the hours after the first weeks of analysis, as did his depression. The feelings of self-loathing from internalized social prejudice lessened in intensity as he experienced some measure of accep-

tance and regard from my attitude toward him. Frantic anonymous
sex decreased in frequency, in part because he was aware of AIDS, but
in large measure because he no longer needed to act out angry, spiteful
transference wishes in a masochistic way. He also became much more
successful in his work, partly for the same reason.

Another illustration is of a young man I saw in analysis for
several years, who differed from the previous patient in the severity of
his masochism and the manner in which he used it to evoke expressions of disgust, rejection, and attack.

> B. had felt homosexual since childhood and had actively en-
> gaged in homosexual sex since early adolescence. He had neither
> heterosexual experience nor sexual interest in women. B. related
> to his previous therapist, along with other aspects of his history,
> many sexual incidents that he felt were sordid, and he portrayed
> them as such, along with his shame and disgust over being
> homosexual. He did this frequently, and on more than one
> occasion inquired if the therapist felt B. would be better if he
> gave up his homosexuality. His therapist's agreement and subse-
> quent well-intended admonitions made the patient increasingly
> desperate, disillusioned, lonely, and enraged. He eventually left
> treatment and came to me wanting to become heterosexual,
> although skeptical of the possibility.

B.'s masochism was severe. It derived from early injury to his narcissism and the resulting self-directed, spiteful rage, from his identification with a hostile, masochistic mother; from the expression of passive
sexual longings for an emotionally distant father; and, very importantly, from critical social attitudes perceived, identified with, and
internalized when B. was quite young. In the transference, these
wishes were expressed as a need to be humiliated, dominated, and
rejected. I did not always succeed in my attempts to maintain an
accepting and positive attitude toward him because his needs to
disgust me and to evoke my rejection were so persistent. Nevertheless,

my reciprocal responses to his transference were both manageable and useful to our understanding, and I believe I was generally successful not only in maintaining a neutral attitude but in conveying my acceptance and positive regard for him.

I do not view B.'s homosexuality as his problem. Because he had an exclusive, or nearly exclusive, homosexual fantasy life since childhood and because of his long-standing homosexual activity with little or no real heterosexual interest, I consider him to be gay. I do not believe, therefore, that there is any clinical justification for attempting to change his basic homosexual behavior, nor do I expect to be able to change his sexual orientation. This attitude has enabled us to analyze those aspects of his wish to be heterosexual that are related to the passive acquiescence to and acceptance of internalized critical social values, and it has made it possible for us to understand unrealistic projections of these social attitudes in the transference. We can now begin to have a less cluttered view of early conflict and other determinants of his masochism. Some of the angry, destructive, rebellious activity related to his response to social attitudes has diminished.

I am emphasizing the importance of an undeviatingly uncritical, accepting therapeutic stance in which thoughtfulness, caring, and regard for the patient are essential. By so doing I am not underestimating the value of the questioning, uncovering, and usual interpretive work of any analytic or dynamically oriented therapy. Nor am I advocating the unquestioning acceptance of the patient's views and values. Rather, I am attempting to demonstrate that an attitude of positive regard makes analytic work possible because it enables the patient to express and analyze negative transference distortions from both the past and present. This stance has therapeutic value because it is in part through his interaction with the analyst that any patient acquires a new, more positive, and more accepting image of himself (Loewald 1960, p. 20). I believe that neither the positive attitude described nor the therapeutic action is different from that in any other analytic or psychotherapeutic work. Moreover, I want to emphasize the therapeutic danger of a position that is not neutral by virtue of the analyst's being oriented to changing the patient's sexuality. In my opinion, the first analyses of the cases cited above illustrate what Schafer (1983) means when he writes:

> The simplistic, partisan analyst, working in terms of. . . good and bad ways to live is failing to maintain the analytic attitude. In this failure, he or she can only be encouraging the analysand to fixate on some pattern of paranoid and depressive orientations, to persevere in sadomasochistic fantasizing and acting out, or to engage in wholesale repression of disturbing factors. [p. 5]

I now turn to those patients who have worked with well-intentioned, therapeutically zealous analysts who have managed to accomplish the mutually acceptable goal of curtailing homosexual behavior. Claims of achieving behavioral change in a highly motivated population of male and female homosexual patients have varied from about 20 percent to 50 percent with every variety of therapeutic modality (Marmor 1980, p. 277). Bieber and colleagues (1962), who viewed homosexuality in terms of an underlying fear of heterosexuality, reported a 19 percent change of exclusive homosexuals to heterosexuality, using what was probably a modified psychoanalytic technique (p. 276). Socarides (1978) claims that of "forty-four overt homosexuals who had undergone psychoanalytic therapy, twenty patients, nearly 50 percent, developed full heterosexual functioning" (p. 406).

I intend to illustrate the emotional and social consequences of the attempted and seemingly successful change from homosexuality to heterosexuality for three patients whom I have seen in a long-term, psychoanalytically oriented psychotherapy beginning ten to fifteen years after the completion of their prior analyses. These three patients, according to the definition previously given, were homosexual when treated by their previous analysts. There appear to have been few of the "blighted germs of heterosexuality" in any of these men. In each case, sexual behavior was temporarily modified, but the patients remained homosexual in that their sexual orientation, as expressed by the predominance of homosexual fantasy, remained unchanged. When I treated them, they either previously or currently had the additional difficult social and personal complication of a family.

When C. consulted me, he was 47 and the father of two adolescent girls. He had married in his late twenties shortly after the completion of a five-year analysis. Before the analysis, he had had an active homosexual life, including a relationship with a young man who he said was the only passion of his life. He had never enjoyed sex with women prior to his analysis and *learned* (patient's emphasis) to enjoy sex with them in his analysis. Although sex with men was not specifically prohibited, the love affair was proscribed and sex with women was prescribed. There had been no homosexual sex since his marriage. He sought therapeutic assistance because of persistent depression, no zest for living, low self-esteem, apathy in his work, and no sexual interest in his wife, with whom he had not had sexual relations since the birth of his last child. His masturbatory and other sexual fantasies were exclusively homosexual. He longed for the lost love of his youth.

This man was a devoted father and husband. His wife knew nothing of his past homosexual life. He had no regrets over the change in his sexual behavior, except that he felt something was missing in his life—he called it a "passion." C. was still homosexual: he had a conscious erotic preference for other men, still had an active homosexual fantasy life, and continued to long for the love of other men.

C. did not wish to resume analysis, but he did enter into analytically oriented therapy. He expressed a great deal of anger (which he had previously been unaware of) at his analyst for "manipulating" him. He grieved over having given up the passion that he spoke of so often. Over the course of two years of therapy his life felt less burdensome as his depression decreased. He became more tolerant of his homosexual fantasies and impulses and was able to think of himself as homosexual. He never resumed sex with his wife, nor did he resume his homosexual life because he felt it would disrupt his marriage.

C. always believed that his previous analysis had been successful. He had a wife and children from whom he gained enormous pleasure. He liked the conventionality, the relative lack of stress in his life, and his professional success. It became clear in our work, however, that the denial, repression, and unanalyzed acquiescence that had been necessary in order for him to achieve the renunciation of his homosexual behavior had affected his capacity to enjoy and achieve to the fullest extent possible, and that the failure to analyze these defenses and transference manifestations were in part responsible for the depression that motivated his return for further treatment. The question of whether or not he would have been happier living an active homosexual life is unanswerable. But it would appear that the analyst's health values (Hartmann 1960) made it impossible for either the patient or the analyst to consider this other sexual and social option.

> D. was in his late thirties and had previously been in analysis for about five years, during which time he both married and separated. According to his recollection, he had felt homosexual since early adolescence and had engaged in homosexual sex since that time. He entered analysis in his twenties because of several unhappy relationships with other men, and because of depression and ambivalence about being homosexual. He met his wife during the analysis, and she was the first woman he had ever had sex with. Although his sexual relationship was not "great," he perceived it as adequate, and he gave up for a time all homosexual activity. Subsequently, however, his work became increasingly tedious, and he felt depressed, argumentative, and apathetic. He resumed occasional surreptitious homosexual sex; the relationship with his wife continued to deteriorate and finally ended in separation. He stopped his analysis at the time of the separation from his wife, ostensibly because he felt the analyst was unempathic and rigid. He sought consultation several years later because of continuing depression connected with low self-esteem.

When I saw this man, he had very little or no interest in women and not much more interest in having sex with other men, although he readily acknowledged he was homosexual. He wanted a stable relationship, which he felt was possible only in a conventional marriage. During three years of therapy, he mourned the loss of his wife and the probability that he would never have children, and he began to have an active sex life with other men. This patient's analyst had made essentially the same technical modifications as C.'s analyst: questioning homosexual behavior without actually prohibiting it, and encouraging dating and any heterosexual involvement. In both of these cases, the homosexual behavior was inhibited by the analyst's positively reinforcing the more acceptable heterosexual behavior and by his use of a probably unconscious, disapproving attitude that served as a negative reinforcement of homosexual behavior. Transference manifestations of wanting to be loved, the need to acquiesce, and the patients' passive longings were all used in the service of helping these patients to suppress their homosexual behavior.

The next patient, E., had had an analyst who, unlike the analysts of the two previous patients, gave the appearance of being noncoercive, nonjudgmental, and unmanipulative. Because the patient had not engaged in homosexual sex prior to or during his analysis, no apparent modifications in analytic technique or obvious violations of analytic neutrality were necessary to discourage such behavior. The observation afforded by E.'s subsequent long analysis suggested, however, that the analyst's social values had interfered with this patient's treatment. I want to illustrate with this case the ways in which the interpretation of homosexuality as a defense can convey the analyst's bias.

> E. started his analysis when he was in his early twenties because of conflict about his homosexual fantasies and a lack of interest in girls. Homosexual masturbation fantasies and daydreams had persisted since before adolescence. When he entered this analysis, he had never engaged in homosexual activity, except for very occasional adolescent sexual play that was clinically insignificant. Throughout the analysis, the analyst consistently interpreted the homosexual fantasies as a defense against assuming

aggressive male roles, which included having heterosexual sex. The analyst's view implicitly and comfortingly conveyed to the patient that he was not really homosexual and that what appeared to him to be homosexuality and what he feared was homosexuality could be analyzed and would disappear. He continued to have exclusively homosexual fantasies; but, because of a powerful positive transference, he did engage in occasional sex with girls, although he was frequently impotent. Shortly after the termination of the analysis, he married. Sexual interest in his wife rapidly waned, and after several years of marriage, he began to have homosexual sex for the first time. When E. came to me in his late thirties, he was depressed, agitated, despairing, and confused. He was "wandering between two worlds" and wanted to find a way to bring them together.

The analyst's heterosexual bias was expressed largely and repeatedly in the interpretation of homosexual fantasy as defense against fears of heterosexuality and of competition, that is, as the unsuccessful resolution of oedipal-stage conflict. When I began to treat E., it was clear that he had a need to feel enraged and to see his analyst as negligent and uncaring. Nevertheless, his perception of his former analyst's intolerance of homosexual behavior, expressed in the interpretation of E.'s homosexuality as a defense against heterosexuality, also appears to have been accurate. The analyst's inability to help the patient discover this aspect of his identity contributed to E.'s later symptoms and to the painful social situation he found himself in at the beginning of his subsequent treatment.[3]

In the three preceding illustrations each patient's transference wishes were unconsciously used by the analyst, because of the analyst's

---

[3]Fantasies of a homosexual nature and homosexual behavior may, of course, be used at times defensively by some patients who are predominantly heterosexual. Homosexual men may use homosexual behavior, just as heterosexuals may use heterosexual behavior, to ward off intolerable affects (Isay 1986).

countertransference needs, to attempt to change his patient's sexual orientation. This, of course, made it impossible in these initial efforts for any of these patients to understand those essential conflicts that were expressed in the transference. For example, C. had acquiesced to what he perceived as his analyst's wish for him to behave heterosexually out of an attempt to be the good sibling. His brother had been the actively rebellious one. C. won his place by being acquiescent and agreeable. D. came to his subsequent therapy with an enormous un-analyzed rage connected with early narcissistic wounds. He had the feeling that he had been a replacement for a sibling killed in the war. As a child he had felt neither understood nor appreciated, perceiving that he had been treated as if he were his deceased older brother. He, of course, felt that his analyst had, like his parents, a need of his own in treating him as if he were "straight," and, feeling a similar lack of empathy in his analyst, believed he had again been misunderstood and unappreciated. E. had been rebellious as a child out of a longed-for love that he never received. His passivity and acquiescence expressed this deep longing for the love of both parents. Pleasing his analyst by at-tempting to be heterosexual, he could win a long-sought and always elusive love.

The exploitation of transference for hoped-for therapeutic gain is, of course, not new. Many of the gains of the brief analyses of the 1920s and the crisis-oriented and focal therapies today were and are in part based on such techniques. Those analysts who advocate, as mentioned earlier, the introduction of encouragement to overcome what they feel to be the homosexual's phobic avoidance of sex with women make conscious use of the transference for attempted thera-peutic gain. My concern here, however, is with the analyst's uncon-scious exploitation of transference wishes as an expression of the analyst's value system and countertransference, which adds a measure of insidious conviction to the patient's long-standing belief in his being intolerable or evil.

Not only had the understanding and exploration of conflict been limited in each of the previous therapies by the use of the patients' transference wishes in order to attempt to change their sexuality, but subsequent analytic exploration was made even more difficult by their ensuing marriages. In the cases of C. and E., the two men who remained married, it was more difficult to obtain a full understanding of underlying conflict because of the degree and extent of their defenses. In saying this, I am not questioning whether marriage and children were worthwhile compromises for these homosexual men. I am only pointing out that the subsequent therapy was made more difficult by their social situation and by such factors as the denial, repression, reaction formation, and readiness to acquiesce that led them into marriage and, perhaps, to remain in their marriages (see also Person in Panel 1977, p. 189). Furthermore, had there been a stronger bisexual orientation in any of these patients, the outcome of treatment might have been more successful.[4]

DISCUSSION

In emphasizing the problems that many analysts have in treating homosexual patients, I am not implying that psychoanalysis cannot help gay patients. On the contrary, I feel that both psychoanalysis and analytically oriented psychotherapy can be helpful to these patients in ways in which they are helpful to heterosexual patients and for the same spectrum and distribution of character problems, and symptomatic neurotic and psychotic reactions (Bieber et al. 1962). My experience suggests that the usual analytic attitude of positive regard and neutrality may be enormously, perhaps especially, helpful to any patient who has internalized the critical, deprecatory attitudes of a prejudiced society by helping him to acquire a more positive, accepting image of himself. It is at present, however, because of the

---

[4]I believe it is likely that observations of the successful conversion of "homosexual" patients to heterosexuality over an indefinite or extended period of time are, in fact, due to the successful suppression of the homosexual component in men who have a strong bisexual orientation.

"moral value irradiation" of our work, difficult to measure the true potential of psychoanalysis for the treatment of gay patients.

The difficulties that many analysts, as well as other therapists, have had in treating homosexual patients, I believe, derive from the confusion of health ethics with moral values, so that "empirically subjective values are posited as if they were 'objective' and accessible to empirical validation" (Hartmann 1960, p. 67). These health ethics, interacting with countertransference, have skewed our data and interfered with our perception and comprehension of the many ways that homosexuality, like heterosexuality, can be expressed, some of which are healthy and some of which are not.

Freud implicitly recognized the problematic influence of social values when he responded to a letter by Ernest Jones of December 1, 1921, in which Jones asked for advice on the matter of accepting a homosexual applicant for psychoanalytic training: "The Dutch asked me some time ago about the propriety of accepting as member a doctor known to be manifestly homosexual. I advised against it, and now I hear from Van Emden that the man has been detected and committed to prison. Do you think this would be a safe general maxim to act on?"

In the Circular Letter of December 11, 1921, Otto Rank, in collaboration with Freud, officially responded from Vienna:

> We would not want to answer your question, dear Ernest, concerning possible membership of homosexuals as you suggest; that is to say, we do not on principle want to exclude such persons because we also cannot condone their legal persecution. We believe that a decision in such cases should be reserved for an examination of the individual's other qualities.[5]

Psychoanalysts have also inadvertently contributed to social bias, as well as partaking of it. Psychoanalytic theory and practice have

---

[5]This letter was discovered by Dr. Hendrick Ruitenbeek, and can be found in the Rare Books and Manuscript Library of Columbia University. It was reprinted by Marmor (1980, p. 395). I want to thank Lottie M. Newman for reviewing the original letter and providing this translation.

promulgated a theory of developmental aberration and illness that has
been used by the neo-traditionalist theologians of all churches to
reinforce the view that homosexuality is evil. This position is predicated on the idea that homosexual acts are intrinsically evil and are
perfectible and correctable. For example:

> . . . the evidence is still too fragmentary to unseat the prevailing
> scientific appraisal of homosexuality as the living-out of sick and
> stunted emotions. The odds are still high that the average individual
> who chooses homosexual behavior will be choosing a sick, immature
> way of life. The odds should determine the ethical decision, it seems to
> me, at least for the individual for whom professional analysis has
> confirmed his emotional sickness. [Batcheler 1980, p. 69]

Or:

> What troubled people need—either singly or in combination—is to
> learn to take serious responsibility for their attitudes, behavior and
> circumstances . . . every failure to take a possible maturational step has
> moral significance and falls under the rubric of original sin . . . we have
> also seen that this is true even if the person's responsibility is mitigated
> by the process having taken place unconsciously. . . . It is impossible
> for homosexuality not to be included in this category. [p. 83]

Or:

> To the degree that they can hold the impulse in rein and fail to do so,
> they are committing a sin, a violation of the will of God or, in secular
> terms, an aberration from the norm. [p. 58]

The essential clinical issue for us as analysts and therapists is the
extent to which we can help our patients to be as free as possible of
those conflicts that interfere with their capacity to live gratifying and
happy lives as it is within their grasp to live. I believe that we must act
to lessen the burden of the instinctual sacrifices that society imposes
on gay patients (Freud 1927), and to help them resolve those conflicts
that interfere with the most gratifying expression of their sexuality.
Again, to quote Hartmann (1960):

It would be absurd to expect that only what has survival value for the individual or species would actually be called "good," or that everything called "evil" must have the opposite effect. . . . It is, however, particularly difficult to determine how far "good" contributes to happiness—happiness being a highly complex psychological phenomenon, and the concept being ambiguous. [p. 66]

REFERENCES

Batcheler, E., ed. (1980). *Homosexuality and Ethics*. New York: Pilgrim.

Bayer, R. (1981). *Homosexuality and American Psychiatry*. New York: Basic Books.

Bergler, E. (1956). *Homosexuality*. New York: Hill & Wang.

Bieber, I., Dain, H., Dince, P., et al. (1962). *Homosexuality: A Psychoanalytic Study*. New York: Basic Books.

Ford, C., and Beach, F. (1951). *Patterns of Sexual Behavior*. New York: Harper.

Freedman, A., Kaplan, H., and Sadock, B. (1975). *Comprehensive Textbook of Psychiatry*. Baltimore: Williams & Wilkins.

Freud, S. (1927). The future of an illusion. *Standard Edition*, 21:5–56.

_____ (1935). Letter to an American mother. Reprinted in *Homosexuality and American Psychiatry: The Politics of Diagnosis*, by R. Bayer, p. 27. New York: Basic Books, 1981.

Friedman, R., and Stern, L. (1980). Juvenile aggressivity and sissiness in homosexual and heterosexual males. *American Academy of Psychoanalysis* 8:427–440.

Glover, E. (1932). The relation of perversion formation to the development of reality-sense. In *On the Early Development of Mind*, pp. 216–234. New York: International Universities Press.

Great Britain Committee on Homosexual Offenses and Prostitution (1963). *Wolfenden Report*, Authorized American edition. New York: Stein and Day.

Hartmann, H. (1960). *Psychoanalysis and Moral Values*. New York: International Universities Press.

Hooker, E. (1957). The adjustment of the male overt homosexual. *Journal of Projective Techniques* 21:18–31.

Isay, R. (1986). Homosexuality in homosexual and heterosexual men.

In *The Psychology of Men*, ed. G. Fogel, F. Lane, and R. S. Liebert, pp. 277–299. New York: Basic Books.

Kinsey, A., Pomeroy, W., and Martin, C. (1948). *Sexual Behavior in the Human Male*. Philadelphia: Saunders.

Kolb, L., and Johnson, A. (1955). Etiology and therapy of overt homosexuality. *Psychoanalytic Quarterly* 24:506–515.

Loewald, H. (1960). On the therapeutic action of psychoanalysis. *International Journal of Psycho-Analysis* 41:16–33.

Marmor, J., ed. (1965). *Sexual Inversion*. New York: Basic Books.

———— (1980). *Homosexual Behavior*. New York: Basic Books.

Ovesey, L. (1965). Pseudohomosexuality and homosexuality in men. In *Sexual Inversion*, ed. J. Marmor, pp. 211–233. New York: Basic Books.

Panel (1954). Perversion. J. Arlow, reporter. *Journal of the American Psychoanalytic Association* 2:336–345.

———— (1960). Theoretical and clinical aspects of male homosexuality. C. Socarides, reporter. *Journal of the American Psychoanalytic Association* 8:552–566.

———— (1977). The psychoanalytic treatment of male homosexuality. E. Payne, reporter. *Journal of the American Psychoanalytic Association* 25:183–199.

Person, E. (1983). Review of *Homosexualities* by A. Bell and M. Weinberg. *Journal of the American Psychoanalytic Association* 31:306–314.

Rado, S. (1949). An adaptational view of sexual behavior. In *Psychosexual Development in Health and Disease*, ed. P. Hoch and J. Zubin, pp. 159–189. New York: Grune & Stratton.

Riess, B. (1980). Psychological tests in homosexuality. In *Homosexual Behavior*, ed. J. Marmor, pp. 296–311. New York: Basic Books.

Schafer, R. (1983). *The Analytic Attitude*. New York: Basic Books.

Socarides, C. (1968). *The Overt Homosexual*. New York: Grune & Stratton.

———— (1978). *Homosexuality*. New York: Jason Aronson.

Wiedeman, G. (1974). Homosexuality. *Journal of the American Psychoanalytic Association* 22:651–696.

3

Dynamic Psychotherapy of Gay Men: A View from Self Psychology

CARLTON CORNETT, LCSW

Self psychology is currently a popular model in dynamic psychotherapy. It is a model that stresses the importance of self-esteem and identity cohesion. It is also a model that recognizes the deleterious effects that the external environment can have on self-esteem and cohesive identity development. Both of these qualities make self psychology a model with enormous potential to aid in the dynamic understanding of gay men and help the psychotherapist respond more effectively to her/his gay patients.

NARCISSISM, SELF-ESTEEM, AND THE GAY MAN

Although initially strongly criticized by the traditional mainstream, self psychology has found a place of prominence within psychoanalysis. Although there are still a number of critics (e.g., London 1985, Rangell 1982, Wallerstein 1985), every analyst and analytically oriented psychotherapist currently in practice is familiar with and influenced to some extent by concepts from Kohut's work.

The current popularity of self psychology is predicated largely on its inclusion of self-esteem in the legitimate foci of clinical work. It is out of the development of self-esteem that the human capacities to value the self and to value others (i.e., love) ultimately develop. Traditional ego psychologically oriented clinicians have long maintained that narcissism has been a focus of psychoanalysis since Freud's (1914) seminal paper on the topic. However, it has only been since the advent of self psychology that the term narcissism has *begun* to lose some of its pejorative connotations. Further, self psychology has attempted to elucidate differing types of narcissism. Although perhaps initially appearing esoteric, this differentiation has important clinical ramifications, especially in the context of psychotherapy with gay men. Much traditional (e.g., Socarides 1978) psychoanalytic clinical theory regarding male homosexuality has been influenced by the idea that the narcissism characteristic of such disorders as schizophrenia is essentially identical to that of homosexuality, except in terms of relative quantity. This notion, combined with the generally devaluing quality ascribed to narcissism as it has been traditionally conceptualized, has resulted in many unsuccessful, even hurtful, experiences for gay men with analysis and analytically oriented psychotherapy. In subsequent treatments, such experiences require great effort to overcome.

Self psychology has embraced narcissism as much more than an unfortunate but unavoidable artifact of human development, to be kept in strict abeyance. Rather, self psychology has illuminated narcissism as the primary element of identity development that influences the ability to love, work, and create. Self psychology has also focused on shame, the antagonistic state of functional narcissism (Kohut 1984). It is noteworthy that self psychology, with its emphases on self-esteem and identity development, has found application in a number of areas of clinical concern and practice, but has had only scant attention paid to its relevance for application to gay men. When self psychology does appear in the clinical literature in conjunction with the treatment of gay men, it is often focused primarily on the illustration of other clinical issues, not on its applicability to this particular patient population (e.g., Shapiro 1985; Trop and Stolorow 1991). However, self psychology does have direct applicability to the understanding of gay men, which can be utilized clinically (Ferguson 1989).

Narcissism and Psychopathology

Freud's (1914) original conception of narcissism focused on the investment of libidinal energy in the internal psychic world in preference to external objects. From the outset, narcissism was linked with pathological conditions, especially schizophrenia. Freud proposed the primary dynamic of narcissism to be a grandiose preoccupation with the self. Even in the earliest psychoanalytic writings, there was a recognition that grandiosity functions as compensation for a fundamental sense of inadequacy. However, therapeutic technique (i.e., when a patient with narcissistic deficits was considered analyzable at all) focused on active redirection of the patient's narcissistic demands. These demands were often judgmentally and pejoratively described as manifestations of a sense of entitlement. Often linked with such severe psychopathology as paranoia or schizophrenia, a narcissistic presentation was often considered a priori evidence that a patient would not benefit from traditional psychoanalysis.

As his thinking progressed, Freud figured narcissism prominently in his (1924a,b) conceptions of paranoid, manic-depressive, and schizophrenic states. The individual manifesting one of these disorders was seen as having decathected external objects in favor of cathexis of the self. Such a patient was, therefore, not analyzable by the classical technique, because he was deemed unable to develop a stable transference relationship with the analyst.

Psychoanalytic theorists soon began to move toward an under-

standing of homosexuality characterized by arguments involving narcissism. Bieber and colleagues (1962) and Socarides (1978) explain
male homosexuality in terms of a number of dynamics. One of the
most important of these dynamics, however, involves the contention
that homosexuality is an expression of blatant narcissism, this asser-
tion resting on the contention that a gay man's attraction to other
men is an expression of self-cathexis or grandiosity. In this argument,
attraction to a member of one's own sex is prima facie evidence of
narcissistic disturbance.

   Clinical technique has been influenced by this conceptualization
as well. Anna Freud (1954) modified the ground rules of treatment
with some of her homosexual patients to include a prohibition against
romantic/sexual contact with other men while the analysis pro-
ceeded. This intervention was primarily designed to frustrate narcissistic resistances, which she believed could be bolstered through such
contacts. With most patients deemed as suffering from narcissistic
disturbances, standard, if not classically pure, technique has generally
involved the frustration of "grandiose" strivings in an effort to redirect
libidinal energy from the self to external objects.

Kohut and Mr. Z.

It was in this milieu of thinking about narcissism and homosexuality
that Kohut (1979) found himself when he began his first analysis with
Mr. Z., a man who might be described as homosexual if this term is
defined by fantasy and affectional orientation (as Isay does in the
preceding chapter) and not limited to sexual behavior. Although
Kohut initially believed this to be a successful analysis, albeit one
characterized by his countertransferential frustration with his patient's feelings of entitlement and need for affirmation, his assessment
of this first treatment following Mr. Z.'s second analysis some years
later was very different.

   By the inception of Mr. Z.'s second analysis, Kohut had moved
from the classical position on narcissism (i.e., an aberrant state of
development) to understanding it as an integral part of normative

development. He had also moved from pejoratively conceptualizing narcissistic manifestations as nontransference reactions and had begun to understand them as intense transference manifestations communicating a hunger and yearning for empathic acceptance, approval, affirmation, and valuation absent from the patient's earliest interactions with primary caregivers. From this understanding, he had elucidated conceptualizations of the mirroring, idealizing, and twin-ship/alterego selfobject transferences. He had also identified the cor-ollary emotional state of shame as the reverse side of the grandiose behavior of some patients, and the universality of shame as a response to sustained and traumatic injuries of the individual's self-esteem. It is a testament to his courage that Kohut recognized in his second analysis of Mr. Z. that his classical approach in the first analysis had inflicted many narcissistic injuries and that the intensification of many of Mr. Z.'s demands for acceptance and unequivocal approval were probably iatrogenic in nature, the result of technical errors.

Kohut's work with Mr. Z. illuminated important considerations regarding psychoanalysis and psychoanalytic psychotherapy that have been refined and elaborated with the maturation of self psychology. The concept of narcissism has been elaborated to more broadly reflect the nature of the individual's capacity to affirm, value, comfort, and soothe the self (i.e., to modulate anxiety and maintain a functional level of self-esteem) both routinely and in times of unusual or dramatic stress.

Development of Self-Esteem and Its Deficits

A cohesive identity and the capacity to maintain a functional level of self-esteem are originally acquired through interactions with parents and other significant caregivers. If these persons are reliably empathic, they function as affirming selfobjects for the child. Through their function as mirroring selfobjects, they stimulate the child's sense of pride, assertiveness, and grandiosity so that mature confidence is possible. They aid the child in developing the ability to modulate and manage anxiety by allowing him to merge with their strength and calmness through idealization. They also aid the child in developing a

sense of connection to the rest of humanity and a social sensitivity
through their twinship functions. Development of these spheres of the
self forms the foundation of the child's identity.

The developing child's identity is also shaped by the internalization of characteristic patterns of interaction with parents; these
internalized patterns form the basic context of his belief as to what
should constitute the nature of his interpersonal interactions (i.e., the
ways others should treat him throughout life). Patterns internalized
from interactions with unempathic parents lead to development of an
expectation of unempathic responses as a given in life or as what is
due. Later, intimate relationships then take on similar unempathic,
even narcissistically injurious, characteristics (cf. Kernberg's [1980]
view of this phenomenon from an object relations perspective).

It is the caregivers' inability, due to their own self-deficits, to
reliably offer empathic contact in one or more of these spheres of the
self that yields deficits in the child's ability to soothe himself and/or
make use of selfobjects in later life during times when the equilibrium
of his self-esteem is threatened (Kohut 1977, Rowe and Mac Isaac
1989, Wolf 1988). However, self psychology also proposes that the
individual never fully gives up hope that he is entitled to more
satisfying, reciprocal relationships. This hope may move underground
and out of awareness, but later forms the basis for a "curative fantasy,"
which sustains the patient as he begins the process of psychotherapy
(Ornstein 1988).

Throughout life, the individual routinely makes use of selfobjects
to maintain self-esteem and does so more intensively during periods of
increased stress. Self psychology is interpersonal in its emphasis on the
individual as inseparable from his selfobject matrix (Wolf 1988), an
idea congenial to both the American object relations and interpersonal traditions (e.g., Imber 1984, Jacobson 1975).

The Importance of Self-Esteem in Thinking about the Gay Man

Self psychology's emphasis on identity cohesion and self-esteem is
helpful in understanding gay men. No other group faces as many

assaults on its collective self-esteem as do gay men. Alienation from selfobjects, and ultimately the self, is often a part of the homosexual boy's world from his earliest years (Green 1987, Isay 1989).

A number of theorists (e.g., Friedman 1991, Green 1987, Isay 1989, Leavy 1986) propose that homosexuality is constitutional in origin. This is not a view wholly supported by the American Psychoanalytic Association, which finds the constitutional argument unconvincing (Moore and Fine 1990). However, most gay men report being unable to remember a time that they did not experience themselves as somehow different from other boys, even if this difference is only later identified as homosexuality. This suggests that whether or not a hormonal, genetic, or other physiological component can be isolated to account for homosexuality, this orientation is experienced as inborn by the gay man. The controversy as to whether or not homosexuality is constitutional in nature is obviated by this experience, because the subjective world of the person is the field of interest. Any alternate explanatory model (e.g., scientific Reality) is secondary to the person's experienced reality.

The sense of being different as a child, which adult gay men articulate as their homosexuality, is also detected by others in their selfobject matrices during development. Fathers seem to sense homosexuality in their sons, perhaps even in their earliest interactions. They certainly seem to sense it when the boy reaches the age range of 3 to 6 (Isay 1989).

Isay (1989) proposes that in this age range an erotic orientation toward the father develops, as an erotic orientation toward the mother develops in heterosexual boys. He suggests that they may adopt nonconforming masculine gender attributes to interest the father. These attributes include ". . . gentleness, sensitivity, and a lack of interest in aggressive sports" (p. 19).

> I believe that they develop these characteristics for the same reason that heterosexual boys develop certain of their *father's* attributes — in order to attract first the mother's interest and then someone like the mother. These identifications in homosexual children appear to follow the

manifestation of the sexual orientation and the erotic attachment to the father and not to precede them. [p. 19]

The homosexual boy's peers and other adult males in his life also detect this gender nonconformity (Friedman 1991, Green 1987). Not invariably, but overwhelmingly, this nonconformity meets first with fear (often not easily articulated) and then derision, contempt, devaluation, and rejection from the father and other males. Friedman (1990) also notes the higher probability that homosexual boys will be abused as a result of gender nonconformity. When rejection by the father occurs, it may be either subtle or overtly cruel. However manifested, this rejection represents a traumatic (and generally sustained) insult to the boy's self-esteem and self-cohesion.

For the homosexual boy, gender nonconformity does not represent a rejection of being male, and, from the perspective of self psychology, rejection by the father, male peers, and the larger patriarchal culture can create particular vulnerability in the twinship sphere of the self (Cornett 1990). As the boy yearns for the twinship selfobject experience of sharing masculinity with his father (i.e., being a male among males), his sense of rejection, disappointment, and alienation intensifies with an increasing sense of his father's lack of connection.

It is important to note that while this perspective concerns the relationship between the boy and his father (superficially resembling the distant father of traditional psychoanalytic theories), it begins with the assumption that homosexuality is a constitutional first fact. Rather than the father's rejection of the boy "causing" homosexuality, it is the fundamental, albeit not necessarily conscious, awareness of the boy's homosexuality by his father that leads to the rejection. There is no support in this position for the argument that homosexuality is the result of flawed heterosexual development. Rather, the pain that brings many gay men to psychotherapy can be more accurately described as an artifact of normative homosexual development in a primarily heterosexual culture.

Rejection by the father is echoed by practically every other system and symbol in our society to which the boy could look for feelings of similarity (twinship), strength (idealization), and affirmation (mirroring). The selfobject experiences available to heterosexual boys, if not from their fathers then through institutions and systems, are unavailable to the homosexual boy. There are no institutions in this culture that celebrate homosexual masculinity. Heterosexuality is the most basic assumption of the systems with which the boy comes into contact, and a sense of alienation is inescapable. Miller (1981) proposes that our culture is becoming increasingly narcissistically depriving for everyone. This, however, has always been and continues to be true for the homosexual boy.

As an adult, the gay man continues to face denigration and devaluation religiously, legally, medically, politically, socially, and economically. The devaluation that gay men experience has been heightened by the advent of AIDS. Known originally as GRID (Gay Related Immune Deficiency), this disease has often been equated as synonymous with male homosexuality and has been used as an explanatory argument in the continuing societal rejection of gay men.

The natural cumulative result of the massive devaluation and rejection most gay men experience throughout their development is shame and self-alienation. A yearning for consolidating and affirming selfobject relationships (which has often resulted in disappointment and rejection in the past) encompasses the basic complaint that brings most gay men to psychotherapy.

The insights of self psychology can be especially useful in clinical work with the gay man. The emphasis placed on ameliorating shame and facilitating the development of functional and durable self-esteem and self-cohesion is particularly applicable to the difficulties many gay men present to the psychotherapist.

PSYCHOTHERAPY: AFFIRMING THE SELF

Overview

Prior to discussing psychotherapeutic technique, it will be important to address one question that may legitimately arise for some readers.

This question could simply be asked: Is not the technical stance of the self psychologically oriented psychotherapist the same regardless of the sexual orientation of the patient? The answer to this, in the main, is yes. Self psychology is not a patient population specific model. If it were, its usefulness generally would be diminished. However, I have chosen to emphasize certain of its technical qualities that are especially important in clinical work with gay men. There are self psychologists (e.g., Chernus 1992) who believe my technical emphases to be more existential than self psychological. Since I do not make a sharp distinction between an existential versus a self psychological stance, it will be up to the reader to decide if emphasis becomes exaggeration. I have also specifically noted why I assert that a specific point is important for work with gay men and where self psychology, existentially oriented or not, may lend itself more readily to the concerns of gay men.

For self psychology, one of the primary goals of psychotherapy involves the creation of an environment that can rekindle the hope for growth and then nurture it. In this environment, the therapist serves as both a reliably empathic selfobject and a participant observer of the therapeutic process. The therapist as a reliable, albeit imperfect, empathic selfobject provides a milieu that aids the patient in experiencing a recrudescence of his developmental needs for mirroring, idealization, and/or twinship. As these needs arise during psychotherapy, however, they are met by sensitivity and empathy that affirm the patient's self and rekindle hope—often dormant since earliest childhood—that the patient is worthy of reciprocal, empathic, and affirming relationships. The internalization of this relationship pattern with the therapist leads to a replication of this pattern with selfobjects outside the therapist's office. Through the experience of therapy, the patient essentially learns to value himself, to feel deserving of relationships that value him, and to slowly discard the previous recurrent, interpersonal patterns driven by self-deficits (Cornett 1992a).

Chapter 5 deals extensively with a resistance that frequently occurs in the psychotherapy of gay men: the fear of hope. Because Chapter 5 deals extensively with this issue, the discussion on technique that follows will touch only peripherally on this area. There is a danger of oversimplification and reductionism when resistance is not considered; however, for clarity I have chosen to separate an examination of resistance from a discussion of technique more generally. I do this with the acknowledgment that resistance is an integral part of the psychotherapy that must effectively be addressed for the patient to receive the most available from the treatment.

"Technique": The Empathic Milieu

Clinical technique and the curative functions of self psychology unfold along three primary avenues: creation of an empathic ambiance, amplification of expressions of the self, and transmuting internalization. As was alluded to above, the primary "technique" (a term Rowe and Mac Isaac [1988] subtly suggest may have only marginal application for self psychology) is the therapist's assumption of an empathic stance vis-à-vis the patient. Such a stance is created through the internal processes of the therapist coming to life in verbal responses to the patient, but also through the overall ambiance created by the therapist in interaction with the patient.

There has been much written concerning the optimal setting for psychotherapy. Langs (1973, 1982) has been a prolific writer in this area. Others (e.g., Hollender and Ford 1990) have also presented schemas for understanding the setting of psychotherapy, including such basic issues as how the furniture should be arranged. Langs (Langs and Stone 1980) proposes that empirical clinical evidence dictates that a specific type of universally applicable setting is necessary for successful analytic work to unfold. Stone (Langs and Stone 1980) argues that a universally applicable setting exists only theoretically and, even then, is subject to the idiosyncrasies of the individual conceptualizing it (which, of course, negates its universality).

Self psychology maintains a more relaxed attitude toward the basic setting of psychotherapy. There is a single goal to the setting, and that is to create an environment that facilitates empathic understanding by the therapist. There is no preset formula for creating such an environment. Indeed, Wolf (1988) proposes that

> Patients know that their analysts are human beings with idiosyncratic interests. Trying to pretend otherwise is bound to fail sooner or later. But, worse, attempting to be someone other than oneself contradicts the whole spirit of the analytic endeavor, which, I believe, is to acknowledge and strengthen the self and its expression. [p. 88]

He goes on to propose that the primary function of the setting of treatment is to communicate the analyst's ". . . availability as a potential carrier for the selfobject function without forcing himself or herself upon the analysand" (p. 88).

Within the empathic setting created by the therapist and patient, the patient allows the therapist to hear his story. He reveals his hopes, wishes, dreams, and disappointments. As the therapist responds empathically, a yearning for selfobject nurturance (i.e., transference) is allowed to emerge in the patient. Transference manifestations may be in the mirroring, idealizing, and/or twinship spheres; one may emerge as the primary transference theme in the psychotherapy, or a combination of the three may alternate in intensity at different points. Singly, or in combination, these transference manifestations give voice to a hunger for that which is lacking in the self.

This understanding of transference is in contrast to the more classical position that transference manifestations represent complex displacements and/or projections. Transference in the classical model has emphasized distortion of the relationship between therapist and patient. The heart of traditional analytic technique has been delineation, exploration, and, ultimately, interpretation of the complex system of displacements and projections that coalesce around a central, primarily oedipal, theme coloring the patient's relationships. With the interpretation of these distortions in the therapeutic relationship, the patient understands the previously unconscious expectations that he carries into relationships. This interpretation and understanding ultimately break the compulsion to repeat unsatisfying relationship patterns based on unresolved oedipal yearnings and defenses against those yearnings. Although generally less concerned with the vicissitudes of oedipal strivings than object relations, Strupp and Binder (1984) capture the traditional view of transference: ". . . [Transference] is based on rigid proclivities to interpret events in a certain way without the flexibility to consider alternatives" (p. 137). Transference interpretation offers the patient an opportunity to consider alternatives, or as Reik (1948) proposes, to show the power of ". . . fantasy working in broad daylight" (p. 111).

For self psychology, transference is seen as having a richer content than that afforded by the classical conceptualization. Without discarding the idea that displacements and projections are involved in transference, self psychology challenges the idea that the primary content of transference is embodied in these mechanisms. It also calls into question the proposition that transference represents a distortion of the relationship between therapist and patient. Rather, transference phenomena are seen as adaptive attempts to solidify the self, to complete the self by filling deficits (Tolpin 1985). As viewed from this perspective, transference is a re-creation of past interpersonal patterns, but this re-creation has as its goal the acquisition of something previously missing from the self, rather than satisfaction of the compulsion to repeat.

Amplification over Interpretation

The implications of this view of transference for psychotherapy with gay men are important. Primarily, the idea of transference interpretation (i.e., focused on illuminating the distortions that the patient creates in the therapeutic relationship) as the central healing factor of treatment is questioned. Interpretation has been the technical activity by which analytic treatment endeavors have been defined and their success judged; the classical analyst has often fairly narrowly defined her or his role as that of interpreter (e.g., Moore and Fine 1990). From this perspective: "What the analyst communicates to the patient becomes a way for the patient to think about and define his inner experiences and comes to constitute the form his new self-knowledge will take" (Levy and Inderbitzin 1992, p. 101). An inherent danger in this view of interpretation is destructive heterosexualization. In working with gay men, the heterosexual (and often homosexual) therapist must continually struggle against the tendency to hetero-sexualize interpretations. The heterosexual foundation of our culture, whether subtly or blatantly expressed, is an undeniable part of any psychotherapy. Socarides (1992) gives voice to this phenomenon in more overt form:

> Scientists, psychologists, psychiatrists, political leaders, public officials and others with vested interests today ransack literature for bits of fact and theory which can be pieced together into a pro-homosexual or bisexual concept of nature, man and society. Some of the individuals say that homosexuals are healthy, society is sick and that science should cure society. Others raise false or outdated scientific issues in their war with *traditional values* (emphasis added). [p. 322]

Other analysts (e.g., Schoenewolf 1990, Strean 1984) are equally blatant in their position that a heterosexual orientation should be *the* orientation for everyone. Schoenewolf (1990) further proposes that psychoanalysts should be ". . . both medicine men and moral arbiters" (p. 221). Of course, such a stance places the therapist in the role of ensuring social conformity and compliance. This seems to be a partic-ular problem for therapists working with gay men (e.g., Davison 1976, Dulaney and Kelly 1982, Halleck 1971, Rochlin 1982) and sounds a cautionary note regarding the use of interpretation as it is traditionally defined as the preeminent tool of treatment with gay men.

Self psychology redefines interpretation as an *experience* rather than a therapist *activity* and relegates the importance of the act of interpretation to a lesser domain. It challenges the classical assump-tion that "All but the most disturbed patients need more to correct their distortions than they need a real object in the therapist" (Blanck and Blanck 1974, p. 187). Instead, Ornstein and Ornstein (1985) assert that the most important aspect of treatment ". . . is not what the analyst says, or thinks he says, but what the patient experiences in connection with what the analyst says" (p. 50). The experience of the treatment is thus raised to the level of greatest importance (Cornett 1992a). If that experience is empathic it is healing because it stands in stark contrast to the chronic unempathic responsiveness of caregivers (including for the gay man, social culture) that gave rise to the original self-deficits. Through the experience with the therapist, the patient internalizes the capacity to treat himself more empathically. Through utilization of the therapist as a selfobject who responds with more consistent empathy, the patient fills voids in the mirroring, idealizing, and/or twinship sphere(s) of the self. The development that was previously stunted in one or more of these spheres is, in this way, stimulated again. The patient also gains, through the experience with the therapist, familiarity with an empathic selfobject that offers a model for replication of this experience in the patient's life outside the therapist's office.

An important verbal aspect of the therapist's responsiveness as an empathic selfobject is the process of understanding and explaining (Ornstein and Ornstein 1985) or the empathic assignment of meaning (Tolpin 1985). These two conceptions of the therapist's verbal activities with a patient describe interactions that are superficially similar to, but fundamentally different from, interpretation in its traditional sense (Kohut 1984).

As it is classically conceived, interpretation brings about psychic change by bringing to the patient's awareness ". . . elements of psychic conflict that were formerly unconscious or known to the patient only in incomplete, inaccurate or otherwise distorted form" (Moore and Fine 1990, p. 103). Awareness and integration of this previously repressed material liberates the patient from its grasp. Freud (1913), however, cautioned that interpretations should not be offered to a patient ". . . until he has only one short step more to make in order to get hold of the explanation for himself" (p. 140).

The difficulty this position offers from a self psychological perspective, even given Freud's cautious approach, is that it holds out the therapist as expert on the psychic life of the patient, thus decreasing the patient's sense of his own expertise regarding himself (Cornett 1992b). It is important that the gay man, who has experienced dramatic external definition and moral judgment throughout his life, experience a sense of expertise about defining himself. External arbitration of the patient's reality (e.g., when, what, and how he learns about himself) does not serve to increase the cohesion and integrity of the self. Indeed, at some times it can serve as an iatrogenic injury to the self, experienced as blaming, rejection, or devaluation by the patient, re-creating past shameful experiences (Henry et al. 1990).

As it is conceptualized by self psychology, the process of understanding and explaining functions as an amplification of the patient's experience. It serves to identify, clarify, coalesce, and organize what the patient is communicating, rather than translating or externally defining deeper meanings in the communication (Kohut 1984). It may take a number of forms, including reconstruction, clarification, questioning, and confrontation.

This technical stance also focuses on self-esteem. Expressions of the patient's view of himself are amplified by the therapist. A gay man's statements are often critical, judgmental, and reflective of familial and cultural experience. Statements of his feelings, wishes, desires, and so on, are often negated by harsh self-criticisms. Commenting on these types of criticisms and judgments offers the patient an opportunity to explore their applicability and can gradually lead to the patient attempting to understand, rather than condemn, self-expressions. It should also be noted, however, that the therapist can and should, while amplifying these expressions, acknowledge the critical nature of them to the patient. This could be considered a form of confrontation, but the goal of such comments is not to stop the patient from discussing himself in these terms. Rather, the goal is to differentiate the therapist as selfobject from previous selfobjects whose expectations gave life to and then maintained expressions of self-criticism, self-loathing, and shame.

This type of empathic amplification of the patient's experience strengthens the integrity and cohesion of the self and encourages the patient to search for deeper awareness. Ornstein and Ornstein (1975) propose that the entire experience of treatment, if reliably empathic, fosters an interpretive attitude on the part of the patient. There are, of course, always interpretations made by the therapist in any psychotherapy, because the patient's communications are heard and organized by the therapist into a schema that is understandable for her or him. Such interpretations can serve an empathic function when shared with the patient if the patient's experience is the guide to their use.

Transmuting Internalization

Any unempathic response (if not traumatic or part of a chronic pattern by the therapist) can serve a healing function in that it promotes transmuting internalization. One of the more persistent, albeit inaccurate, criticisms of self psychology (e.g., Levine 1979) is that it is an overly gratifying system of treatment that does not provide for internal structural change in the patient (which I'm defining broadly and not in reference to the patient's sexual orientation). Inherent in this criticism is the notion that change should be a goal of psychotherapy. This is a particularly risky notion to bring to psychotherapy with gay men who have received the message that they should change throughout their lives. If a therapist brings the assumption to the therapy that change is the primary goal, she or he risks exerting a pressure, of which she or he may be unaware, that can reactivate old narcissistic wounds. One of the fundamental challenges that self psychology offers for dynamic psychotherapy is to question this notion that change is the primary goal. Psychotherapy can result in change, although this is a secondary goal to creating an experience of empathic contact for the patient, whether or not change takes place. Obviously, however, some form of change or growth often does take place because the experience of contact with an empathic selfobject allows the self to grow beyond previous deficit-based constraints. In addition, self psychology proposes that growth can occur through imperfect empathic responsiveness by the therapist, which results in transmuting internalization, the exercise of the patient's developing or expanding capacity to soothe and comfort the self.

Transmuting internalization, like most tenets of self psychological technique, is based on the analogy of the optimal development of
a child in responsive, empathic selfobject milieu. If the child's caregivers are predominantly reliably empathic, the child develops the
capacity to retrieve cognitive and affective memories of empathic
interactions when the caregivers lapse in responsiveness. The child
learns that the world is imperfect in its empathy, and gradually he
refines the capacity to soothe and comfort himself based on internal
models of interaction with the generally empathic selfobject(s). In this
area there are obvious parallels to Winnicott's conceptions of transitional phenomena as facilitating structural development (Bacal 1989).

Effective psychotherapy follows the same developmental line.
Psychotherapists, no matter how skillful or empathically attuned, are
imperfect. If the therapist is generally reliably empathic, however, the
patient makes use of empathic lapses (i.e., provided that they are not
massively traumatic) to develop the capacity to comfort himself.
Growth resulting from this process shows durability after treatment
ceases.

With the gay man this phenomenon takes on a special importance. The total selfobject milieu in which the gay man developed was
generally reliably unempathic. As a result, empathic resonance and
responsiveness by the therapist are of particular importance. Paradoxically, when the therapist responds empathically, the patient often
negates the genuineness of the interaction. Empathic lapses are con-
strued as the real constitution of the therapeutic relationship. This is
one expression of resistance as a fear of hope which will be subsequently discussed in more detail. Such expressions, however, are
based on actions by the therapist that are, at least in part, unempathic
in nature. Under these circumstances, transmuting internalization is
facilitated by the therapist taking note of such moments of lapse and
acknowledging them apologetically, even if they do not constitute
errors in the strictest sense.

Apologies and countertransference disclosure are also controversial areas (e.g., Burke and Tansey [1991] caution careful exploration of
apologies and other moments of countertransference disclosure), but

are crucial to successful psychotherapy with gay men. The shame that gay patients feel is often manifested in accepting responsibility for painful experiences that are externally prompted. An empathic lapse by the therapist often becomes a source of self-criticism for the patient. At these times it is helpful for the therapist to note the patient's self-criticism and, if it follows a remark or intervention by the therapist, to explore the interaction for empathic disjunction. If there has indeed been an empathic lapse, an apology from the therapist can be therapeutic.

Some analysts are concerned that apologetic interactions between therapist and patient give action to masochistic countertransference. There are masochistic elements to any apology, but an apology is also an empathic act. It acknowledges both the impact that one's behavior has on the patient and the fact that the therapist has no need to foster a grandiose image of perfection. It is also a manner of displaying respect, which offers the patient a view of the therapist as one who is respectful of others because he holds her/himself in respect (Strupp and Binder 1984). This small act is often powerfully therapeutic because it stands in antithetical contrast to the gay patient's experiential history with both his parents and the larger culture.

Internalization of these interactions can lead to significant internal structural expansion and cohesion. It often leads to increased assertiveness and a sense of the self as valuable and worthy of respect. Further, with this gradual development of a sense of self-value, the therapist's empathy comes to be experienced as equally genuine to moments of disjunction. This development then represents the increased capacity to experience love, respect, and valuation in relationships generally as genuine and natural.

MICAH

Although it is never possible to capture the nuances of psychotherapy in a clinical presentation, general themes are discernible. The following vignette of a young gay man is offered to illustrate theoretical material in a clinical situation.

Micah: I know this sounds crazy, but I'm not really sure why I'm here. I mean things are pretty good in my life. I have a lover and it's a really good relationship. But sometimes I just get down. I can't really explain it and it sounds kind of stupid. I go through these periods when I just feel kind of, you know, blue. I guess it's called depression. I know that sounds crazy and kind of stupid, but at those times I really feel sad.

Therapist: Uh, huh. Sometimes you feel sad, even though you're not sure what that's about. This kind of sadness seems crazy.

Micah: Yeah, but it's more than that, and this is the *really* crazy part; sometimes I feel really angry and I don't know why. Little things like driving or something that Bill [the patient's lover] does that doesn't amount to anything, they can make me really angry. I slam doors, I hit things, I've even wanted to hit Bill. I know that probably sounds bad. I tell myself a lot that what I'm feeling is really very dumb. Do you think it's dumb?

Therapist: Do I think it's wrong or dumb to feel angry sometimes?

Micah: No, to be angry without really knowing why. I guess I just feel angry sometimes and I don't know why and it makes me feel out of control.

So began the first session with Micah, a 26-year-old gay man. The therapist had invited Micah to talk about the difficulties that brought him into therapy. What ensued did indeed offer a great deal of information about the difficulties prompting Micah's appointment. The therapist took note of the fact that Micah disparaged himself throughout his discussion of how he felt. It was obvious that he had a great deal of difficulty in allowing himself to talk about his feelings without simultaneously judging those feelings. Subsequent sessions followed this pattern. Micah became more aggressive with his judgments toward himself, and the therapist intervened by calling his attention to this in the fourth session.

Therapist: You know, Micah, I've noticed, and I wonder if you've noticed, that you often follow descriptions of how you think or feel by statements with words like "dumb," "crazy," and "wrong,"

Micah: Well, they are all those things. Sometimes it is dumb to feel the way I feel.

Therapist: Is it?

Micah: Yeah, don't you think so? Don't you think sometimes it's wrong or stupid to feel angry and not even know why, or to feel depressed and not know why? After all, I have a good relationship and a good job. I'm not living out on the street. I have a lot of friends. It seems like I ought to be happy with my life and not bitching about it.

Therapist: You seem to feel not entitled to be angry, like you're imposing by talking about being angry. I'm not aware that I've heard you "bitching" about anything. I've heard you talking about how you feel about things. It also seems that when you feel strongly about something, you tend to judge it and call it "stupid."

Micah: Well, sometimes things are just stupid. Especially the way I feel.

The next several sessions went along in a similar fashion. Micah would talk about something of obvious importance to him and disparage and devalue his feelings about it. The therapist would respond empathically, attempting to understand Micah's feelings and sense of himself but also noting the harsh judgments that were often applied to these feelings. Micah was initially very reticent in accepting the therapist's observation that he was harshly critical of himself.

In this initial period of the therapy, the therapist and Micah began looking at Micah's harshly critical perspective toward himself. It could be argued that the therapist may have cut off exploration of some areas by introducing the idea so early that Micah was being critical of himself. However, it is often more helpful to begin early in the therapy to note the ways that the patient experiences and treats himself. This is not an attempt to cut off those experiences, but to amplify his descriptions of them. This approach also offers the patient the possibility that the therapist may be a different kind of selfobject in his life. The therapist may be interested in hearing the patient's feelings without judging them (for a gay man, sharing feelings and having those feelings judged are often inseparable phenomena).

Over the course of the next several weeks, Micah detailed a relationship with his lover, Bill, which was very conflictual. Although he maintained that this relationship was "very good" he often described instances in which his needs went unmet in the relationship. He found himself unsatisfied sexually and often experienced Bill as financially taking advantage of him. Micah made a substantial salary as an engineer and often reported that Bill, who was two years younger than he, would expect him to pay for all of the couple's expenses and activities. During sex, Micah played the role of satisfying Bill. Sometimes this was satisfying for Micah, but more often it left him feeling vaguely frustrated and longing for some reciprocity within the relationship. In the fifth month of therapy the following exchange took place.

> *Micah:* I think Bill is a wonderful man and we have a wonderful relationship.
>
> *Therapist:* Uh, huh.
>
> *Micah:* But sometimes, I get tired of having to pay for everything. Sometimes I'd like him to pull out his wallet when we're at a restaurant or grocery shopping. Sometimes I'd like him to volunteer to pay an extra bill. Sometimes I'd like for him to buy me a little gift for no reason.
>
> *Therapist:* Like you do for him?
>
> *Micah:* Yeah. I don't really get any presents. It would be nice occasionally just to come home and find a little card or a box of candy or something.

Therapist: Bill doesn't respond to you financially in the way you'd like him to. You'd like it if he would be more willing to pay some and also if he'd surprise you occasionally by spending some time thinking about a gift for you and then surprise you.

Micah: Yeah. Don't get me wrong. Bill's a great guy. It's just sometimes he isn't as thoughtful as I'd like him to be. I don't ask for a whole lot. I just want him to do some of the things for me that I do for him.

Therapist: You know, you've described Bill over the last couple of months and he sounds like a guy that you genuinely love and like in many ways. He sounds like a man who has a lot of qualities you respect. But it also sounds like there are a lot of times when you would like for Bill to be more reciprocal in the relationship that the two of you have. It sounds like sometimes you'd like for him to maybe put his needs in second place to yours. And this may be a bit of a stretch, because you haven't said this, as such, but maybe sometimes it feels like Bill is somewhat exploitative of you, both financially and sexually.

Micah: I'm not sure I've ever really thought about it just like that. But sometimes it does feel like he takes me for granted and believes that I owe him money and sex. And I don't really get the feeling that he feels like he owes me the same consideration in return.

Therapist: It maybe makes sense then, doesn't it, that you find yourself angry with Bill sometimes?

Micah: Yeah, I guess it does. I guess I'm having a hard time, though, accepting the idea that it's OK to be angry with Bill because he is so wonderful in other ways.

In this interaction, Micah began to describe an awareness that his current relationship was neither fully reciprocal nor satisfying. He began to express a yearning for affirmation from his lover. From this early material it appeared to the therapist that Micah could be yearning for mirroring ("show me I'm important to you by reciprocating") and/or idealizing ("let me rely on you some") selfobject responses. The therapist's responses offered Micah a space where he could feel (and even talk about) his yearnings without attack, censure, or arbitration. He could begin to experience himself.

Micah's therapy continued to unfold as he talked about his development and his relationship with his parents. He described both his parents as emotionally unavailable to him unless they needed something from him. However, each description of his parents was followed by a reminder to himself that "that's just the way they are and I need to accept it." He gave no real indication that he would allow himself to *feel* what he was feeling before demanding that it be accepted.

His relationship with his father was especially difficult for Micah to discuss. He presented his father as a man who took no pride in his son's activities. Micah was seen as being a sissy and "one of the girls." Much of Micah's shame could be easily understood in light of the father's devaluations. His father had great difficulty in responding to Micah empathically. Micah presented a number of instances in the therapy in which he had approached his father with an accomplishment and a sense of pride only to be told that it was "not good enough." It was clear that after enough such interactions he stopped feeling pride. He also talked about instances in which he had gone to his father terrified, seeking reassurance. At these times his father would say to him, "There's all sorts of people who have it lots worse than you do right now." The times that he had sought reassurance, affirmation, and strength, especially from his father, he had been rejected and his feelings devalued. As a result of this, he also learned to devalue himself and disparage his feelings.

Micah also learned another important lesson from the unempathic interactions with his father. He learned that times of success and pride (self-esteem) were times to be denigrated. This was a lesson that he carried throughout his life, and he found himself most depressed during times when he was achieving some kind of success.

The evidence that his father sensed his homosexuality ("sissy," "one of the girls") made sense to Micah as exploration of the family dynamics progressed. The father's inability to mirror Micah's accomplishments or allow him to merge through idealization began to become emotionally understandable in this light as the father's limitations rather than Micah's. Similarly, his father's rejection of his twinship stirrings became clearer. This particular area became an important one transferentially.

Micah became very curious about the therapist, whom he knew to be gay. Often he compared his thoughts, feelings, wishes, and so on, with those of the therapist. The therapist generally affirmed these comparisons by listening and striving to understand them (rather than disavowing or rejecting them as the father had done). On occasion he would also confirm Micah's perceptions of him, directly or indirectly. Small acts of therapist self-disclosure, provided they do not overwhelm the therapy, can be powerfully therapeutic for deficits in the twinship sphere, and especially so for gay patients working with gay psychotherapists (Cornett 1990).

It could be argued that mirroring transferences are endemic to self psychologically oriented psychotherapy because the therapist's empathic availability stimulates the patient's pride and invites more assertive communication of his unique wants, as well as his accomplishments. For Micah this was the case. The therapist's simple availability to resonate to Micah's internal world led to an increase in Micah's desire to talk about his accomplishments and a decrease in his shame about this.

In the ninth month of therapy, the twinship and mirroring spheres began to show new vigor and to assert themselves in anger toward intolerance. This also offered Micah the opportunity to challenge his shame regarding his homosexuality. Micah had previously presented his homosexuality derogatorily as "just the way it is, there's nothing I can do about it." However, he arrived for one session enraged after seeing a television news special that focused on the controversy surrounding the Boy Scouts' rejecting gay men as scoutmasters.

Micah: It just made me so mad to see them talk that way. Hypocrites. I used to be a Scout and lots of the leaders were gay. It just infuriates me that they could sit and look down on good people who have something to offer. Who do they think they are kidding? Who do they think they are hurting? It's the kids. It's always the kids who get hurt. Gay men have a lot to offer. Why does who we sleep with have to have anything to do with how we function in the rest of our lives?

Therapist: Does it have anything to do with how we function in the rest of our lives?

Micah: What do you mean? What are you talking about?

Therapist: Well, you sound like you're really mad about the fact that the Boy Scouts are discriminating against gay men.

Micah: Yeah?

Therapist: You also seem to be demanding to know if your sexuality has anything to do with how you are as a person in other areas of your life. And it seems like the demand is mostly to know for yourself.

Micah: You mean, I'm wanting to know whether or not I believe that I'm inferior?

Therapist: Well, that's a little stronger than I was trying to say it, but if that's your experience it certainly fits. I think my observation was that you seem to be really angry about the behavior of the scouting administration and wondering whether or not it's valid.

Micah: [after appearing thoughtful for a moment] Yeah, I guess I'm wondering if part of the way the Scouts are behaving is sort of the way we've talked about my doing myself so much.

Therapist: You mean the devaluation?

Micah: Yeah. It seems like I'm really mad about the way the Scouts are doing, but I've had a hard time accepting myself being gay, too.

Therapist: Maybe now what you're describing is a sense of pride in being gay and some anger that others would treat you and other gay men in the way your father did.

Micah: Maybe I'm beginning to feel good about myself as a gay man, but now sort of looking for my father in everybody else.

Therapist: This is another event in your life that is a source of pride and you're expecting some devaluation for it.

Micah: Yeah, that's what I was talking about.

In this exchange, the patient moved through a sequence of self-experiences. First, he was angry about the discriminatory policy assumed by the Boy Scouts of America regarding gay men as scout-masters. This led to exploration of the possibility that one of the frustrating things about the position that the Scouts had taken was that it reflected some of the ways his father, and subsequently he, had treated himself. Next, it led to looking at the possibility that he might be experiencing some pride in being gay and that his feelings of anger might be an expression of this pride. Self psychology, rather than seeing anger as a vicissitude of aggression, proposes that anger is often an assertive demonstration of the self. It is a self-state that signifies, albeit sometimes in indirect fashion, a striving or belief in juxtaposition to other strivings or beliefs. In his anger about the discrimination of the Boy Scouts, Micah asserted his ability to now see himself as a gay man among gay men. The twinship selfobject yearnings that had gone unsatisfied with his father were fulfilled in the relationship with the therapist, and Micah could now see himself as belonging to a group of men similar to himself. The twinship selfobject experience with the therapist, to whom he felt similar, expanded to include gay men in general.

Micah's psychotherapy extended over a two-year period. In the course of the two years, his relationship with Bill gradually became more distant and Bill eventually moved in with another man. By this point, however, Micah was ready for the relationship to take a different course. He found himself involved with another man who was more sensitive and compassionate toward him. He spent some months wondering about the genuineness of this man who found him enjoyable and valuable; however, by the end of his therapy he was able to genuinely believe that he had found someone who appreciated him and that this was deserved appreciation.

When Micah terminated his therapy he was settled into a reciprocal and affectionate relationship. He reported greater comfort with himself, and his closing therapy hours were less dominated by his critical self-attacks. He talked of hope and made plans for the future. His termination, as are most terminations, was tentative, and he related that there might be a time when he would return, but that he felt confident enough to leave the therapy with the gains he had made.

CONCLUSION

Self psychology is a dynamic model with wide application. It would be anathema to the spirit of the model to suggest that it is only or always applicable to any particular patient group. It is, above all, a way of viewing the therapeutic process that acknowledges and even cele-brates the uniqueness that each patient brings to the therapeutic encounter. It places the empathic vantage above all others, which makes it enamored of individual differences and intolerant of formula-driven conceptions of the human being. It is a way of thinking about psychotherapy rather than a specific set of techniques.

Self psychology, however, like any theoretical model, has some basic tenets that make it unique from other dynamic models. But it is still in its relative infancy as a theoretical model in the dynamic family. It is still encountering and expanding the parameters of its applicabil-ity. With its emphasis on self-esteem enhancement and cohesive identity development, this way of thinking can be particularly useful in psychotherapy with gay men.

Kohut (1971) noted that "the reliability of our empathy . . .

declines the more dissimilar the observed is to the observer . . ." (p. 37). The goal of this chapter has been to highlight the aspects of self psychology that hold special promise for understanding gay men, and to bring the observed into closer proximity and, therefore, closer similarity to the observer. From this proximal vantage point, dynamic psychotherapy with a gay man becomes, first, more helpful to the patient but, not inconsequentially, also more rewarding for the therapist.

REFERENCES

Bacal, H. (1989). Winnicott and self psychology: remarkable reflections. In *Self Psychology: Comparisons and Contrasts*, ed. D. Detrick and S. Detrick, pp. 259–271. Hillsdale, NJ: Analytic Press.

Bieber, I., Dain, H., Dince, P., et al. (1962). *Homosexuality: A Psychoanalytic Study*. New York: Basic Books.

Blanck, G., and Blanck, R. (1974). *Ego Psychology: Theory and Practice*. New York: Columbia University Press.

Burke, W., and Tansey, M. (1991). Countertransference disclosure and models of therapeutic action. *Contemporary Psychoanalysis* 27:351–384.

Chernus, L. (1992). The "corrective emotional experience" revisited: response of an "orthodox" self psychologist. *Clinical Social Work Journal* 20:225–228.

Cornett, C. (1990). The "risky" intervention: twinship selfobject impasses and therapist self-disclosure in psychodynamic psychotherapy. *Clinical Social Work Journal* 19:49–61.

_____ (1992a). Beyond words: a conception of self psychology. *Clinical Social Work Journal* 20:337–341.

_____ (1992b). Intimations and echoes of the divine: self psychology, existentialism, and psychotherapy with the gay man in the AIDS era. Paper presented at the sixth clinical conference of the Institute for Human Identity, New York City, February.

Davison, G. (1976). Homosexuality: the ethical challenge. *Journal of Consulting and Clinical Psychology* 44:157–1 6 2 .

Dulaney, D., and Kelly, J. (1982). Improving services to gay and lesbian clients. *Social Work* 27:178–183.

Ferguson, M. (1989). City of night: a self psychological perspective on male homosexuality. *Journal of Gay and Lesbian Psychotherapy* 1:47–61.

Freud, A. (1954). Problems of technique in adult analysis. *Bulletin of the Philadelphia Association for Psychoanalysis* 4:44–70.

Freud, S. (1913). On beginning the treatment. *Standard Edition* 12:123–144.

_____ (1914). On narcissism: an introduction. *Standard Edition* 14:67–102.

_____ (1924a). Neurosis and psychosis. *Standard Edition* 19:147–153.

_____ (1924b). The loss of reality in neurosis and psychosis. *Standard Edition* 19:181–187.

Friedman, R. (1990). Book review of the *Psychoanalytic Theory of Male Homosexuality* by Kenneth Lewes. *Archives of Sexual Behavior* 19:293–301.

_____ (1991). Contemporary psychoanalysis and homosexuality. *Experimental and Clinical Endocrinology* 98:155–161.

Green, R. (1987). *The "Sissy Boy Syndrome" and the Development of Homosexuality.* New Haven, CT: Yale University Press.

Halleck, S. (1971). *The Politics of Therapy.* New York: Science House.

Henry, W., Schacht, T., and Strupp, H. (1990). Patient and therapist introject, interpersonal process, and differential psychotherapy outcome. *Journal of Consulting and Clinical Psychology* 58:504–511.

Hollender, M., and Ford, C. (1990). *Dynamic Psychotherapy: An Introductory Approach.* Washington, DC: American Psychiatric Press.

Imber, R. (1984). Reflections on Kohut and Sullivan. *Contemporary Psychoanalysis* 20:363–380.

Isay, R. (1989). *Being Homosexual: Gay Men and Their Development.* New York: Farrar, Straus, & Giroux.

Jacobson, E. (1975). The regulation of self-esteem. In *Depression and Human Existence*, ed. J. Anthony and T. Benedek, pp. 169–181. Boston: Little, Brown.

Kernberg, O. (1980). Some implications of object relations theory for psychoanalytic technique. In *Psychoanalytic Explorations of Tech-*

nique, ed. H. Blum, pp. 207–239. New York: International Universities Press.

Kohut, H. (1971). *The Analysis of the Self.* New York: International Universities Press.

––––– (1977). *The Restoration of the Self.* New York: International Universities Press.

––––– (1979). The two analyses of Mr. Z. *International Journal of Psycho-Analysis* 60:3–18.

––––– (1984). *How Does Analysis Cure?* Ed. A. Goldberg and P. Stepansky. Chicago: University of Chicago Press.

Langs, R. (1973). *The Technique of Psychoanalytic Psychotherapy.* Vol. 1. New York: Jason Aronson.

––––– (1982). *Psychotherapy: A Basic Text.* New York: Jason Aronson.

Langs, R. and Stone, L. (1980). *The Therapeutic Experience and Its Setting.* New York: Jason Aronson.

Leavy, S. (1986). Male homosexuality reconsidered. *International Journal of Psychoanalytic Psychotherapy* 11:155–174.

Levine, F. (1979). On the clinical application of Kohut's psychology of the self: comments on some recently published case studies. *Journal of the American Psychoanalytic Association* 6:1–19.

Levy, S., and Inderbitzin, L. (1992). Interpretation. In *The Technique and Practice of Psychoanalysis*, vol. 2, ed. A. Sugarman, R. Nemiroff, and D. Greenson, pp. 101–115. New York: International Universities Press.

London, N. (1985). An appraisal of self psychology. *International Journal of Psycho-Analysis* 66:95–107.

Miller, A. (1981). *The Drama of the Gifted Child.* New York: Basic Books.

Moore, B., and Fine, B., eds. (1990). Interpretation. In *Psychoanalytic Terms and Concepts*, pp. 103–104. New Haven, CT: The American Psychoanalytic Association and Yale University Press.

Ornstein, A. (1988). The conduct, method, and process of psychoanalytic psychotherapy. Audiotape produced and distributed by Smith, Kline and French Pharmaceuticals.

Ornstein A., and Ornstein, P. (1975). On the interpretive process in psychoanalysis. *International Journal of Psychoanalytic Psychotherapy* 4:219–271.

Ornstein, P., and Ornstein, A. (1985). Clinical understanding and explaining: the empathic vantage point. In *Progress in Self Psychology*, vol. 1, ed. A. Goldberg, pp. 43–61. New York: Guilford.

Rangell, L. (1982). The self in psychoanalytic theory. *Journal of the American Psychoanalytic Association* 30:863–891.

Reik, T. (1948). *Listening With the Third Ear*. New York: Farrar, Straus, & Giroux.

Rochlin, M. (1982). Sexual orientation of the therapist and therapeutic effectiveness with gay clients. *Journal of Homosexuality* 7:21–30.

Rowe, C., and Mac Isaac, D. (1989). *Empathic Attunement: The "Technique" of Psychoanalytic Self Psychology*. Northvale, NJ: Jason Aronson.

Schoenewolf, G. (1990). *Turning Points in Analytic Therapy: From Winnicott to Kernberg*. Northvale, NJ: Jason Aronson.

Shapiro, S. (1985). Archaic selfobject transferences in the analysis of a case of male homosexuality. In *Progress in Self Psychology*, vol. 1, ed. A. Goldberg, pp. 164–177. New York: Guilford.

Socarides, C. (1978). *Homosexuality*. New York: Jason Aronson.

———— (1992). Sexual politics and scientific logic: the issue of homosexuality. *Journal of Psychohistory* 10:307–329.

Strean, H. (1984). Psychosexual disorders. In *Adult Psychopathology: A Social Work Perspective*, ed. F. Turner, pp. 316–344. New York: The Free Press.

Strupp, H., and Binder, J. (1984). *Psychotherapy in a New Key: A Guide to Time-Limited Dynamic Psychotherapy*. New York: Basic Books.

Tolpin, P. (1985). Discussion: the primacy of preservation of the self. In *Progress in Self Psychology*, vol. 1, ed. A. Goldberg, pp. 83–87. New York: Guilford.

Trop, J., and Stolorow, R. (1991). A developmental perspective on analytic empathy: a case study. *Journal of the American Academy of Psychoanalysis* 19:31–46.

Wallerstein, R. (1985). How does self psychology differ in practice? *International Journal of Psycho-Analysis* 66: 391–404.

Wolf, E. (1988). *Treating the Self: Elements of Clinical Self Psychology*. New York: Guilford.

4

Psychotherapeutic Implications of Internalized Homophobia in Gay Men

ALAN K. MALYON, Ph.D.

Certain aspects of the prevailing cultural ethos have profound developmental consequences for most gay men. In particular, the emphatic antipathy that distinguishes contemporary social attitudes toward homosexuality tends to bias the socialization process and, in turn, the intrapsychic development of gay men. This chapter outlines some of the specific psychological effects of biased socialization and notes several of the clinical issues and psychotherapeutic implications arising from these developmental variations.

This report is based upon research and clinical data derived only from samples of gay men. For this reason it would not be prudent to generalize these findings to women. Careful extrapolation would, doubtless, lead to meaningful parallels, but the danger of misrepresenting the developmental differences between lesbians and gay men is too great to warrant such inductive inferences at this time.

THE SOCIALIZATION OF THE
HOMOSEXUAL MALE

Socialization can be described as the internalization of the values, symbols, regulations, beliefs, and attitudes that are inherent to the developmental milieu (Schafer 1968). Because homophobic beliefs are a ubiquitous aspect of contemporary social mores and cultural attitudes (Weinberg 1972), the socialization of the incipient homosexual nearly always involves an internalization of the mythology and opprobrium that characterize current social attitudes toward homosexuality.

Internalized homophobic content becomes an aspect of the ego, functioning as both an unconscious introject and a conscious system of attitudes and accompanying affects. As a component of the ego, it influences identity formation, self-esteem, the elaboration of defenses, patterns of cognition, psychological integrity, and object relations. Homophobic incorporations also embellish superego functioning and, in this way, contribute to a propensity for guilt and intropunitiveness among homosexual males.

The psychological processes that compose internalization become differentiated and operational during the pregenital era. According to Money (1963) the precursors of sexual orientation are also established by the end of latency. It is not until the adolescent era, however, that distinct and conscious homosexual desires become manifest and that the potential for homosexual self-recognition evolves. Thus, the subjective realization of homoerotic motivation is preceded by the introjection of a miasmic antihomosexual bias. This sequence of developmental events contaminates the process of adolescent identity formation. The internalization of homophobic partiality renders homosexual desire unacceptable even before the process of attribution begins. As a result, the maturation of erotic and intimate capacities is confounded by a socialized predisposition that makes them alien to the ego and militates against their integration. This, in turn, precludes a satisfactory resolution of the developmental conflicts that define psychological adolescence.

The primary psychological task of adolescence is that of identity formation (Erikson 1950). Identity develops in an interpersonal context. Therefore, the adolescent requires extensive opportunities to engage in experimental psychosocial behavior. Primitive and undifferentiated primary ties of dependency with parents must be transformed, through maturation and experience, into the capacity for eroticized and empathic attachments to peers. Under optimum psychological and social conditions, the evolution of identity, with concomitant changes in the dynamics and content of object relations, eventuates in the capacity for mature intimacy.

The peer group provides the primary social context for this process. Peer group validation is of fundamental importance in the development of autonomy and self-esteem. Conformity brings acceptance, whereas differences, especially stigmatized divergences, result in alienation. To consolidate an identity there must be the freedom to engage in peer interactions that incorporate the expression of needs, values, interests, and proclivities. In other words, adolescent object relations should nurture the development of all adaptive aspects of the self. This ideal is, of course, never fully realized for any adolescent, but self-actualization and psychological integrity are even more severely inhibited for the homosexual adolescent.

Peer-group norms and prevailing social attitudes are not compatible with the fixation of same-sex erotic and intimate capacities, especially during the latter aspects of the adolescent era. Thus, the already complex developmental task of forming an identity is further complicated for the homosexual adolescent by the conflict between cultural expectations and deviant psychosexual promptings. Disparate object choice, then, leads to atypical adaptational demands. Homoerotic ontogeny is shaped by a heterosexual socialization process. As a result, the adolescent psychosocial and ideational environment is not conducive to psychosexual congruency for the incipient homosexual. Instead, the adolescent homosexual is encouraged to obtain peer-group validation through the development of a false identity, that is, by the suppression of homoerotic promptings and the elaboration of a heterosexual persona.

The intrapsychic consequences of this adaptation are varied and unfortunate. The most likely developmental outcome is an interruption (sometimes temporary, but often lasting a decade or more) of the process of identity formation and epigenesis of ego integrity. Conformity to role expectations consistent with the prevailing heterosexual standard precludes psychological integrity. The ego must necessarily be fragmented, and those parts that significantly define the self-concept, and furnish the basis for intimacy, must be suppressed or denied. This adaptation is inherently conflictive. As a result, psychological defenses become highly elaborated to bind the accompanying chronic anxiety and to maintain a tenuous and brittle false identity.

Other aspects of ego development may continue, but the rejection of homosexual proclivities truncates the process of total identity formation. It is resumed whenever conflicts over homosexual urges change or diminish enough to allow for the acknowledgment and partial acceptance of same-sex desires, a process known as "coming out." Coming out is the precursor to a reemergence of many of the issues, intrapsychic conflicts, and psychological resources that were preeminent during primary adolescence. This rather unique developmental pattern is an aspect of the process of identity formation (Cass 1979). Thus, psychological differentiation and identity consolidation is a biphasic process for most gay males (Malyon 1981, 1982). During the second epoch of identity formation, previous conflicts are attenuated and the possibility of further ego development is enhanced. With the completion of this second phase, the natural vicissitudes of the ego are restored and the maturation of intimate capacities can proceed, less impeded by developmental fixation and psychological inhibition.

The foregoing has been a summary of certain of the possible consequences of biased socialization. It should not be assumed, however, that all homosexual males are affected to the same degree or in the same way by the cultural influences described. The developmental significance of any particular aspect of the socialization experience is determined by the special vulnerabilities, needs, and defensive strategies of each individual. Furthermore, no two people function in exactly the same developmental context. Thus, not every homosexual male becomes symptomatic. Nevertheless, the psychological and so-cial phenomena described above can be very potent, and their psy-chosocial consequences must be appreciated in the assessment and treatment of gay males who do enter psychotherapy.

CLINICAL ISSUES AND PSYCHOTHERAPEUTIC GUIDELINES

Several diagnostic and clinical considerations are implied by the developmental circumstances just outlined. Certain of these will be noted in the discussion of treatment that follows. A gay-affirmative point of view forms the clinical perspective for the psychotherapeutic guidelines to be described. This theoretical disposition regards homo-sexuality as a nonpathological human potential. The goals of gay-affirmative psychotherapy are similar to those of most traditional approaches to psychological treatment and include both conflict resolution and self-actualization. But while the traditional goal of psychotherapy with homosexual males has been conversion (to het-erosexuality), gay-affirmative strategies regard fixed homoerotic predi-lections as sexual and affectional capacities that are to be valued and facilitated. In addition, gay-affirmative approaches to therapy appre-ciate the psychological effects of the developmental anomalies noted above. Thus, one of the primary objectives of gay-affirmative psycho-therapy is to provide corrective experiences to ameliorate the conse-quences of biased socialization. Gay-affirmative psychotherapy, how-ever, is not reductionistic: it does not regard homophobia as the singular pathogenic element in the evolution of symptomatic condi-tions among gay men. Instead, gay-affirmative approaches to psycho-therapy consider oppression and antihomosexual attitudes to be just two of the many factors that influence the process of personality formation and psychological adaptation.

The following description assumes a thorough set of clinical skills, a basic knowledge of psychodynamic principles, and a sophisticated understanding of the intrapsychic and behavioral consequences of atypical socialization. This is not a prescription for how to do psychotherapy. Instead, it is a frame of reference for the accomplished clinician.

The approach to gay-affirmative psychotherapy presented here has a psychodynamic orientation. It conceives of psychotherapy as a developmental process that aims at facilitating both conflict resolution and self-actualization. The therapeutic process consists of four stages, as follows: (1) the phase devoted to building the therapeutic alliance, (2) the analytic phase, (3) the identity consolidation phase, and (4) the existential phase. The basic framework for this model is derived from Wolman's (1975) description of *interactional psychotherapy*, although the phases outlined here are significantly modified to fit the special psychotherapeutic needs of the homosexual male.

Before discussing each phase of the model, it is necessary to note that conflict resolution is never complete, nor is psychological growth a process with finite limits. Dynamic and reconstructive psychotherapy always consists of several phases, whether or not they are formally articulated. The phases overlap each other; at any point in the treatment process there may be a return to levels of clinical or therapeutic issues from an earlier phase. As increasing levels of psychological reorganization and integration are achieved, there is often greater access to repressed material and an accompanying availability of additional ego strengths and resources that would enhance problem resolution and self-actualization.

The phases which are described below are somewhat reified and artificial. They do, however, represent the typical issues that must be resolved in psychotherapy with homosexual men. In addition, they serve as a general guide for the sequence of treatment.

Phase One

The initial objective for any kind of psychological treatment is to establish an effective therapeutic rapport. The first phase of treatment, then, must be concerned with promoting trust and establishing the responsibilities of both client and therapist. Most often, a nondirective or client-centered approach can achieve this. The person entering therapy must be helped to regard the therapist as a person of special knowledge, competence, and genuine goodwill, who will come to care about and help the client.

When building rapport, the issue of values must be addressed, since these have such a profound influence on the therapeutic process. In the past, psychotherapy was regarded as value-free; it is no longer presumed to be so (Roman et al. 1978). Values and attitudes influence virtually every aspect of the treatment process, from what is interpreted to how it is interpreted. They determine what is considered a problem and can even have a bearing on how well the therapist likes the patient. For this reason, it is important for the therapist to consider which of her or his own values should be discussed with the client during the first phase of treatment. For example, with gay male clients, it is usually prudent for clinicians to indicate their therapeutic bias with respect to homosexuality and to discuss how this bias will influence the content and goals of therapy. Open discussion can protect against iatrogenic potentiation of internalized homophobic material.

The issue of therapist self-disclosure must also be pondered carefully during the first phase of treatment. If the clinician is gay, it is often of therapeutic value to reveal this early in the treatment process in order to help assure the client that the details of his homosexual feelings and behavior will be understood and accepted by the therapist. In addition, this revelation increases the likelihood that the therapist will, at some point, become the focus for projection, displacement, and stereotypical perceptions. This therapeutic augmentation of internalized antihomosexual attitudes creates an opportunity for interpretation, cathartic attenuation, and cognitive reworking of these attitudes and introjects. After the resolution of homoerotic conflicts, the known homosexual orientation of the therapist often helps the client to model attitudes and adaptations consistent with psychological integration and a positive gay identity. There are instances when early therapist disclosure would be countertherapeutic, particularly if the client has not yet come out and is deeply conflicted over his homoerotic promptings. In this instance, therapist disclosure might be too threatening to the client and result in a premature termination of treatment.

The first phase of psychotherapy with gay men should not be limited to building the therapeutic alliance. It is also the most propitious time for information gathering and assessment. In taking a developmental history, it is useful to focus on the evolution of homosexual self-awareness and, particularly, on the conflicts, self-perceptions, and adaptations associated with it. Current attitudes and adjustments to homosexuality also need to be assessed. It is especially important to identify the presence and nature of internalized homophobia and its derivatives, both conscious and unconscious.

Because the personality is a dynamic system, any developmental input, such as homophobia, has diffuse intrapsychic consequences; that is, exogenous homophobia, once internalized, usually functions as an unconscious introject with elaborations throughout the personality structure. Its very tenacity and pervasiveness, however, should be a caveat to the clinician. It is tempting to deal with the bewildering complexity and innate imperviousness of the unconscious by relying on a single dynamic or pathogenic explanation. Therefore, the reductionistic inclinations of the therapist must be mediated by an astute appreciation of the overdetermined nature of *all* psychological states and adaptations. During the early stages of treatment, the task is more one of assessment than one of intervention. Therefore, it behooves the therapist to restrict diagnostic formulations to hypotheses, and to resist attributing too much psychological determination to oppression. The initial diagnostic aim should be to delineate a tentative developmental profile that gives credence to the full range of formative variables.

Phase Two

The analytic phase of therapy is devoted to conflict resolution and cognitive restructuring (Lazarus 1974). The client–therapist relationship is the generic element of this stage of treatment. As Silverman (1974) points out, the transference is a fundamentally important aspect of all forms of psychotherapy. The repeatedly tested empathic psychotherapeutic relationship encourages an attenuation of defensive operations. This allows for the emergence of repressed material, including forbidden impulses, infantile fantasies, and irrational beliefs.

This is an insight-oriented phase of therapy; its purpose is to assist the client in relating to the unconscious in a conscious way. Thus, the primary form of intervention is interpretation, and the basic goal is an attenuation of the conflicts and neurotic adaptations derived from earlier pathogenic experiences.

There is a particular focus on homophobia, the purpose being to infer unconscious homophobic content and to identify conscious homophobic ideation. The object is to shift the ego-dystonic focus from homosexuality to homophobia.

Conscious attitudes are rather easily modified. Repressed anti-homosexual material, however, is much more difficult to apprehend and change. The derivatives, elaborations, and developmental consequences of introjected homophobia are as pernicious as the original internalized attitudes. Therefore, an important goal of this stage of psychotherapy is to illuminate the many complex secondary and tertiary adaptations that are abstractions of homophobia, for example, low self-esteem, lack of psychological congruity and integration, overly embellished and ossified defenses, problems with intimacy, and a particular vulnerability to depression.

The initial awareness of more-than-incidental homosexual promptings usually has profound psychological implications. It is nearly always accompanied by feelings of intense anxiety, despair, and intrapsychic conflict. This affective response brings about a dramatic potentiation of suppressive defenses. Conflict over burgeoning homosexual self-awareness also activates the process of stimulus generalization. This augments a gradual stigmatization of all intense affective phenomena (Clark 1977), prompting an even more profound elaboration of the already established defensive motif (suppression, denial, and overcompensation). This, in turn, leads to an inhibition and compartmentalization of all eroticized impulses. This psychological fragmentation of sexual and affectional proclivities interferes with the developmental process; that is, an integrated and positive identity cannot be established so long as eroticized desires and capacities are repugnant and, consequently, estranged. In the absence of identity consolidation, further development cannot take adequate advantage of the maturation of more differentiated and complex psychological and interpersonal capacities. Thus, one of the more significant outcomes of homophobic bias is an arrest of the developmental process. The other major consequence is a contamination of self-concept.

The analytic phase of psychotherapy addresses both of these aberrant conditions. The transference situation is particularly well suited for reworking biased socialization experiences and consequent developmental variations. The empathic aspects of this special relationship encourage the abreactive release and affective reworking of the exquisite psychological pain associated with the profound alienation, loneliness, and self-contempt engendered by the homophobic ethos. Alexander and French (1946) and Ferenczi and Rank (1925) emphasized that reparative success often can be accomplished only through the emotional relationship with the therapist. For example, the therapist's unconditional acceptance of homoerotic capacities is a necessary countervalence for earlier antihomosexual cultural conditioning. In turn, this acceptance enhances the possibility of a cognitive restructuring (Lazarus 1974) of the ideas, perceptions, and beliefs that form the self-concept. Through the use of direct confrontation, interpretation, and the principles of reinforcement, fixed homophobic ideation and homosexual conflicts can be modified. In addition, if the therapist is gay and has worked through her or his own homophobic prejudice and self-contempt, a uniquely auspicious opportunity exists for utilizing the client's capacities for identification, introjection, and modeling to modify his self-perceptions and the symbolic meaning he attributes to homosexual desire. Modeling is one of the active and empirically verifiable factors in effective psychotherapy (Bandura 1969). The gay clinician is in a position to provide a counterstereotypic model for the homosexual client.

Phase Three

This period of psychotherapy is distinguished by its concern with identity consolidation (viz., a gay identity) and with facilitating the capacity for intimacy. Although the therapeutic goals are quite definite, this is the least discrete stage of the treatment process, for identity formation is a rather continuous process, occurring over the duration of psychotherapy and beyond. Nevertheless, it involves a special constellation of issues and conflicts in gay-affirmative psychotherapy. As already noted, biased socialization complicates identity formation and the development of intimate capacities for homosexual men. Specifically, the aspect of ego development that concerns the resolution of identity issues is interrupted during primary adolescence and is resumed only after homosexual self-disclosure occurs. The biphasic process is a developmental variation that creates certain unique diagnostic and treatment issues in clinical work with gay men.

Gay-affirmative psychotherapy places a special emphasis on the issues associated with second-epoch adolescence. The goal is to aid in the development of an integrated, congruent, and positive identity. In addition, efforts are made to analyze and modify the defensive operations that were constructed to suppress unwanted sexual and affectional impulses. The purpose is to make the defenses less inclusive and tropistic.

It is uncomfortable and confusing to experience the full press of adolescent needs and impulses as an adult. As a result, psychotherapy can be especially poignant during this era. The adult who experiences second-epoch adolescence often needs guidance in selecting and understanding those experiences that will lead to accurate self-definition and positive self-acceptance. Psychotherapy provides support that helps to soothe the internal chaos experienced at this stage; astute interpretations give meaning and direction that attenuate the bewilderment.

In order for the individual to benefit fully from this second phase of primary identity formation, insight must accompany impulse and behavior. To this end, the analytic and cognitive aspects of psychotherapy are of considerable utility to the homosexual male who has just begun to establish a gay identity. Knowledgeable and sensitive interventions can mitigate the subjective bias created by internalized homophobia. Even after conscious attitudes have changed, however, the unconscious homophobic lament continues to influence interpretive processes. As a result, there is a proclivity for evaluating homoerotic experiences in a negative or self-denigrating manner. Effective therapeutic correctives can change this.

Once a mature and realistic identity—a positive gay identity—has been established, the client enters the stage of ego development that is concerned with intimacy (Erikson 1950). Intimacy is more complicated for the homosexual male than for the heterosexual. Antihomosexual attitudes (both exogenous and internalized), masculine sex-role stereotypy and conditioning, insufficient eroticized and affectional preintimacy involvements with other males, and the relative unavailability of models of male intimacy all interfere with the development of the capacity for long-term and mutually satisfying love relationships among gay men. Thus, psychotherapeutic enhancement of this capacity is often beneficial. For example, it is sometimes necessary that conflict resolution, deconditioning, and cognitive restructuring precede intimate involvement. The transference relationship has a special efficacy in this regard. It provides an affective interpersonal milieu in which the homophobic and neurotic misperceptions and conflicts that are sometimes stimulated by intense emotional involvement can be made manifest and transformed.

The issue of intimacy presents another clinical situation in which therapeutic advantages can be derived from the clinician being of the same sexual orientation as the patient. The gay male clinician, because he is both male and homosexual, is likely to elicit intense projection, homophobic hostility, and sex-role identity conflicts in the gay male client. In general, client–therapist similarities invite the very distortions and conflicts that are likely to operate in an empathic and eroticized relationship with a male lover.

It is not true, however, that competent psychotherapy with homosexual men can be conducted only by gay male clinicians. Other therapist variables can outweigh biological sex and sexual orientation in successful treatment outcomes. Nevertheless, a gay male clinician working with a gay male client can provide important opportunities for enhancing therapeutic gains.

Phase Four

During the last stage of psychodynamic gay-affirmative psychotherapy the primary issues are existential: the task is to establish a sense of personal meaning and purpose. Although identity problems are again paramount, this psychological era involves, in addition, issues that transcend sexual orientation and object relations. At the same time, homosexuality, by virtue of its cultural stigmatization, influences the question of personal meaning and the options available for establishing a sense of purpose and significance to life. Once again, homophobic bias influences individual psychological development.

This existential phase of psychotherapy usually follows the resolution of more primitive intrapsychic conflicts and the differentiation of identity. It deals with developmental issues that are more evident once psychological maturity has been achieved. These issues usually become most critical when the client is in his forties and fifties, for only after pregenital and adolescent fixations have been attenuated do existential questions tend to arise.

In Erikson's model of ego epigenesis, the psychological conflicts that are addressed during this psychotherapeutic era are generativity (as opposed to self-absorption) and ego integrity (as opposed to despair). These are postnarcissistic concerns dealing with matters of productivity, creativity, and social responsibility—with the search for personal meaning, dignity, and integrity in one's life.

This phase of psychotherapy is a psychological/philosophical/spiritual state of inquiry. The resolution of the "significance dilemma" is associated with making a conscious and freewill commitment to those values, priorities, activities, or goals that one experiences as subjectively meaningful. The culture provides the heterosexual individual a wide range of well-understood and highly valued purposes for life. These cultural guidelines, however, tend to be exclusively heterosexual in nature. Traditions such as the nuclear family, orthodox religious beliefs, rigid sex-role models, and conservative morality are not relevant reference points for most adult gay males in search of personal meaning and integrity. As a result, the existential crisis can be especially potent for gay men.

Gay-affirmative psychotherapy can be particularly helpful during this phase, because even under the most ideal psychosocial circumstances the question of purpose can be complicated and frightening. The support provided in psychotherapy helps to diminish feelings of despair and confusion. In addition, therapy can encourage self-exploration that, in turn, helps the client to identify that which is important to him and brings satisfaction. Gay-affirmative psychotherapy recognizes the necessity of establishing individual rather than collective solutions to these questions of meaning, direction, and purpose for men. An affirmative approach to psychotherapy facilitates the courage and integrity necessary when inner peace cannot be achieved through social conformity.

CONCLUSIONS

The foregoing discussion has been a cursory and very generalized description of one model of gay-affirmative psychotherapy. Frequently, the course of psychotherapy includes variations on the phases described. For example, sometimes special phases must be devoted to crisis intervention or attenuating refractory symptoms.

Gay-affirmative psychotherapy is not an independent system of psychotherapy. Rather, it represents a special range of psychological knowledge that challenges the traditional view that homosexual desire and fixed homosexual orientations are pathological. Gay-affirmative therapy uses traditional psychotherapeutic methods but proceeds from a nontraditional perspective. This approach regards homophobia, as opposed to homosexuality, as a major pathological variable in the development of certain symptomatic conditions among gay men. The special complications and aberrations of identity formation that have been described in this article are considered to be the result of social values and attitudes, not as inherent to the issue of object-choice.

Gay-affirmative psychotherapy has an abiding concern with the developmental consequences of biased socialization. It also appreciates the equally salient contributions of other pathogenic variables. Thus, gay-affirmative psychotherapy is not reductionistic; rather, it attempts to address the full range of developmental conditions that can lead to pathological adaptations.

REFERENCES

Alexander, F., and French, T. (1946). *Psychoanalytic Therapy*. New York: Ronald.

Bandura, A. (1969). *Principles of Behavior Modification*. New York: Holt, Rinehart and Winston.

Cass, V. (1979). Homosexual identity formation: a theoretical model. *Journal of Homosexuality* 4:219–235.

Clark, D. (1977). *Loving Someone Gay*. Millbrae, CA: Celestial Arts.

Erikson, E. (1950). *Childhood and Society*. New York: W. W. Norton.

Ferenczi, S., and Rank, O. (1925). *The Development of Psychoanalysis*. New York: Nervous and Mental Disease Publishing Company.

Lazarus, A. (1974). Desensitization and cognitive restructuring. *Psychotherapy: Theory, Research and Practice* 11:98–102.

Malyon, A. (1981). The homosexual adolescent: developmental issues and social bias. *Journal of Child Welfare* 60:321–330.

_____ (1982). Bi-phasic aspects of homosexual identity formation. *Psychotherapy: Theory, Research and Practice* 19:335–340.

Money, J. (1963). Factors in the genesis of homosexuality. In *Determinants of Sexual Behavior*, ed. G. Winokar. Springfield, IL: Charles C Thomas.

Roman, M., Charles, E., and Karasu, T. (1978). The value system of psychotherapists and changing mores. *Psychotherapy: Theory, Research and Practice* 15:409–415.

Schafer, R. (1968). *Aspects of Internalization.* New York: International Universities Press.

Silverman, L. (1974). Some psychoanalytic considerations of non-psychoanalytic therapies: on the possibility of integrating treatment approaches and related issues. *Psychotherapy: Theory, Research and Practice* 11:298–305.

Weinberg, G. (1972). *Society and the Healthy Homosexual.* New York: St. Martin's Press.

Wolman, B. (1975). Principles of interactional psychotherapy. *Psychotherapy: Theory, Research and Practice* 12:149–159.

5

"Resistance" in Dynamic Psychotherapy with Gay Men

CARLTON CORNETT, LCSW

INTRODUCTION

Donald was a 27-year-old gay man who presented neatly attired and smiling for the first session with his clinic therapist. He shook the therapist's hand with a nod and took the chair that he was offered. He appeared anxious, and his green eyes seemed to convey a sense of desperation. The therapist's emotional response to Donald was sadness. He also sensed a strong internal desire to do something for his new patient. He smiled and asked Donald what events had prompted his scheduling the appointment and then sat back quietly, ready to listen. A faint, anxious smile crossed Donald's face and he said quietly: "I don't know why I'm here." This was followed by a giggle that expressed more weary desperation than mirth. The therapist again found himself aware of an intense desire to help Donald, but he also felt powerless and impotent simultaneous with this desire. This first session ended at the same point of contact between both parties. Donald left this first hour still exuding a sense of pain that was only minimally articulated. The therapist was left looking, even hoping, for a means of helping. The hour was a disquieting one for the therapist, who later sought out a clinic supervisor to make some sense of the interaction. The supervisor offered a number of comments about projective identification and the difficulty of a first interview, but finally explained the therapist's sense that there had been little or no movement in the session as "resistance."

The interaction between Donald and his therapist is not an uncommon one. First sessions are often, perhaps typically, anxiety-provoking events for both participants. The patient searches for a role in the interaction that will give expression to his difficulties but not leave him indefensibly vulnerable. The clinician seeks to respond helpfully, to begin forging a therapeutic alliance and to engage the patient in the psychotherapeutic endeavor (Greenson 1967). The climate of first sessions, perhaps of many hours of a psychotherapy, is tinted by what has traditionally been called resistance. This concept, however, can be a problematic one for those clinicians working with gay men. The very word *resistance* conjures images of one party working against the other. In this chapter the concept of resistance will be discussed initially from two different perspectives. The first perspective proposes that resistances in psychotherapy are attempts by the patient to postpone or halt progress in treatment that are motivated by a fear of discontinuity and change. The second perspective proposes that resistances are the patient's adaptive attempts to protect himself from narcissistic injury. This chapter will focus on integrating these two perspectives, which are not mutually exclusive, through a theme of primary importance in the gay man's life: the fear of hope. Donald's treatment will illustrate clinical intervention in the resistances of a gay man. Although *resistance* is a particularly ill-suited term, it will be used to maintain clarity because it has a familiarity and currency that invest it with the clearest communicative power.

RESISTANCE AS MOTIVATED
BY A FEAR OF CHANGE

The concept of resistance is ubiquitous to dynamic psychotherapy. Freud (1914), in fact, came to identify transference and resistance as the two defining phenomena of psychoanalysis and psychoanalytically oriented psychotherapies. He proposed that any psychotherapy that recognized the centrality of these two phenomena in the treatment process could legitimately be called psychoanalytic in nature.

Freud's early writings are colored by his notion of resistance as an obstacle to be overcome. Resistance, in this context, was seen as the patient actively, albeit without conscious awareness, blocking the return of unconscious material (e.g., memories, fantasies, etc.) that could elaborate the pathogenesis of a neurotic symptom. As "cure" was originally conceptualized as the resolution of symptomatology through the emergence of such unconscious material and its subsequent integration into conscious awareness, resistances could also be seen as actively militating against the success of treatment generally.

Fine (1979) credits Freud's self-analysis as the initial field of observation for resistance. Freud (1900) found himself reluctant to acknowledge discomforting feelings, fantasies, and memories that arose, especially those in his dreams. He also began to notice the same phenomenon in his work with patients. This observation of a reluctance to know certain material was correlated with a lack of therapeutic change. Some patients showed little, if any, improvement or improved only slowly and with much effort on the part of the analyst. From these observations Freud developed the idea that while the patient undertook psychoanalytic or psychotherapeutic treatment to dispense with troubling symptoms (i.e., to change) there was a simultaneous and fundamental fear of the loss of the neurotic difficulty and its secondary gains, but also a fear of change generally. With the elaboration of this understanding came the integration of resistance as a core tenet of psychoanalysis: "The resistance accompanies the treatment step by step. Every single association, every act of the person under treatment must reckon with the resistance . . . " (Freud 1912, p. 103).

Even as the psychoanalytic movement fragmented, with various analysts outlining different developmental and clinical emphases, resistance remained a cornerstone of dynamic thinking about treatment. In some models, resistance assumed a more prominent place than it had held in even Freud's thinking. Reich (1972), for instance, developed character analysis from an interest in the form(s) of resistance offered by particular patients that ultimately elaborated their character structure. Ferenczi's (1976) active technique (see also Stanton 1991) similarly focused on resistance as a path of insight development, potentially richer than that obtained through interpretation of the transference.

Both Reich and Ferenczi elaborated what had previously been only an undercurrent in Freud's conception of treatment, that resistance could be a valuable ally to the analyst and to the treatment. Their views clearly moved technique away from the notion that resistance served only as a hindrance to clinical improvement.

American ego psychology has traditionally maintained an interesting balance between these two views of resistance. Greenson (1967) reviewed the evolution of resistance as a concept in classical dynamic thinking and emphasized the necessity of seeing patient resistances both as obstacles to successful treatment and as information regarding the nature of the patient's ego. Like many American analysts, however, he gave greatest weight to the view of resistance as an active attempt on the part of the patient to avoid change:

> Resistance means opposition. All those forces within the patient which oppose the procedures and processes of analysis . . . which interfere with the patient's attempts to remember and to gain and assimilate insight, which operate against the patient's reasonable ego and his wish to change; all of these forces are to be considered resistance. . . . [pp. 59–60]

He further explains the primary function of resistance to be . . . "defend[ing] the *status quo* of the patient" (p. 60). This notion that resistance primarily works against the therapist/analyst and opposes change is an important theme in contemporary dynamic thought.

One of the most articulate proponents of this view of resistance has been Castelnuovo-Tedesco (1989, 1991a,b). He proposes the fear of change to be intrinsic to the psychoanalytic and psychotherapeutic situation. He further contends that patients generally perceive the prospect of change as a potential experience of discontinuity of the self. In this manner, he proposes that the fear of change, which presents itself as resistance, may serve a narcissistically protective function as well.

Gay (1989) supports this view by exploring the fear of change as a common experience underlying many spiritual and religious traditions. He traces the fear of change to a more general fear of death or cessation of the self. This fear is an ever-present dynamic in psychotherapy. Gay views the dynamic theory of cure as one of a progression through mourning: "Freud's basic theory of cure . . . is best seen as a variation on the theme of mourning stated in his essay, 'Mourning and Melancholia' . . . " (1989, p. 26).

Gay also sees the fear of death/change in the emphasis on transformation over change in many religious traditions. Many of these traditions propose a redemptive savior who offers transformation of the self rather than change of the self. Transformation avoids change and ensures continuity of the self, albeit generally on a different plane of existence: "An actual change of the self is more frightening than transformation of the self because change requires one to give up one's fantastic unconscious hopes to find a heaven as conceived by the infantile ego" (p. 41).

Change also potentially represents an interruption in identity. By its very nature, change represents a redefinition of the self. This position ultimately argues that psychotherapy patients hope for transformation (improvement of circumstances requiring little or no personal change) and fear change.

As Reich and Ferenczi reconceptualized resistance in early psychoanalytic writings, contemporary self psychology has also attempted to propose a different view of the function(s) of resistance. This view emphasizes resistance as adaptive and protective.

SELF PSYCHOLOGY AND RESISTANCE
AS FEAR OF FURTHER INJURY

Kohut (1984) charged that the traditional view of resistance is adversarial; it stands the therapist (attempting to facilitate change) in opposition to the patient (resisting change). He asserted that: "All these so-called resistances serve the basic ends of the self; they never have to be overcome . . . rather, they are healthy psychic activities, in all their ramifications, because they safeguard the . . . self for future growth" (p. 235). He also preferred ". . . to speak of the 'defensiveness' of patients—and to think of their defensive attitudes as adaptive and psychologically valuable—and not of their 'resistances'" (p. 114). He proposed that patients seek to preserve the cohesion of the self through defensive maneuvers. The patient resists experiences that threaten the coherence and integrity of the self. Such experiences arouse fragmentation or disintegration anxiety, this state being analogous to the experience of psychologically dying. Shane (1985) sums up this position by asserting that ". . . the operative principle regarding the function of resistances and defenses . . . [is] the principle of the primacy of self-preservation" (p. 76).

Evident in both views of resistance is the idea that the prospect of change engenders a fear of loss of the self, or death. However, while both perspectives converge on this theme it is also in this convergence that the basic antagonism between the self psychological view of resistance and the more traditional view lies. The fundamental friction between perspectives involves the importance of change to the conception of treatment and, more generally, "cure." For self psychology, change is not intrinsic to the conception of treatment. The goal of psychotherapy from a self psychological perspective is to aid the patient in strengthening the cohesiveness of the self. Discontinuities of self-experience or identity (i.e., change) are anathema to the fundamental goal of the therapist serving as an empathically attuned selfobject. The emphasis on the therapist as *self*object itself eschews change in that it emphasizes the primacy of the patient's experience rather than the therapist's skills to bring about a difference in the patient.

Moments of resistance or defense-resistances (a term Kohut preferred) are seen in this context as adaptive means of essentially correcting a treatment that has strayed off course. The patient is making the therapist aware, through defensive maneuvers, of empathic disjunctions. These disjunctions are often founded upon a therapist's desire to bring about change (although a host of other countertransferential intrusions can create empathic lapses as well). For self psychology, resistances are the patient's adaptive attempts to protect the self from narcissistic injury.

While self psychology can be especially helpful in clinical work with gay men, this view of resistance is incomplete, as is the more traditional view, in addressing the dynamics of resistance that gay men bring to psychotherapy. Castelnuovo-Tedesco (1986) acknowledges that most psychotherapy patients are seeking affirmation over change, but he still emphasizes helpful psychotherapy as fundamentally an endeavor of change. Shane (1985), in discussing a case presentation, explains:

> Such congenital vigor of the nuclear self promoted in the patient an innate capacity to form *compensatory* structures, that is, *the capacity to hope for a satisfactory selfobject that would in the future enable him to consolidate the structures he had already formed in childhood.* [final emphasis added, p. 75]

Self psychology subordinates change to affirmation; however, it does not adequately emphasize a potential resistance inherent in affirmation: the fear of hope.

GAY MEN AND RESISTANCE AS AN EXPRESSION
OF THE FEAR OF HOPE

For gay men, as for most other groups of people who experience massive and chronic rejection and devaluation, the two conceptions of resistance outlined above integrate well through an emphasis on the fear of hope. It is a fear of hope, containing elements of both a fear of change and a dread of further narcissistic injury, with which a therapist must contend when working with gay men.

As has been discussed throughout this volume, gay men face dramatic rejection and devaluation on both familial and societal levels. The repeated experience of being rejected and devalued leads to a belief that these two corollary experiences are what one can expect and, more importantly, what is due from life. The gay man's world-view is often constructed on this experiential history. Relationships are, for the most part, narcissistically injurious. Because of this, moments of affirmation are the disjunctive exception rather than the rule. Overt attempts by a therapist (or most anyone else) to respond empathically are interactions that can threaten identity cohesion.

When the gay man is approached with affirmation rather than derision an important ambivalence arises that can ultimately appear in the clinical situation as resistance. This conflict and subsequent defensive reaction can best be understood through an integration of the self psychological and traditional views of resistance.

An affirming and empathic approach by the therapist is at first overtly appreciated and valued by the patient. It touches a generally dormant chord of hope in the patient that he will be responded to as someone of value, worthy of respect. However, affirmation can also represent a discontinuity in his experience (i.e., a change) and is therefore anxiety-provoking. In addition, such affirming interactions also hold the potential for disappointment and loss (i.e., further narcissistic injury). The therapist who offers affirmation through an empathic stance could also potentially denigrate and deride. After all, the willingness to accept affirmation may invite derision. The patient must balance his hope against his history. The result of this balance is often much like that presented by Donald. He communicated a wish and hope to be understood. He also, paradoxically, communicated through his silence and vagueness both a fear that he would be understood and a fear that the affirmation of being responded to empathically would tantalizingly lead to disappointment.

There are a number of ways through which this complex ambivalence can find expression. One is the sense of vagueness that permeated the first hour with Donald. Others include an overtly questioning but covertly devaluing approach to the therapist (e.g., her or his skills, office, etc.). A patient may talk about his difficulties and his feelings in the third person or offer telegraph descriptions of his story. Often, as a part of the initial fear of hoping, the patient will ascribe to the therapist a range of negative roles and motives (traditionally conceived of as negative transference).

Within any of the infinite varieties of expression that a resistance based on a fear of hope may find in the clinical setting there is often a common theme. This theme concerns the therapist's willingness to accept and value the patient *as a homosexual*. Sophisticated patients will sometimes directly question whether or not the therapist has biases toward homosexuals. Some, although not as many as might be expected, question the therapist's sexual orientation. Some ask if the therapist is ". . . one of those who believes in making gays straight."

This concern is understandable in light of the basic homophobia present in both the psychoanalytic community and the larger society. Psychotherapists, particularly those of a psychoanalytic orientation, often conceptualize homosexuality as a flawed or failed outcome of heterosexual development and adaptation, thereby pathologizing it (Cornett and Hudson 1985). Unfortunately, psychoanalysts and analytically oriented psychotherapists have often been the most vocal in their opposition to homosexuality being considered a healthy sexual variation. The gay patient has good reason to inquire about whether or not the therapist has an unspoken agenda.

This inquiry, however, is also based on an expectation that the encounter with the therapist will be reflective of the experiences the patient has had with the larger culture. The therapist could be a more affirming presence than many others have been for the patient, but there is every reason for the patient to believe that satisfaction of the hope for acceptance and affirmation is unattainable. There is much more reason to believe that the experience with the therapist will be another one of rejection and disappointment. The concern for being accepted as homosexual is both a realistic attempt to avoid an experience of devaluation and the external manifestation of an internal challenge the patient is offering to his hope.

RESPONDING THERAPEUTICALLY
TO THE FEAR OF HOPE

In the vignette opening this chapter, Donald showed one way that resistance can be manifested in the first hour. It is important to note that this is only one form that such resistances can take. It is also worth noting that such resistances are not confined to the first hour, but are a part of the psychotherapy of gay men from start to finish. As is generally true in dynamic psychotherapy, how the therapist responds to resistance can mean the difference between success and failure in the endeavor.

In light of this form of resistance, the relationship between therapist and **patient** must be characterized by respect, sensitivity, and courtesy for psychotherapy to proceed successfully. Although these qualities seem obvious, they may require some definition as they are proposed for the gay patient.

Respect in this discussion refers to the therapist's willingness to be honest and candid with the patient. Not all therapists work well with all types of patients. Certainly not all heterosexual therapists work well with homosexual patients. I have observed in some otherwise very sensitive and well-meaning therapists an inability or unwillingness to understand relationships by any other than a heterosexual model. They conceptualize gay relationships as involving one partner who plays the masculine role while the other partner plays the feminine role. They see monogamy as the ideal for every relationship, even while dismissing the extrarelational affairs of heterosexual friends or patients. Finally, they have a fundamental revulsion to descriptions of gay sex. This obviously interferes in their willingness to hear a gay patient discuss sexual issues. It also interferes in their being able to hear important expressions of shame, guilt, or other complex conflicts in sexual behavior. In the age of AIDS, when much shame and guilt are expressed through unsafe sexual practices, the therapist's unwillingness to hear about a gay patient's sexual life can have life-threatening consequences.

Obviously, my contention would be that psychotherapists who see homosexuality as pathological and would replace it with heterosexuality have no business treating gay men. Beyond this, however, therapists must have the fundamental honesty with first themselves and then with their patients to avoid working with gay men if they are limited by their own internal dynamics. They must be willing to refer to psychotherapists who are comfortable with gay men.

Some therapists may accurately point out that such an honest discussion culminating in a referral represents a rejection of the patient. Referrals from one therapist to another invariably result in a feeling of rejection by the patient. Rejection in this manner, however, is preferable to the sustained rejection that results from a psychotherapy in which the therapist finds her- or himself blocked from valuing the patient because of an immutable part of the patient's identity. Provided, of course, that the therapist–patient interaction is characterized by tact on the therapist's part, the honesty of the therapist is a form of respect that is a quiet, but in the long-term incontrovertible, way of challenging the patient's fear of hope. This form of respect truly eschews devaluation. It is also a form of respect that often lessens the expressions of resistance that will be enacted with the therapist to whom the patient is being referred.

The second quality, *sensitivity*, is closely related to the first. In this chapter, it refers to the therapist having some notion of the gay subculture. We are becoming increasingly aware that acculturation plays an important role in human development. There are very few therapists whose practices are solely composed of white, middle-class, Protestant, college-educated men and women. Yet we are still amazingly willing to apply developmental theories originating from this type of patient to all our patients. As a group, dynamic psychotherapists must be able to move from the paradigms that primarily define one culture (i.e., generally the therapist's) to those that reflect the context in which patients of divergent cultures developed and function as adults.

There is an important gay subculture that must be understood by the therapist for him or her to be of optimal help to a gay patient. It is a subculture of symbols, words, rituals, and practices that are not identical to those used in and by the larger culture. It is striking that psychotherapy, which relies so heavily on words and symbolism, often assumes the meanings of these are equivalent to those used in all groups and cultures of people.

For psychotherapists who wish to work with gay men it is imperative that they learn something of the context in which their patients live their lives. Obviously, much of this must be learned from each individual patient. However, it is naive to assume the stance that everything is understandable only from the patient's perspective and that this obviates the need to understand the larger acculturation of his life. For every group of people there are stresses, ambitions, political struggles, and so on, that are shared by that group and are basically unique to that group.

The logical extreme of this position would encourage stereotypical tunnel vision, and that is not the intent here. It is also not possible to specify exactly what the gay male subculture is because it is different in every locale. It is helpful for the therapist working with gay men to read local and national popular publications directed toward the gay community. It is also helpful for the therapist who is truly wishing to be sensitive to her or his gay patients to count among friends gay men to whom she or he can direct questions and who can, if he or she is interested, show aspects of the local gay community (e.g., bars, restaurants, reading clubs, community centers, political organizations, etc.). Many stereotypes, which would potentially interfere with effective psychotherapy, can be laid to rest with this type of sensitivity.

This type of sensitivity is a second quiet confrontation to the fear of hope. It communicates a willingness on the therapist's part to truly attempt immersion in the patient's experience and offers some affirmation to the patient (i.e., as someone worthy of being understood as a part of a larger context). But sensitivity, like respect, works in a way that does not threaten overwhelming discontinuity to the patient's experience of self.

The final component of the therapist's approach to the gay man, *courtesy*, is an integral part of psychotherapy with any patient. However, it is often amazing how subtly discourteous we dynamically oriented psychotherapists can be to all our patients (in the guise of therapeutic neutrality, anonymity, etc.). Greenson (1967) addresses this issue at length in regard to the analyst/therapist's responsiveness, or lack thereof, to questions. Sullivan (1953, 1956) was also deeply concerned with the need to extend common courtesies to patients as an important part of the total treatment (i.e., not just as part of developing a therapeutic alliance). Many of Sullivan's lectures and seminars (e.g., Kvarnes and Parloff 1976) are concerned with the need to acculturate the patient to psychotherapy for it to be a successful endeavor. It is probably not coincidental that Sullivan, himself gay, was concerned about this aspect of the therapist's clinical functioning.

Strupp and Binder (1984) and Luborsky (1984) discuss the need to socialize the patient to the psychotherapy relationship. It is a specific and unusual type of relationship that is dramatically more effective if the patient is educated as to how and why the therapist envisions the process working. It is discourteous for the therapist to insist that the patient assume a particular seating arrangement, or refuse to answer questions, or cut the patient off in midthought as the hour ends, without at least explaining how the therapist conceptualizes the importance of this or any other act idiosyncratic to the psychotherapeutic situation.

Discourteous behavior of this type offers narcissistic injury to every patient, but is especially injurious to the gay man because it reenacts former patterns of discourtesy. The obverse is, however, also true: socializing the gay man to the process of psychotherapy is therapeutic because it challenges his fear of hope.

One of the dynamics that brings about the fear of hope is the cluster of experiences that involve a rejection in multiple ways by the larger culture. The path to cultural acceptance is blocked for a homosexual by a number of factors in Western society. The gay man often does not experience integration into the larger culture typically because so many of the symbols and rituals of socialization are heterosexually based. As an adult he can become a part of a vibrant gay subculture, but many men avoid this experience out of shame or guilt. But whether they become an active part of their local gay community or not, there is still a yearning for experiences of affirmation and acceptance that are part and parcel of the socialization experience. This yearning, however, is also a component of the fear of hope.

The therapist's simply acculturating the patient to the process of psychotherapy is an act of courtesy. It is also a challenge to his fear of hope in that it offers a previously yearned for, but rejected as unattainable, experience of acceptance. This challenge, however, is offered without massive disjunction. There are also, of course, myriad other ways that the therapist may demonstrate courtesy to the patient. Each time the therapist successfully does so, the patient's view of self as unworthy of courteous treatment and/or as shameful is nontraumatically challenged.

The three interrelated qualities of respect, sensitivity, and courtesy form an integral part of the therapist's response to the patient's fear of hope. Another important means of responding to this dynamic, however, is to comment on it as it is encountered throughout the course of the therapy.

In Chapter 3 I discussed the issue of amplification/affirmation versus interpretation and generally subordinated the latter to the former. It is in the area of working with the fear of hope, however, that interpretation (i.e., linking the patient's verbalizations or other behavior with motivations of which he may be only partially aware) can be helpful in psychotherapy.

For this type of interpretive (i.e., which many more classically oriented therapists might label as a clarifying) intervention to be successful, the therapist must be willing to conceptualize resistance as an expression of the fear of hope. This conceptualization eschews the generally adversarial nature ascribed to resistance. Put simply, for this type of intervention to be most helpful the therapist must relinquish the mindset that the patient is opposing her or him or the treatment in general. If this adversarial perspective is maintained, interpretations of the resistance are not only unheard but are often perceived by the patient as painful acts of rejection.

Another important aspect of this view of resistance, which minimizes its adversarial aspect, is the therapist's willingness to avoid seeing change as the goal of the therapy. As psychotherapists we all wish for improvements in the lives of our patients. However, that wish can become an opportunity for rejection, especially for groups like gay men, who have been found wanting by their families and/or the larger culture all their lives. The therapist's hope must not become the central dynamic of the therapy or she or he may be perceived as another potentially accepting and affirming figure that ultimately would not accept the patient unless he changed.

To conclude this brief discussion of clinical intervention in resistance in psychotherapy it may be helpful to return to Donald, who began the chapter, to look at this view of resistance in clinical application. The psychotherapy to be discussed was a relatively brief one, lasting about two years. Donald was initially seen once weekly and subsequently twice weekly in a public mental health clinic by a heterosexual therapist in supervision with a gay therapist.

RESISTANCE OVER THE COURSE OF A PSYCHOTHERAPY

After the initial hour with Donald, Mr. B., the therapist, had sought out a clinic supervisor. His regular supervisor was on vacation, so he met with another with whom he was familiar and comfortable. As the supervisory session progressed and Donald's resistance became the focus, the supervisor encouraged Mr. B. to interpret Donald's resistance from the outset as a way to maintain his symptoms and, thus, his world-view (i.e., the fear of change).

Armed with this guidance, Mr. B. saw Donald for a second time the next week. Donald was as pleasant but as vague as he had been during the initial session. Mr. B. found himself again wanting to help Donald, but this began to give way to a more frustrating sense of impotence. During a couple of long pauses, Mr. B. found himself growing somewhat impatient and finally burst out a demand to know why Donald was in his office. Donald appeared stunned and stumbled to explain a sense of sadness, lack of fulfillment, loneliness, and desperation. His description was, however, hard for Mr. B. to follow, and, toward the end of the hour, he interpreted Donald's resistance as: "Not really wanting to let me know enough about your difficulties that I can help you change them." Donald quietly accepted this and, in the closing minutes of the session, related: "I guess I'm just tired of tricks. I want a relationship."

After this second hour, Mr. B.'s regular supervisor had returned from vacation, and later in the week met with Mr B. Mr. B. was vaguely dissatisfied with his interaction with Donald and the content of their last hour. Prior to approaching the more general area of the theoretical foundation of Mr. B.'s technical approach, his supervisor asked what Mr. B. thought Donald had meant by his being tired of tricks and wanting a relationship. Mr. B. had understood this to mean that Donald was tired of playing games in relationships and wanted a genuinely caring and reciprocal relationship. The supervisor pointed out that, although this could be a large part of what he meant, Donald might have also meant that he was tired of brief sexual encounters ("tricks") and wanted a more stable relationship. Mr. B., a fairly young and inexperienced therapist, was unaware that "trick" was a term with a specific and unique meaning in the gay community. The supervisor proposed that he read the local gay paper to get a feel for other deficits in his knowledge base about gay men.

The supervisor then also shared an alternative view of the resistance Donald had shown in the first two hours of the session, that is, that he might be afraid of hoping. This was a novel idea to Mr. B. who was, nevertheless, interested in it. The supervisor asked how Mr. B. had acculturated Donald to the psychotherapy relationship and found that Mr. B. had followed an accustomed method (leaving the field of observation ambiguous, protecting his neutrality and anonymity). The supervisor proposed that Mr. B. outline how he saw psychotherapy (which was more traditional in orientation than his supervisor) with Donald and offered an explanation of the importance of this. Both also talked about Mr. B.'s early negative countertransference (i.e., his impatience) as potentially being part of an interpersonal pattern that Donald had often experienced previously.

In the third session Mr. B., interested in testing out the supervisor's hypotheses, met with Donald. He began by apologizing that he had not initially explained the therapeutic situation and broadly explained his role as that of a listener — drawing parallels between relationships in Donald's life, especially as they were manifested in the relationship between the two of them — and as that of an observer who brought new ideas to Donald's attention. He described the role that Donald would have: arriving for appointments, talking about whatever came to mind, and paying his bill. He noticed a reduction in the tension that had permeated the room in the first two hours. He then explained that he had not clearly understood what Donald had meant by his reference to "tricks." Donald explained tricks as sexual encounters. He seemed both disappointed that Mr. B. did not initially understand this, and pleased that he had asked for clarification.

During this third hour Donald was more at ease in talking about his desire for a relationship but fearing himself unworthy of one. He described himself as "boring" and "unattractive." For much of the session Mr. B. listened quietly as Donald described a wish for a loving and reciprocal relationship, his conviction that this was and always would be out of reach, and the compromise he made in this conflict through brief sexual encounters with men that would never lead to the kind of relationship he wanted.

Over the next several weeks Donald seemed to become more at ease with Mr. B. and talked extensively about a history of rejection. A wisp of hope that his future would not always be full of rejection seemed to follow his lamentations but was never quite articulated directly. During his supervisory hours over these weeks Mr. B. talked about his sense of the dynamics of the case, and he and his supervisor continued to look at this as organized around the central dynamic of Donald fearing his hope. Mr. B. was encouraged to respond empathically (i.e., affirmingly). Intrigued, he agreed to modify his more classical and austerely interpretive approach.

During the third month of his therapy Donald arrived late for his regularly scheduled hour. He sat down and appeared to be angry. The content of the hour concerned a graphic description of a sexual encounter he had had the previous night. In uncharacteristically plain language Donald talked about "blowjobs," "rimming," and "getting fucked." Mr. B., aware of his own vague sense of discomfort about the entire topic and its presentation, at one point uncomfortably asked what "rimming" meant. Donald lashed out that he was tired of having a therapist who did not understand him and then became quiet. Mr. B. conceptualized the interaction as involving a negative transference to a harshly critical father but did not offer the interpretation. Rather, he attempted to empathically reflect Donald's anger with him. Nevertheless, he felt the session had been mishandled and was frustrated with the outcome.

During his next supervisory hour Mr. B. discussed the possibility that Donald might be right in his assessment that he needed a therapist who understood gay men and gay sex more completely. The supervisor suggested that it would probably be important for Donald to talk about sex. He also emphasized, however, that not knowing everything about gay sex was not equivalent to not wishing to hear about gay sex. The former was not necessarily a problem that would derail the therapy, although the latter could be. Mr. B. decided that this was an issue for his own self-growth, that he was willing to listen to Donald talk about sex, and that much of his discomfort involved his lack of knowledge about what Donald meant by his terms. They then talked about Mr. B.'s understanding of the anger Donald had demonstrated toward him. The supervisor encouraged Mr. B. to think of this from the perspective that had been the focus of their work thus far together, that perhaps Donald's anger represented a fear that the therapist he had found who tried to understand, albeit imperfectly, was "too good to be true."

The next hour found Donald still angry with Mr. B. He talked about a man he had met the night before who was a "leather queen," a combination of terms with some ambiguity for Mr. B. He inquired as to what this meant. Donald again exploded about Mr. B.' s lack of knowledge about the gay world. After this barrage, Mr. B. quietly offered the possibility to Donald that he might be afraid that he (Mr. B.) was trying to understand. He linked this with the many other relationships in Donald's life that had been disappointing and suggested that it was understandable that Donald did not want to repeat that disappointment. He added: "Maybe you're afraid that I do want to understand you, because that gives you some hope and hope is a thing you can't afford." Donald was thoughtful and ultimately cried, talking further about the many painful rejections and disappointments that he had suffered in relationships.

The months progressed with Donald becoming more assertive and confident in his relations with others. His "tricking" turned into dating, and he was pleased that he was meeting men who could potentially meet some of his needs. His hope, however, continued to be powerfully frightening. As he began to experience less frequent depressive episodes and more satisfaction interpersonally, he began to fear that he would soon die. Mr. B. emphasized the ways that this fantasy both re-created his world-view (i.e., ultimately he would never get what he wanted) and also kept him "from getting too excited and hoping too much."

There were numerous incidents of resistance throughout these months that included not telling Mr. B. about men he particularly liked, attempting to keep all discussions on a sexual level, and teasing Mr. B. about his lack of knowledge about gay men. (This lack of knowledge remained considerable, although Mr. B. became quite interested in the gay subculture and often asked both his supervisor and other gay clinic employees about the usage of terms, etc.) The last major resistance appeared, however, at the end of the first year of Donald's therapy.

As Donald completed his first year of therapy, he related a desire to "speed things up," which was initially puzzling to Mr. B., who heard Donald's valuation of the therapy but was unclear as to what "speeding it up" meant. In one session Donald reported a dream in which he saw Mr. B. driving down a familiar street and felt ashamed that he had seen him outside the office. Mr. B. initially conceptualized this as a dream relating to Donald's vulnerability in letting Mr. B. know so much about his romantic, especially sexual, life.

Mr. B. related the dream to his supervisor and found that, by this time not surprisingly, the supervisor linked it to the theme of hope and its dangers. Mr. B. approached the dream in the following hours with a gradual interpretation of it as elaborating Donald's wish to move things along. The familiarity of the dream communicated a desire to see the affirming and accepting therapist more frequently, which was immediately followed by shame for having hoped and wished for more time with the therapist and, thus, more acceptance and affirmation. Donald confirmed that he had wanted to increase his sessions to twice weekly, but that he had been afraid that this would change the relationship with Mr. B., who might become "tired of [him] or bored." Over the next several weeks elements of both transference and resistance were explored in this complex wish-fear sequence.

Donald spent approximately ten months in twice weekly psychotherapy. He ended therapy relating a sense of increased confidence and hope for the future. Indeed, his final hours were concerned with future plans and wishes. He terminated therapy feeling a sense of affection for Mr. B., which Mr. B. reciprocated. In addition, Mr. B. left his relationship with Donald with much more knowledge about gay men. He later reported to his supervisor a fear that he would have missed out on a very satisfying and educational therapy relationship with Donald if he had maintained his initial approach to Donald's resistances.

CONCLUSION

Resistance has been one of the core concepts of psychodynamic theory almost from its inception. It has been a problematic concept, however, in that it has often been seen as part of an adversarial relationship between patient and psychotherapist. The idea that resistance is primarily a fear of change (i.e., "getting better") has contributed to this adversarial relationship. Self psychology's emphasis on resistance as a means of avoiding narcissistic injury has been a step away from this fundamental difficulty.

In clinical work with gay men, however, an integration of both conceptions of resistance proves helpful. The philosophical stance that change is a by-product (if it occurs at all) of psychotherapy rather than its goal underlies this integration. Such an integration builds upon the fundamental dynamic that oppressed and persecuted groups are frightened of hoping for improvement. Hope may result in two opposite but equally uncomfortable outcomes: new, affirmative relationships (i.e., change and identity discontinuity) or further disappointments (i.e., narcissistic injury). The fear of hope is a resistance present in the psychotherapy of gay men throughout its course and often is an organizing principle of an entire therapy.

Divergence in psychodynamic theorizing has often resulted in factionalism with competing theories using the clinical situation as a proving ground. Resistance is a concept in which different perspectives can be usefully combined to improve clinical work. It is a concept of particular importance in understanding the dynamics of treatment with gay men, a group of people in our culture who feel the adversarial nature of our society on a daily basis and who seek acceptance from the psychotherapist rather than another adversary.

REFERENCES

Castelnuovo-Tedesco, P. (1989). The fear of change and its consequences in analysis and psychotherapy. *Psychoanalytic Inquiry* 9:101–118.

———— (1991a). Fear of change as a source of resistance in analysis. In *Dynamic Psychiatry: Explorations in Psychotherapy, Psychoanalysis, and Psychosomatic Medicine*, pp. 243–259. New York: International Universities Press.

———— (1991b). Psychotherapy and the fear of change. In *Dynamic Psychiatry: Explorations in Psychotherapy, Psychoanalysis, and Psychosomatic Medicine*, pp. 119–128. New York: International Universities Press.

Cornett, C., and Hudson, R. (1985). Psychoanalytic theory and affirmation of the gay lifestyle: are they necessarily antithetical? *Journal of Homosexuality* 12:97–108.

Ferenczi, S. (1976). On forced fantasies: activity in the association-technique. In *The Evolution of Psychoanalytic Technique*, ed. M. Bergmann and F. Hartman, pp. 118–125. New York: Basic Books.

Fine, R. (1979). *A History of Psychoanalysis*. New York: Columbia University Press.

Freud, S. (1900). The interpretation of dreams. *Standard Edition* 4/5:1–625.

———— (1912). The dynamics of transference. *Standard Edition* 12:99–108.

———— (1914). On the history of the psychoanalytic movement. *Standard Edition* 14:7–66.

Gay, V. (1989). Philosophy, psychoanalysis and the problem of change. *Psychoanalytic Inquiry* 9:26–44.

Greenson, R. (1967). *The Technique and Practice of Psychoanalysis*. Vol. 1. New York: International Universities Press.

Kohut, H. (1984). *How Does Analysis Cure?* Ed. A. Goldberg and P. Stepansky. Chicago: University of Chicago Press.

Kvarnes, R., and Parloff, G., eds. (1976). *A Harry Stack Sullivan Case Seminar: Treatment of a Young Male Schizophrenic*. New York: W. W. Norton.

Luborsky, L. (1984). *Principles of Psychoanalytic Psychotherapy: A Manual for Supportive-Expressive Treatment*. New York: Basic Books.

Reich, W. (1972). *Character Analysis*. Third Ed. Trans. V. Carfagno. New York: Simon and Schuster.

Shane, M. (1985). Summary of Kohut's "The Self Psychological Approach to Defense and Resistance." In *Progress in Self Psychology*, vol. 1, ed. A. Goldberg, pp. 69–79. New York: Guilford.

Stanton, M. (1991). *Sandor Ferenczi: Reconsidering Active Intervention.* Northvale, NJ: Jason Aronson.

Strupp, H., and Binder, J. (1984). *Psychotherapy in a New Key: A Guide to Time-Limited Dynamic Psychotherapy.* New York: Basic Books.

Sullivan, H. (1953). *The Interpersonal Theory of Psychiatry.* New York: W. W. Norton.

_____ (1956). *Clinical Studies in Psychiatry.* New York: W. W. Norton.

6

The Borderline Personality Disorder and Gay People

CHARLES SILVERSTEIN, Ph.D.

OBJECT RELATIONS THEORY

The Borderline Personality Disorder (BPD) is a diagnostic construct that originated in the modern psychoanalytic interest in object relations theory (Kohut 1971). This theory proposes that pregenital problems, particularly during the phase of separation-individuation of the child (18 to 36 months of age), lead to severe personality disorders in adulthood. It is a theory that primarily implicates the mother as the culprit of the child's later problems by her refusing to allow her child to develop firm psychological boundaries between the child and others, including herself. She does this, it is hypothesized, by withdrawing her love from the child if the child attempts to separate, or by overgratification at the symbiotic stage. This withdrawal produces an abandonment depression in the child, a type of depression that will be experienced throughout the child's life (Masterson 1981). The theory is an extension of Freud's description of an anaclitic depression (Freud 1914). Presumably, the child's attempt at separation is experienced by the mother as a parallel abandonment depression.[1] As Rinsley (1982) noted, "The mother is available if the child clings and behaves regressively, but withdraws if he attempts to separate and individuate" (p. 36).

SYMPTOMATOLOGY

Perhaps the sine qua non, symptomatically, of the BPD is the concept of splitting, whereby all objects (i.e., people) are bifurcated and identified as either all good or all bad.[2] Good objects are safe ones, whereas bad objects are dangerous and bring on the reexperience of the early abandonment depression. This person perception never allows for ambiguity or differentiation because that would lead to confusion, anxiety, and frustration. A bad object may change, and often does, but when it changes, it does so completely and at once, becoming good, so that the person experiences a series of alternations of perception and, hence, alternations of affect. A veridical perception of the assets and liabilities of another person is almost impossible, so that the good becomes bad, and back again. Technically, the person is said to lack object constancy. The same process is said to occur in self-perception as well, in which a partial self-image inaccurately reflects the person's whole self. Therefore, the person relates to others as parts of a larger and unintegrated ego, rather than as a whole. Kernberg (1975) believes that this good/bad split was originally a simple defect of integration, which then in adulthood is used as a defense of the ego, protecting it from conflicts between libidinal and aggressive identifications.

---

[1] There is a tendency on the part of some psychoanalysts to lean heavily upon the mother as the cause of all future dire consequences that befall the child. One cannot help wondering whether hidden amid all this theory is a rage toward mothers on the part of the theorists.

[2] This is Kernberg's definition of splitting. Splitting to Kohut and Masterson is more complicated and tied to etiological theory.

Kernberg further stated that a person with a BPD fears his own aggression. Good objects protect the person from bad ones, so that he can't be destroyed by self-aggression. It is, therefore, a projection, an externalization of the all-bad aggressive self upon other people. Although the borderline person may believe he is protecting himself from the attacks of others, he is really attempting to control them in order to prevent them from, as he sees it, attacking and destroying him. What he does not see is that the aggression he perceives in others is but a mirror of himself.

Kernberg suggested that the syndrome of the BPD is composed of four symptom groups: diffuse anxiety, multiple phobias, little constancy of sexual behavior, and impulsive and/or addictive states or both. In addition, the BPD person is perceived as compliant and dependent, but often alternates between dependency and self-assertion, depending upon his perception of the benevolence or potential harm of significant people in the environment. Kernberg further identified the BPD as a stable, yet pathological, form of personality disorder. To him the "border" was a state between neurosis and psychosis, but he also believed that under stress or the influence of drugs a transitory psychosis can occur.

In practice, people classified as borderline have tended to be quite varied, with some functioning quite well, and others holding on to the barest threads of ego strength. Therefore, Kernberg (1975) suggested a twofold classification of the BPD into "upper" and "lower" levels. An upper BPD is one in which the principal fear is abandonment and the principal defense is clinging to another person. In the lower level BPD, the principal fear is engulfment and the principal defense is distancing from others. The lower level BPD person is clearly the more disorganized of the two, with feelings of depersonalization and frequent but temporary psychotic episodes that include paranoid ideation. A good review of the dynamics of upper and lower level borderline people can be read in Meissner (1983). Through this dichotomous classification Kernberg noted that the borderline diagnosis includes an unusually large range of individuals, including those, as in the upper level, whose reality testing is fairly good and who learn to function acceptably, and those whose level of functioning is extremely limited, who are labile in temperament to the extreme, and in whom transitory but frequent psychotic episodes appear throughout life.

At this point even the casual reader may note that the invention of the BPD as a diagnostic category has led to diagnostic boundaries as diffuse as the people it is said to identify, and may soon be said to include an ever-expanding segment of the population previously diagnosed as suffering from a variety of neuroses, character disorders, and psychotic reactions. In a book review, Ziesat (1983) noted the potential for using the label as a wastebasket category for cases that were difficult to diagnose. He noted that some psychoanalysts thought of the BPD as including essentially neurotic people, with sporadic evidence of psychosis, whereas others thought them to be psychotic with a neurotic veneer. He stated:

> If we are going to retain the word "borderline" as a diagnostic term describing this group of patients, we should be clear about which border we are referring to, to wit: Does borderline personality straddle schizophrenia and neurosis, as was originally thought, or affective disorders and character disorders? Or is it a mild form of schizophreniform illness? Or is it simply a type of affective disorder? The reason that such questions are important is that the answers may eventually point to practical treatment strategies. [p. 666]

Even Meissner (1983), who supported the new classification, was cognizant of the hazardous diagnostic foundation of the BPD, and wrote: ". . . the borderline description is so nonspecific that it embraces an as yet unspecified differential diagnosis covering a wide range of disorders" (p. 180).

It is beyond the scope of this chapter to argue the validity of the BPD diagnosis, particularly with respect to the etiological beliefs held by object relations theorists. As we find true of all diagnoses, they can be used as descriptors of behavior without subscribing to the etiological components suggested by theorists. That is precisely what is proposed for the rest of this chapter and the case to be presented. Toward that end, we may accept the descriptive statement of the BPD as a diagnostic category listed in the third edition of the *Diagnostic and Statistical Manual of Mental Disorders* (American Psychiatric Association 1980):

> The essential feature is a personality disorder in which there is instability in a variety of areas, including interpersonal behavior, mood, and self-image. No single feature is invariably present. Interpersonal relations are often tense and unstable, with marked shifts in attitude over time. Frequently there is impulsive and unpredictable behavior that is potentially physically self-damaging. Mood is often unstable, with marked shifts from a normal mood to a dysphoric mood or with inappropriate, intense anger or lack of control of anger. A profound identity disturbance may be manifested by uncertainty about several issues relating to identity, such as self-image, gender identity, or long-term goals or values. There may be problems tolerating being alone, and chronic feelings of emptiness or boredom. [p. 321]

THE CULTURAL BACKGROUND

What seems to this author to have been ignored by object relations psychoanalysts is the question of why the BPD has attained such prominence in the past thirty or forty years. This question invariably suggests the introduction of cultural factors that have created environmental stressors that increase the likelihood of the kind of personality disorder we now call the BPD. This is not a unique idea. Diagnoses come and go as the times and theories change (Silverstein 1976–1977, 1984). Although conversion hysteria was all the rage at one time, hardly any clinicians today meet "glove anesthesia" in a lifetime of practice. Nor is masturbation now listed as a mental disorder. In their places have gone mental disorders that were never listed before, such as anorexia nervosa and bulimia. Also newly listed are those behaviors (e.g., the sexual dysfunctions) that existed in the past but were never labeled mental disorders.

The great increase in the use of the BPD within recent years is unlikely to be the product of inadequate mothering (Chodorow 1978). Mothers are no less competent today than their mothers or grandmothers were in previous generations. It can even be argued that today's mothers are better educated and more knowledgeable of child-rearing practices. The effects of mothering (and, one would like to think, fathering) are certainly the foundation for adulthood. But other influences come to bear on the child that can ameliorate or aggravate the effects of early childhood. This is particularly true with respect to issues of sexual identity and gender identity.[3] It is in these areas that our society has changed most severely, and this fact, it is maintained, is the reason for the increase in the incidence of the BPD.

Parenting has changed dramatically in this century. In previous generations parents were role models for their children, and this was as true of sexual and gender identities as it was for all other areas of adult behavior. In a sense, it was a vertical system in which one generation modeled themselves after the generations that came before them. It was an easy system, and one that produced stability and dependability within the family and the social structure. Moral rules proscribed one's sexual behavior to a relatively small number of acts, with violations of the rules handled harshly. There were rarely conflicts of gender identity, and where they did occur, they were kept secret (Faderman 1981). In a well-structured society that eschewed ambiguity, few personal choices were made, for few were required. Within the confines of such a system, the BPD was unlikely to appear because one's society created an external structure that ameliorated family inadequacies.[4]

---

[3]These two are often confused. Sexual identity refers to one's sexual orientation—homosexual, heterosexual, or bisexual. One's gender identity, on the other hand, is one's concept of male, female, or androgyny (Bem 1974). Either can be confused in a person.

[4]One should also note that the extended family was the norm in previous generations, whereas today the nuclear family keeps other relatives

HOMOSEXUALITY AS A CULTURAL VARIATION

Previous to the nineteenth century, homosexual behavior was not a significant problem for society. Whatever transgressions may have occurred, men and women married, had children, and fulfilled their social roles as parents. In 1869, the ground was broken to change all that. In that year the word *homosexual* was invented (and its counterpart, *heterosexual*) (Lauritsen and Thorstad 1974, Steakley 1975). The implications of this fact are seldom discussed. This leads to the suggestion that both sexual identities are artifacts of modern society (MacIntosh 1968). A social role, in contrast to mere genital behavior, began to emerge for those men and women whose emotional and sexual desires were directed toward the same sex. Confined almost exclusively in the late nineteenth and early twentieth centuries to the realm of medical abnormality (if not curiosity), homosexual couples, what few there were, usually mirrored the social and sexual roles of heterosexual marriage, with one member of the pair playing a rigidly defined male role, and the other a female role, clothes and all (Kiernan 1884). Many of these relationships lasted for a lifetime, though they would probably have been mystified by a word such as *homosexual* (Faderman 1981).

It was only after the Second World War that homosexual love became a possibility for most people, and the rise of the modern gay liberation movement created the environment that encouraged long-term coupling between gay people. Three forces combined to instruct men and women that personal choices were not only possible but necessary in our modern society.

Alfred Kinsey's Research

The first impact was Alfred Kinsey, whose monumental sex research profoundly affected our notions of normal and abnormal sexuality

---

at a distance. Previously, extended family members could make up for the deficiencies of a child's parents.

(Kinsey et al. 1948). The sexual revolution that he and his colleagues helped to create is often misunderstood. The result is not that people had more or less sex after his work than before. He went after more dangerous game than the mere counting of orgasms. He demonstrated the frequency of various forms of sexual behavior at different ages and at different socioeconomic and educational levels. The very best example of this was his documentation of the normative aspects of masturbation at a time when many medical authorities still diagnosed it as abnormal, and the frequency of homosexual behavior, also condemned as pathological. From a psychological point of view, Kinsey's books were permission-giving for people to experiment sexually.

The Women's Liberation Movement

The women's liberation movement (Flexner 1975) fought against the traditional social role of women and demanded the same opportunities as our society provides its men. Women were encouraged to join the professions and the business world, and to delay childbearing if they wished. At the same time, a concerted attack upon the traditional hardnosed image of men was instituted, and a new masculine standard was suggested: the androgynous man who developed his sensitive qualities as well as the customary masculine ones.

The Gay Liberation Movement

The changes initiated by the women's movement led directly to the modern gay liberation movement that began after the Stonewall riot in 1969 (Katz 1976, Weeks 1977). This movement is the third force in our discussion of sexual and social choices. The gay liberation movement was at once an attack upon traditional notions of masculine and feminine, and upon the sexual conservatism of the psychiatric profession. Gay liberation was instrumental in helping millions of gay people to *come out*, in the organization of a gay service network.

These three forces,[5] the work of Kinsey and his colleagues, the women's liberation movement, and the gay liberation movement, have been the foundations of the sexual revolution of the 1970s and 1980s. This revolution, so supportive of individualism, has implicitly instructed the young that a myriad of choices are possible about one's social and sexual roles throughout life. Models from the past have been judged as archaic so that one cannot be instructed, but must learn empirically through experience. But if the individual has been freed from outmoded social and sexual roles, he is nonetheless forced to exact a price for his freedom—to make choices—and this freedom invariably results in personal confusion and conflict.[6]

One needs to remark here that traditional notions of male and female were constructive in society. Everybody knew what was expected of him or her, and knew what to expect from others. There may have been no choice, but there was certainly dependability. The reader should avoid judging this belief as an atavistic call for a return to Victorian standards. It is just the proposition that freedom is not being free, and that some of us are incapable of creating empirical standards for ourselves and first become confused and finally disoriented.

It is the point of view of this chapter that the BPD is a direct result of these changing social norms in the twentieth century, that it is, in a sense, a social dilemma created by freedom.

The BPD has increased in frequency because the social structures present in previous generations have vanished. Individuals are now forced to make a considerable number of choices over sexual behavior, sexual identity, and gender. It is a task wherein a person is asked to create order out of confusion, and from that ordering of personal and

---

[5]One could reasonably argue that "the pill" was another force, but it is not relevant to a discussion of homosexuality.

[6]One might hypothesize that the failure of the churches to control their members, particularly those who live in large urban areas, has contributed to the insecurity and confusion of us all.

social alternatives evolves a psychological structure that is the modern
equivalent of the rules from, say, the Victorian era, but one that is
empirically derived. Therefore, the most important responsibility for
each person in today's society is to create this personal psychological
structure as a replacement for the former social and religious regulations. If one fails to do so, then all subsequent alternatives will be met
with even greater confusion. In those who suffer the greatest confusion, disorientation occurs and ego defenses are created to prevent
total psychological breakdown. These ego defenses are the symptoms
of what is now called the BPD.

This idea is not at all radical. *DSM-III* (APA 1980) notes that
certain personality disorders "have a relationship to corresponding
categories in the section Disorders Usually First Evident in Infancy,
Childhood, or Adolescence" (p. 305). It goes on to associate the
Identity Disorder of Adolescence with the adult diagnostic category of
BPD.

DSM-III (APA 1980) states that the Identity Disorder is most
common in adolescence, and further states that:

> The disorder is apparently more common now than several decades
> ago, however, perhaps because today there are more options regarding
> values, behavior, and life-styles open to the individual and more
> conflict between adolescent peer values and parental or social values.
> [p. 66]

What we see today from this perspective and call BPD is a group
of people who are incapable of making choices and suffer confusion
because of it. Most certainly, childhood factors predispose them to
confusion. The symptoms of BPD are unlikely to occur in loving and
caring families. Disordered nuclear families are a necessary, but not
sufficient, reason for the rising incidence of the BPD.

But let us now consider the life of a gay man, Gerard, and follow
that with a discussion of his personality dynamics and their implications for all gay people.

THE LIFE-STUDY OF GERARD

"The Train" (a dream)

"It is dusk. Even in my dream I can feel a cold wind blowing on my naked arms. I can remember feeling goose bumps even with my coat on. The cold seems like it will never end. I am alone on this grayish platform, with no destination. Where am I and why am I so aware of every detail of my position and yet so totally unaware of where I am? I am confused by the terrain around me.

(People enter the train and it leaves.)

"Now the trains are totally unrecognizable to me. They are definitely subway cars, but their destinations are mysterious. One goes to New London, the other to Boston. Somewhere there is a connection to 42nd Street. But I cannot remember where it is or how to get there.

"I retreat to the men's room and take up residence there. The door is locked, so now I can sleep. It is safe, warm, and, when I wake up I can buy a toothbrush and some shampoo and cleanse my body.

"I awaken and try to recollect the dream. I only remember the train station and the john. And being lost. Everything is so easy, if only I could figure it out!"

Patient Information

Gerard is a 32-year-old white male employed as an executive by a New York City firm, and has been in psychotherapy for the past year. His entry into psychotherapy was by self-referral, and except for a brief hospitalization at the age of 14 for what appears to have been an adjustment problem of adolescence, this has been his first experience with psychotherapy. He has one brother two years older, and a younger brother and sister. He was born to a working-class family who lived in a rural New England town. His father worked sporadically at a local mill, where employment was seasonal, and at odd jobs around town. There is no history of mental illness in the family.

Gerard is gay and has lived with a male lover, Alan, for the past four years. Previously he lived with his first lover, Tom, for twelve years. Gerard reports no discomfort about his sexual orientation, nor does he remember feelings of guilt, low self-worth, or a desire to become heterosexual, although he did have an affair with a woman during late adolescence. Gerard's sexual behaviors are highly specialized. His typical form of sexual activity is "S & M" sex, where one party plays the role of the sadist, and the other the masochist. Gerard is a masochist and here, too, he reports his sexual experiences are ego-syntonic.

Chief Complaints

Gerard brought to the initial interview one chief complaint from which a number of distressing problems had arisen, leading to his current feelings of discomfort. He felt unloved and deceived about love, and these feelings centered almost exclusively on Alan, his current lover. Gerard did not believe that Alan loved him, though the evidence for this was circumstantial. Gerard said that whenever he tried to express feelings of intimacy, Alan reacted coldly. For instance, Gerard would often prepare breakfast on weekends, but Alan would sleep until noon, or Gerard would plan interesting vacations and Alan would refuse to help in the planning, acting as if the idea of a vacation with Gerard was oppressive. Gerard is very organized about household responsibilities, while Alan is less so, and so cleanliness became another area of conflict. Occasions occurred every day whereby Gerard interpreted Alan's behavior as rejecting.

Though both hold executive positions and live modestly, they are always having money problems. Gerard is preparing for his retirement by making financial contributions to a fund that are so large that his and Alan's monthly expenses are not covered by the remainder of their salaries. The excess is put on credit cards and the money conflicts occur as the bills come due. Gerard works hard to budget these bills, while Alan haphazardly throws his into a desk drawer and pays them only when the dunning letters arrive. Alan's laissez-faire attitude is hopelessly confusing to Gerard, who is obsessed with accounting for every dollar spent.

Gerard doesn't trust Alan. No one, Gerard believed, could want to hurt him so often, yet be in love with him. He reacted to these slights in two related ways. At first, Gerard would react with rage directed at Alan, accusing him of dishonesty. Alan remained silent during these assaults, refusing or fearing to engage Gerard in discussion, and these sullen responses of Alan's served as further proof to Gerard of his coldness. Then Gerard would ruminate all the more, become convinced that their relationship was a sham, and decide to leave Alan. At this point, some dialogue would occur and Alan would agree to change his behavior to suit Gerard. After awhile, Gerard's anger would mount once again and the cycle of feeling unloved, mistrustful, and hostile would occur once more. Gerard felt out of control, and because his feelings were so strong, they were, he felt, destroying him. He could not clear his mind long enough to decide whether Alan did or didn't love him.

Gerard also had problems with his job. He felt that his boss didn't appreciate his work and was overly critical. Gerard typically reacted angrily and ruminated about quitting. These periods of anger were cyclical, appearing and disappearing suddenly and mysteriously. Although Gerard was sure that much of his anger was justified, he wondered at the intensity of it. The parallel affective reactions to lover and employer are obvious.

Two other problems were mentioned at the initial interview. First was his relationship to Tom, his first lover. Gerard still spoke to him every day, saw him occasionally, and considered him a person he still loved. This, too, was a source of conflict because he sometimes felt he should give up his need for Tom, but he wasn't sure. Finally, Gerard had problems with his family, who still lived in rural New England. They didn't know that Gerard was gay, though he had been

living with men now for the past sixteen years. He wanted them to
know. Gerard wanted to learn in therapy how to come out to them.
When asked why he wanted to come out to them, he replied that he
wanted to be able to take his lover home on family holidays, instead of
leaving him in New York City. When pressed further, however, he
admitted that Alan didn't want to go anyway. Gerard looked confused at this point, knowing that the issue was important to him, but
not understanding why introducing Alan to his family was so crucial.

Gerard was asked why he had decided to begin psychotherapy at
this time. He responded by first describing some recent transient
sexual activities in which he had allowed himself to be abused
physically. He feared that he was losing control over his own desires
and was inching inevitably toward contacts with sadistic sexual
partners who lacked all impulse control. Gerard described himself as
feeling like Sisyphus, the King of Corinth, who was forever doomed in
Hades to roll uphill a heavy stone that always rolled down again. This
image frightened him.

Developmental History: Early Years

Gerard's memories of early childhood are mostly sad ones. He remembers how often his father hit his mother, and how often he and the
other children would console her afterward. He can remember, too,
how often, and with such suddenness, his father would physically
attack him. One bitter memory is sleeping in bed and suddenly being
awakened by his father, who beat him as punishment for running
away from home. He also remembers an unusual relationship with his
mother. It was her daily routine from the time Gerard was between the
ages of 5 and 15 to bring him into bed with her after her husband had
left for work. With Gerard in either pajamas or underwear, and she in
a slip, she would embrace him and hold him close to her. As Gerard
got older he became aware of the potential sexuality of the situation,
though he reports not being upset by it. There were times, as he
entered adolescence, that he fondled his penis while lying in bed with

her, though he states that at no time was there any overt sex between them.

Gerard felt like Cinderella. He raised his younger brother, and was required to sweep the house each day, make the beds, and wash the dishes. Before supper, Gerard ate in the kitchen with his mother, then served the rest of the family in the dining room. He performed these tasks without complaint, although he seethed at its unfairness. He felt trapped by her, forced to spend so much time fulfilling her demands.

The image of the eroticized mother recently appeared in a dream. In it, Gerard and his mother were in bed together. She had an erect penis that Gerard recognized as his own, and he was sucking it. Interestingly, during the therapy session, he noticed that she was wearing long nylon stockings, which reminded him of his recent fetish for panty hose. The panty hose fetish had begun a few months earlier, had ceased for awhile, and had reappeared recently. He didn't know why, but during the discussion of this dream, Gerard wondered (quite appropriately) whether he was trying to act like his mother, whether he had identified with her sexually.

During this adolescent period, Gerard originated a unique fantasy concerning his parents. He believed that one day his father would come into the bedroom and show Gerard how to have sexual intercourse with his mother, and the sex act between mother and son would be completed with the father watching approvingly.

A number of significant events occurred between the ages of 12 and 14. On two occasions he tried to harm himself. The first one occurred one day as he was walking through the woods. He stopped for a moment, and then picked up a large rock and hammered it against his arm, trying, he remembers, to fracture it. He had no idea why, and ceased only when the pain became unbearable. To this day Gerard does not understand why he did it. He says that he wanted attention from his father (perhaps also to externalize the psychological pain as a sign that he was still alive).

Soon after, Gerard made the first of two suicide attempts. One Sunday morning, Gerard walked to a stone quarry. He tied himself to a rope and jumped into the water expecting to drown, but the water came up only to his chest. He dragged himself back to a boulder, took off all his clothes, and, sitting naked under the warm sun, mastur-bated.

While still sitting on that rock, Gerard decided to run away to New York City. He did so the next day, but was quickly identified by the police as a runaway and sent home. His father was furious and Gerard was beaten and prohibited from returning to school (where he had been an excellent student) and ordered to get a full-time job in a local mill. He complied, but with yet another resentment to be written on his long list of indignities suffered at home.

Gerard ran away a second time and, arriving at the New York City Port Authority Bus Terminal, became a male prostitute. By having sex with men for money and spending the night with them, he lived a marginal but satisfying existence. He never felt abused, and claims to be profoundly grateful to these men who helped him. Within a few months he traveled to Washington, D.C., where he lived briefly with a group of gay college students, again "hustled," and then went on to Myrtle Beach, South Carolina, where he swallowed a vial of pills in his second and last suicide attempt. He ended up at a psychiatric hospital for a few days, and when his parents were called, they told the hospital authorities that Gerard was on his own. He was then 15 years old. He returned to Washington, D.C., where he met his first lover.

Developmental History: Adult Years

At the age of 16 Gerard met Tom, a man of 24. To Gerard, Tom was "a grownup," a man of substance with an education, a responsible job, and a stable home. They became lovers and lived together for the next twelve years. Sex between them wasn't as exciting as the sex that Gerard had had with other men, but it wasn't as important as his needs for love, security, and a home of his own. In the protection of this environment, Gerard finished high school and eventually got his B.A.

For the first nine or ten years, they lived a comfortable life in a New York suburb. Gerard turned over his salary each week to Tom (much as he had earlier to his father). Gerard thought of this relationship as "we," an affair of intimacy and love. But much as Gerard tried, he could not ignore their sexual incompatibility, for Gerard was becoming more passive sexually while Tom was becoming increasingly distant. Gerard fled to anonymous sexual encounters, most often in "t-rooms," almost every day. He never told Tom of this. Gerard's sexual feelings also began to change from conventional ones to masochistic ones involving leather and humiliation. He mentioned these fantasies to Tom, who became anxious and refused to discuss them.

Gerard's sexual fantasies continued to change over time. He found himself walking the streets of New York looking at men dressed in leather, wondering about the kind of sex they had, and soon these men appeared in his masturbation fantasies. Again Gerard tried to discuss the fantasies with Tom, who dismissed them as unimportant. Gerard said nothing more, though the fantasies persisted. Within a year their relationship ended.

Upon moving to New York, Gerard experimented with S & M sex. He knew after his first experience that he was a "bottom man." As he says, "It never occurred to me to be a top man." He had all the sex he wanted, yet missed the intimacy of a love relationship.

A year later, Gerard met Alan. Alan was a few years older and taught at a large urban university. Alan was a "top" and they were sexually compatible. They have lived together for six years. Neither asks for sexual fidelity in a lover. Although they maintain a good sexual relationship with each other, they also participate in encounters with other men.

In some respects Gerard is tyrannical toward Alan. For instance, Gerard believes that lovers must eat all meals together. Also at meals, Gerard does not condone the eating of foods that he doesn't like, even if Alan likes the foods, or even if friends invited to the house for dinner may like them. Not only does he exercise a veritable veto over foods served at home, but he's also offended if Alan orders a taboo food for himself at a restaurant. So Alan is never allowed to eat any of the foods he enjoys. Gerard is the one who plans everything, including vacations, buying furniture, remodeling the house, and balancing finances. In short, Gerard plans and controls all household and personal functions.

PERSONALITY DYNAMICS: THE TRADITIONAL BPD SYNDROME

Let us first note that the case of Gerard is that of a reasonably well-functioning person, certainly a high-level BPD as described by Kernberg. There are none of the psychotic episodes or drug addictions that one often finds in borderline people. He also illustrates many of the personality dynamics that are becoming more common in clinical settings, particularly in gay men.

Splitting: The Good/Bad Dimension

Gerard's affection dimensions are bifurcated, consisting only of extremes and allowing for no differentiation of meaning; they are categorical judgments of either goodness or badness. Such affective dichotomies can be interpreted as developmentally primitive because they first appear in the earliest years of life, and only with later, more mature learning does differentiation occur, and with it a changed perception of the world and oneself.

Splitting refers to much more than just extremes of evaluative judgment. If we had, for instance, a person who was rigid and unyielding in perception, and who judged others as either good or bad, we would not have an example of splitting. Such a person would probably fall under the rubric of a character disorder. He would be certain of his judgments, experience problems as externally caused, and, most important, would not experience any conflict. The bad person is bad—period. But in the case of splitting as a personality dynamic, judgments are fluid, and a sense of certainty is impossible. He who is perceived as good during one moment in time may change suddenly to a bad person, someone who inexplicably is transformed from one who loves to one who hates or is dangerous in some way. A sense of psychological stability is therefore impossible because the world is ever-changing and always carries the potential for threat. It is a psychological plague—and very painful.

Gerard's reactions to present and former lovers, to employers, and to transient sexual partners appear to be all of a kind. One gets the impression that all are invested with the attribute of "father." There is a good/bad affective dimension attached to the concept of father, and Gerard appears to judge potential father figures on the basis of their goodness or badness. In Gerard's history we find an idealized image of a man, say, a lover. To this person, who we may assume has assets and liabilities as any other, Gerard attributes characteristics that represent a fantasy vision of the good and loving father, while ignoring any dissonant information. The perceptual and affectional distortion is twofold: on the one hand he attributes mythical characteristics to the person, and on the other he represses or ignores those characteristics of the person that are incongruent. Though perhaps not intentional, the process is hostile toward the other insofar as it denies to the other the right to his own individuality. The object of this distortion is, in a sense, a metaphorical prisoner of Gerard's search for the loving father.

The object of Gerard's affection, and most recently this has been his lover, Alan, cannot possibly know or understand that he is required to play the dual roles of the good father from the past and the good lover of today. He is bound to balk at the requirements, which are likely to be experienced as confusion, and to make some gesture of rejection toward Gerard. This conflict, often over symbolic material, results in the instantaneous metamorphosis of the good father into the bad one, and having done that, Gerard reacts to the disappointment in his characteristic ways: anger, attack, and running away to have sexual encounters.

Given this developmental sequence, we have every right to assume that the affective dichotomy of good boy/bad boy occurred

earlier than good father/bad father.[7] We may further suggest that
"son" and "father" interact in such a way as to show that Gerard's
judgment of his own, in contrast to his father's, goodness or badness is
in direct proportion to the perceived goodness or badness of the
father. This can be easily illustrated diagrammatically (see Figure 6–1).

Box 1 represents the idealized and fantasized relationship between Gerard and his father, and also his perception of romantic and
authority figures. Box 4, on the other hand, represents the perceived
reality of his relationship to his father, and reasserts itself with each
frustration or conflict with a lover or authority figure. Box 4 is also a
statement of the genesis of depression because it is a hopeless situation
in which love, caring, and intimacy cannot exist. Boxes 2 and 3 are,
for all intents and purposes, insignificant because not enough individuation between father and son has occurred to allow for judgments to
be made of the two independent people.

This repetitive pattern of disappointment in love in adulthood
leads to deep feelings of depression in Gerard, much as the disappointments in childhood led to depression during those early years. A
chronic depression is, in fact, one of the most prominent aspects of
Gerard's personality. The feeling of having been rejected by his father
(who also failed to protect him from his mother) in his early years is
not yet history because the feelings of rejection are continually
reexperienced in adulthood. Though the relationship between any
son and his father is important, it is possible that the relationship
between a gay-to-be son and his father is even more important
(Silverstein 1981). In addition, there are the morning bed experiences
with his mother, a seductive scene to which Gerard acquiesced and
entwined in the fantasy that his father would teach him how to have
sex with his mother. It would be hard to imagine those experiences
and fantasies without the production of guilt. Though he rarely
expresses guilty feelings, one might reasonably hypothesize that beneath the smoke screen of verbal attack lies low self-esteem and

---

[7]One would expect a similar dichotomy to exist with regard to the
mother, but this has not yet emerged.

Father

	Good	Bad
Good Gerard	Box 1 Good father Good son	Box 2 Bad father Good son
Bad	Box 3 Good father Bad son	Box 4 Bad father Bad son

FIGURE 6–1

feelings of guilt. One therefore needs to explain how Gerard defends himself against the feelings of depression, guilt, low self-esteem, and the fear of abandonment.

The dynamics of depression suggest that it can be dealt with in at least two ways: it can be expressed, leading to reduced motoric activity and the feeling of helplessness, or it can be defended against through a form of reaction-formation, leading to increased motoric behavior and the pretense of domination over the environment. In the former, a passive orientation to the environment is suggested, whereas the latter suggests an active orientation. Of these two orientations to depression, Gerard has chosen the latter ego-syntonic approach, whereby he defends himself against depression through acting-out behavior, convinced not that there is something wrong with him, but that he must protect himself from the malevolence of others.

Two events in Gerard's history show how early his defenses against depression began, and how they relate to current adult behaviors: the arm-wounding and the suicide attempt. Self-harm was the result of depression and the feeling of extreme isolation. In the arm-wounding incident, Gerard remembers hoping that his father would take care of him, and so this suggests a manipulation tied to depression. In his suicide attempt, we have for the first time an association between depression and sexual excitement. One might hypothesize that by the age of 14 Gerard had learned to adapt to depression by transforming it into excitement, and then to release the excitement through orgasm. Because the masturbation, a motoric act, substituted for the affect of depression, we are entitled to call it an acting-out behavior and to hypothesize that adult sexuality may share the same characteristics as these early adolescent experiences, namely, manipulation of others by self-harm, and sexuality as an acting-out behavior to camouflage depression. Of course, we would also expect the origins of these dynamics to be placed much earlier chronologically, but those memories are still subject to repression.

This acting-out as a defense against the depression created by feelings of abandonment takes two forms: toward his lover, Gerard attacks, punishing Alan for reminding him of his feelings of early abandonment, and at the same time, Gerard acts out sexually, seeking a new transient love object. The alleviation of depression by sexual release had begun the day when Gerard tried to commit suicide in the quarry, and that dynamic continues. Confusion results because he is at once attacking one man (Alan) while showing love toward another (during anonymous sex). The totality of this behavior would have to be mystifying.

Identity Diffusion

Lack of individuation from both parents is one of the most significant variables in Gerard's depression and acting-out behavior. Although he is clearly aware of his judgments toward his father, Gerard is less aware that they are also a projection of his feelings about himself, and that these feelings are the most significant, therapeutically speaking.

The identity diffusion involves the mother as well, and this is indicated by the incestuous fantasies, his dreams, and his current, though sporadic, interest in panty hose. One gets the impression from Gerard that ego diffusion toward the father concerns goodness and badness, while toward the mother it concerns sensuality, sexuality, and sensitivity. One would also think that over time these ego diffusions toward both parents would lead to resentment on Gerard's part because of his perceived loss of psychological freedom, illustrated so poignantly by him in this recital of the myth of Sisyphus. Gerard reacts toward these identity diffusions differentially; toward those with power, as with lovers and employers, he acts aggressively, as if he were the bad son, and they the bad fathers. Anonymous sexual partners, however, more likely represent the maternal diffusion and hence are more sensual, more pleasing sexually, and interpreted as more intimate. It is now clear why Gerard ran away from home at ages 14 and 15. It was an attempt to find his own identity and to define his own ego boundaries, though he would hardly have understood this at the time. His running away behavior in recent years is merely a repetition of his search for his individuality.

The identity diffusion has markedly affected Gerard's experience of sexuality. Although his sense of being a gay man has always been secure, his specific sexual behaviors have shifted over time. He began with "vanilla" sex, then turned to hustling, and then, during a brief period in adolescence, had an affair with a woman. During his twelve-year relationship with his first lover, he began the period of anonymous sex in t-rooms. After their break-up, Gerard came out once again, this time into S & M sex as a bottom man. He continues his outside sex while in his current love relationship. Most recently, he has experimented having sex while wearing panty hose, a sexual variation that causes him a great deal of anxiety, perhaps because of the fear that a greater propensity toward "drag" lurks not too far from the surface of consciousness. For our purposes, it is not relevant whether Gerard is in "the closet" with respect to women's apparel (he isn't). His anxiety is caused by the feeling of helplessness over his own sexual fantasies.

One needs to be careful here because it's easy to fall into Victorian standards of sexuality. In the modern gay male community, versatility is valued. A gay man can voluntarily choose between a variety of sexual acts to please himself or a partner, or alter his sexual needs to complement a transient mood. This versatility is an asset when under voluntary control, but in the history reported here, it is not so much versatility as it is a dramatic change in sexuality, wherein a past mode is given up and replaced by a new one.

S & M Sex

Gerard's current sexual behavior appears to be another important dynamic in his search for a good father to take care of him. S & M sexuality is ideally suited to Gerard's adoptive behavior because it creates a clear structure around sexuality. In the first place, the "slave" is taken care of by his "master," a responsibility that is taken very seriously by mature advocates of S & M. To Gerard, who certainly plays a child-like, obedient role, the master, not unlike his father, instructs him as to proper behavior, punishes violations, and rewards obedience. All of this is done according to mutually agreed upon rules. Gerard is also punished physically by the "top," as he was by his father many years ago. S & M therefore avoids any ambiguity as to status and responsibility. At the same time it allows Gerard to please his mentor for the night, which, in a sense, makes the top man less threatening. The punishment may also alleviate the feelings of guilt and help Gerard to feel alive and worthwhile.

More recently, Gerard's need to be punished has gotten out of control, perhaps because depressed feelings have been rising to consciousness. His fear that he may allow himself to be seriously abused is well founded. What has happened from a dynamic point of view is that Gerard has sought out impulse-laden sadists who lack control, whereas in the past he was quite adept at choosing sadists who were highly sensitive to his physical and psychological limits. The harmful S & M experiences, then, are a result of the return of depressed feelings to which are attached feelings of guilt, and for which extreme physical punishment for fantasized crimes are arranged. These fantasized crimes are likely to be incestuous mother/son feelings.

Problems in the area of independence/dependence affect all aspects of Gerard's current life, and this conflict is often acted-out in the drama of S & M encounters. The forceful demand for independence from Alan is more likely a defense by Gerard against his own desire for, and fear of, passivity—the desire to be taken care of, and a passivity that is expressed sexually when he plays a dependent role, but not in his love relationship, wherein trust may lead to feelings of abandonment. As independent as he may pretend to be, and as far away as he may be from his family, for Gerard individuation is not yet an accomplished fact, which probably explains why he continues to hold onto former lovers. Another example of Gerard's conflict in the independence/dependence continuum is his compulsive need to return to his parents' home periodically, trying to create a loving relationship with his parents, only to become disillusioned once again and leave in anger.

Finally, we might note the particular effect of anxiety on Gerard, which is, once again, common in the borderline personality. People with BPD are not more anxious than others, nor do they typically decompensate if they experience a high level of anxiety. Kernberg (1975) illustrated this well. Whether the person typically experiences high or low anxiety in day-to-day living, he becomes accustomed to it and copes well with it. It is only when the anxiety reaches a point much higher than the person's norm that anxiety leads to acting-out behavior. For one person, it may be a relatively low level of anxiety, whereas for another person, a very high level of anxiety is needed to lead to acting-out. In low-level borderline people, the overproduction of anxiety may lead to transient psychotic episodes or drug addiction. In high-level people, it leads to depression and, as in this case, to sexual acting-out. Seeking transient sexual experiences is Gerard's characteristic way of coping with higher than normal anxiety levels. These sexual experiences are a good palliative to anxiety, and after them the anxiety level returns to normal. Without them, a slow but steady decompensation results. It should also be noted that sexual versatility is an asset in Gerard, so that his transient encounters are almost always pleasing for him and his partner.

Gerard from a Cultural Perspective

A shifting world is very unpleasant. Even when change is explicable, many people have a hard time feeling competent, but when the change comes from within the psyche, and is experienced as involuntary, confusion results.

Gerard is an excellent example of a person most vulnerable to external change. Early experiences make it difficult for him to perceive the world accurately. What are Gerard's alternatives when finding his experiential world constantly shifting, and when loved ones like family and lovers can take on the lineaments of Dr. Jekyll? How often such a person must wonder, "Can no one be trusted?" The experiential world is, for Gerard and for many gay people today, a dangerous place that must be controlled for the sake of personal safety.

No doubt Gerard has been difficult at home. He demands behavior from his lover that is unreasonable. This is not compulsivity. It results from two things: the first is his fantasy of creating a more stable home than the one he came from, and the other is a reaction against Alan's laissez-faire behavior. The tidiness that Gerard demands of Alan is a mechanism to control internal confusion by creating external order—having everything out there in its proper place relieves the feeling of disorder within.

A metaphorical concept would be helpful now: the idea of an expanding ego. Those of us trained in traditional analytic theories are used to thinking of the ego —the reality testing part of one's personality—as a boundary between the person and the outside world. In textbooks, it is most commonly illustrated by a circle—"*me*" in the center, and everything else outside. We've been taught that the rigidity of this boundary, or its fluidity, typified either the neurotic or the normal person. But for each individual the size of the circle remained essentially the same.

Might we suggest that there are people, like Gerard, whose ego boundaries expand and contract depending upon the individual's perception of safety or threat?

No one can live in a psychological world composed of chaos. Such deterioration could end only in psychosis, suicide, or drug addiction. A person's self-esteem must be restored in some way. If a person's ego lacks the power to control its own impulses and feelings (some colleagues would insist on calling this an id/ego conflict), it can expand into the outside world to control it, thereby restoring for awhile the internal confusion.[8]

It is not unusual for a person with a deficient concept of self to symbolize the internal disorder through projection of the self onto the environment. The boundaries of the self expand, in a sense, marching over the usual demarcation between self and the outside world, and end up treating the immediate external environment as if it were the ego itself. In Gerard's case, the untidiness of home is menacing because it becomes a vivid representation of his own internal untidiness. The laissez-faire behavior of his lover must be controlled because it might magically transport him back to his original home, the one he hated and feared so much. When Gerard no longer feels attacked, and internal order is restored, the ego contracts and he can experience feelings of love toward Alan and others.

Please do not be confused about the expanding ego. It is not an

---

[8]The idea of an expanding ego is a metaphor; it is not a real thing. It is not like a balloon expanding with the introduction of puffs of air. Nor is the ego a real thing; it too is a metaphor. Our present diagnostic system, and previous systems, are also metaphors, albeit complicated ones, for the worries and concerns of a particular society at a particular time in its history. This is as true of early societies that explained human behavior in terms of dybbuks and demons intruding into the consciousness of the victim as it is of our modern society, which explains human behavior in intrapsychic terms. Descriptions of diagnoses, ego defenses, indeed, all psychological jargon, are not characteristics of the person being described. They are merely convenient, and one hopes useful, ways of organizing the observations of the perceiver.

indication of psychological strength. For instance, it does not show the ability to experience intimacy. Intimacy results when an outsider is allowed through a person's ego boundaries and into the person's concept of self—a potential threat—creating an acceptable feeling of vulnerability. This is very different than an expanding ego, whereby the person throws a net around others to capture them, control them, and make them safe. Intimacy allows the others to be free, while an expanding ego encapsulates them like flies in amber.

What an exhausting process this is, remaining vigilant against any sign of external disorder. Someone less capable than Gerard would live a different life-style, fearing the danger of intimate relationships and therefore seeking only serial relationships with others. Gerard's solution is to have serial, time-limited, transient relationships in his outside affairs, in which his partners are experienced as all good, and a stable home life with his lover, who is perceived sometimes as good and at other times bad.

From this cultural perspective, we can see Gerard's behavior as an attempt to create order in the world. To a large extent he has been successful. As a matter of fact, one might marvel at how well he has coped, given his early experiences. He has remained and been successful in his profession for many years, and is now an executive. Gerard has not given up in his demand for a loving gay relationship. His first lasted for twelve years, and his second is now, as of this writing, in its fourth year. He may often want to walk out, but he's never so foolish as to actually do it.

BORDERLINE PERSONALITY AND GAY PEOPLE

There is no question that the concept of the Borderline Personality has important consequences for gay people. It makes no difference whether the etiological theory suggested by object relations analysts is accurate. From a metaphorical point of view, the diagnostic category viewed from a cultural perspective highlights the problems of social change for many gay people.

We all do not come from loving families. Those who do not, and even those who do, are faced with a world that presents a confusion of alternatives. This is true of all of our citizens, homosexual as well as heterosexual. But the heterosexual world, as it is changing, at least is changing from a recognized standard, and the changes from the past can be charted and evaluated. The heterosexual man, for instance, need only ask of himself, "What kind of man do I want to be?" It is unlikely that he would even think of asking, "What kind of heterosexual man do I want to be?"

But the gay individual must solve questions of both gender identity and sexual identity. The levels of potential confusion for gays are, therefore, twice those of heterosexuals. This obviously leads to considerably more alternatives, and hence, more potential confusion. We might hypothesize, therefore—and this is my second point—that the more the innovations in society favor the acceptance of variations in life-style, the greater the confusion in those groups that vary the most from the norm—such as gay people. Again, as discrimination is reduced, we should expect some gay people to experience more confusion. The Bell and Weinberg (1978) study, albeit with data collected before the Stonewall riot, confirms this. Gays attempted suicide five times more often than heterosexuals, and experience more depression and loneliness. One also tends to see this disorganization more clearly in the gay male world than in the lesbian one because men are more visible and open. One also finds it in the difficulty of some gay men to participate in an intimate relationship, and in some lesbians who cannot help from merging with a lover.

This itself may sound confusing. It may sound like the traditional argument that gay people are psychologically disturbed. But that is not the intention. The psychological problems of gays will be different after gay liberation from what they were before it. Let us make the contrast in time periods more clear.

Before gay liberation, self-loathing and guilt were common

enough in the gay community. Depression was probably the single most important psychological dynamic for a number of reasons, with suicide commonly enough the result. Society's oppression took an awesome toll in gay lives.

Now there is less guilt in the gay world. More gay people are open with family, employers, and friends—and reap the rewards of a person who removes the chains of fear from his or her body. Consequently, depression has become less of a problem than it was earlier. But if gays have few, if any, stable standards of behavior from the past and now have more internal problems to solve in order to create a sense of psychological stability, then it follows that more of them will experience confusion, and even sexual fluidity.

Does this argument suggest that gays are "sicker" than heterosexuals? No, it does not. The question "Are homosexuals sick?" was specious twenty years ago, and is irrelevant today. A sexual orientation is not "healthy" or "sick" (Begelman 1977). To perceive it in these terms requires acceptance of the medical model as the only arbiter of social behavior.

What we might expect to find in the gay population is a bimodal curve of social and personal adaptability. On the lower end of the curve are those gay people—like Gerard—whose early experiences limited their capacity to deal with conflict and ambiguity. There are probably many gay people, men and women, in this category.

But we are likely to find another group of gay people who have learned to cope with the newly allowed freedoms, people who probably come from more nurturant families or who for reasons we ill-understand turn society's opprobrium into psychological strength. These gay people may even turn out to be more adaptable to social and psychological vicissitudes than the average heterosexual person.

From this vantage point, we might predict that over time, as standards of conduct become more predictable in the gay community, the curve of adaptability between these two groups of gay people should change to a normal one. It further suggests that a homogenization will occur in the area of sexual identity.

A FINAL NOTE

What should we make of this new diagnostic category, the Borderline Personality Disorder? Does it exist, and if so, what diagnostic areas lie on either side of the boundary? The question assumes that one diagnostic system is more accurate than another, when in fact diagnostic systems are themselves a reflection of the culture, the times, and, though many professionals dislike admitting it, political negotiation and compromise. The battle over the status of homosexuality in the psychiatric nomenclature is a good example of politics and negotiation in diagnosis (Bayer 1981).

What is of importance to those of us who work with gay people is the idea that they are faced with a disproportionate number of problems. The new cultural belief in individualism has its price: taking responsibility and making choices within a confusing array of possibilities. Those gay people who come from disoriented families will face this freedom ambivalently, unconsciously missing the former social structures that ameliorated family deficiencies. It is toward those people, like Gerard, who live and love in a hostile world that we need to direct our professional competence so that the cultural freedom becomes a personal one as well.

REFERENCES

American Psychiatric Association. (1980). *Diagnostic and Statistical Manual of Mental Disorders*, 3rd ed. Washington, DC: American Psychiatric Press.

Bayer, R. (1981). *Homosexuality and American Psychiatry*. New York: Basic Books.

Begelman, D. (1977). Homosexuality: the ethical challenge: paper 3. *Journal of Homosexuality* 2:213–219.

Bell, A., and Weinberg, M. (1978). *Homosexualities: A Study of Diversity Among Men and Women*. New York: Simon and Schuster.

Bem, S. (1974). The measurement of psychological androgyny. *Journal of Consulting and Clinical Psychology* 42:155–162.

Chodorow, N. (1978). *The Reproduction of Mothering: Psychoanalysis and the Sociology of Gender.* Berkeley, CA: University of California Press.

Faderman, L. (1981). *Surpassing the Love of Men: Romantic Friendship and Love Between Women from the Renaissance to the Present.* New York: Morrow.

Flexner, E. (1975). *Century of Struggle: The Women's Rights Movement in the United States.* Cambridge, MA: Belknap Press of Harvard Universities Press.

Freud, S. (1914). On narcissism: an introduction. *Standard Edition* 14:67–102.

Katz, J. (1976). *Gay American History: Lesbians and Gay Men in the U.S.A. – A Documentary.* New York: Crowell.

Kernberg, O. (1975). *Borderline Conditions and Pathological Narcissism.* New York: Jason Aronson.

Kiernan, J. (1884). Insanity: lecture XXVI. Sexual perversion. *Detroit Lancet* 7:481–484.

Kinsey, A., Pomeroy, W., and Martin, C. (1948). *Sexual Behavior in the Human Male.* Philadelphia: Saunders.

Kohut, H. (1971). *The Analysis of the Self.* New York: International Universities Press.

Lauritsen, J., and Thorstad, D. (1974). *The Early Homosexual Rights Movement.* New York: Times Change Press.

Macintosh, M. (1968). The homosexual role. *Social Problems* 16:182–192.

Masterson, J. (1981). *Narcissistic and Borderline Disorders.* New York: Brunner/Mazel.

Meissner, W. (1983). Notes on the levels of differentiation within borderline conditions. *The Psychoanalytic Review* 70:170–209.

Rinsley, D. (1982). *Borderline and Other Self Disorders: A Developmental and Object-Relations Perspective.* New York: Jason Aronson.

Silverstein, C. (1976–1977). Even psychiatry can profit from its past mistakes. *Journal of Homosexuality* 2:153–158.

———— (1981). *Man to Man: Gay Couples in America.* New York: Morrow.

_____ (1984). The ethical and moral implications of sexual classification: a commentary. *Journal of Homosexuality* 9:29–38.

Steakley, J. (1975). *The Homosexual Emancipation Movement in Germany.* New York: Arno.

Weeks, J. (1977). *Coming out: Homosexual Politics in Britain, From the Nineteenth Century to the Present.* London: Quartet.

Ziesat, H., Jr. (1983). Borderline personality: on which border is the line located? (Review of *Borderline and Other Self Disorders: A Developmental and Object-Relations Perspective.*) *Contemporary Psychology* 28:665–667.

7

The Process of Dynamic Psychotherapy with Gay Men Living with HIV

ROSS HUDSON, LCSW
CARLTON CORNETT, LCSW

INTRODUCTION

The human immunodeficiency virus (HIV) and acquired immunodeficiency syndrome (AIDS) have forever changed the practice of dynamic psychotherapy with gay men. The sine qua non of the dynamic perspective has always been an unyielding interest in the internal world of the patient and a relegation of the external world to the role of derivative communication. HIV has necessitated a change in that emphasis. It is impossible for a psychotherapist to make the physical and social concerns of an HIV-infected patient subservient to the internal world of fantasy, dream, and memory. Now, psychotherapy must balance the internal (e.g., guilt, shame, fear, anger, and their associated fantasy and other manifestations) with the external (e.g., deteriorating physical health, social ostracism, isolation, and discrimination). Striking this balance will be a difficult transition for many, especially more classically oriented, psychotherapists, but for those working with gay men living with HIV, it is an unavoidable reality.

One of the variables adding to the difficulty of this transition is the paucity of literature on dynamically oriented treatment of gay men with HIV. Gochros (1992) and Shernoff (1990) have both looked thoughtfully at the impact that HIV has had on social work practice. Bosnak (1989) has poignantly described the psychotherapy of an HIV-infected young man who ultimately died during their work together. Cabaj (1988) has proposed an AIDS neurosis (i.e., the conviction, supported by conversion symptomatology, that one has AIDS in the face of ambiguous or even contradictory evidence). Isay (Chapter 8) discusses some of the countertransference issues involved in the psychoanalytic treatment of gay men with HIV. However, as yet there has been no comprehensive discussion of the process of dynamic psychotherapy with gay men living with HIV.

In this chapter we will focus on the dynamic perspective and skills necessary to offer assistance to this patient group. We will emphasize technical issues in responding to a gay man first realizing that he is infected with HIV, aiding a patient in reviewing his life and planning for the future, and the perspective necessary for helpful dynamic psychotherapy to take place. We will also focus on the countertransference effects that a patient's HIV has on the psychotherapist in her or his clinical work with that patient. Although detailed comparisons of approaches could be entertained, we have attempted to keep the discussion on practical, clinically based issues affecting the conduct of a psychotherapy.

A DYNAMIC PERSPECTIVE

Hearing the Patient without Defensive Distortion

A diagnosis of HIV infection does not begin a life. There are myriad developmental experiences upon which an HIV infection is superimposed. However, a diagnosis of HIV infection brings to the forefront many of the individual's characteristic ways of seeing himself, the world around him, and characteristic methods of problem-solving. As has been stressed in other chapters, these ways of viewing the self, relationships, and the resolution(s) of problems are often influenced by a development characterized by rejection and devaluation. The first task of the psychotherapist is to respond empathically to the diagnosis without being overwhelmed by it. As psychotherapy unfolds she or he will be working with the patient's entire life, rather than with just the circumscribed HIV diagnosis.

The therapist's response to the HIV diagnosis, however, must also avoid being dismissive. Although this point seems obvious, the therapist's responsiveness is subject to her or his own defenses that are often interferences in optimal responsiveness. The initial hour with a patient who has HIV is the first time many therapists face a patient with a life-threatening or physically degenerative illness. There is a possibility of dismissing the emotional and social consequences of the patient's physical condition through blatant denial or through an almost magical belief that psychotherapy may cure the HIV.

For therapists who have worked extensively with people living with HIV, it is possible to dismiss the uniqueness of the diagnosis for the patient because of another defensive need to categorize it as "I've seen it a million times." This posture, an inherent countertransference danger, may be a sign of the therapist's own unresolved grief about losses of former patients and/or friends to AIDS. However many times the therapist feels that she or he has trod the path previously, it is the patient's first sojourn, and his unique experience must be heard.

Whatever motivation may underlie a therapist's need to minimize or fail to recognize the idiosyncratic nature of the patient's response to an HIV diagnosis, such a response can replay significant developmental experiences involving a lack of empathy and regard. Such a response can also set into motion dynamics that might be labeled as "negative transference" when, in fact, they are beholden to a failure in therapist empathy. An iatrogenic injury of this type may

confirm a patient's view of himself as unworthy of being valued or
treated empathically, even at such a traumatic juncture in his life.

HIV and Identity

An integral part of the patient's response to his diagnosis is how it
affects his sense of self. Many patients quickly develop an identity that
revolves solely around the HIV diagnosis; they see themselves as
"sick." Castelnuovo-Tedesco (1991a) notes that a physical ailment /
injury often assumes an important role in the identity of the person
afflicted. Indeed, the physical difficulty can give tangible identity to a
long-term, perhaps life-long, sense of the self as shameful or inadequate (Castelnuovo-Tedesco 1991b). For gay men living with HIV this
can be an important dynamic.

In 1974, when the American Psychiatric Association removed
homosexuality from its official list of mental disorders, gay men began
to experience some hope that they were on the way to achieving
acceptance from an important quarter of society. Their homosexuality
was no longer labeled "sick." With the inception of the AIDS epidemic
in the American gay community, many gay men have felt that their
hard-fought gains have been eroding and that they are once again prey
to labels of sickness, albeit this time in the physical realm. In either
realm, the labels are attached to a most fundamental aspect of their
identities, their sexuality, and the "sick" label again has moral overtones, as it did when homosexuality was referred to as a "perversion."
Further, gay men often experience the HIV diagnosis as a punishment
for sexual behavior (i.e., "something I brought upon myself"). This
sense of the self as morally "sick" and deserving of punishment suggests
an internalization of societal intolerance toward homosexuality; it
enunciates shame and loathing for the self culminating in a need for
atonement, ultimately involving destruction of the self.

For this reason, the therapist is often the first person the patient
tells about his HIV status. One example is Bernie, a young gay man
who had just learned of his HIV infection, who presented for an initial

interview with his therapist acknowledging: "You are the first person I have admitted to that I have AIDS. I want to be released from the secret. I feel like I want to scream, but I'm afraid of doing that; death may hear me. My friends don't know. My family doesn't know. I'm alone, what can I do?" The patient seeks from the therapist the ability to hear his feelings and his story without moral condemnation. He seeks a safe refuge to review his life and to talk about the future. Bernie's belief that death is close enough to hear his cries of pain is not unusual, and most patients recently diagnosed as HIV positive are convinced that death is a constant and impatient companion.

Psychotherapy and "Cure"

One hope that the patient brings to the therapist in a first meeting is that there is some sense, some meaning that he can discern from both his history and the future (although the future is often seen as very limited). Dynamic psychotherapy, by its very nature, can potentiate the patient's review of his history while joining him in obviating the need to plan for the future. The challenge to the psychotherapist is to maintain a balance in her or his attention to life review and hope for the future.

It is at this initial point of contact with the patient that the therapist must also come to terms with the possibilities and limitations of psychotherapy. We have known colleagues and supervisees who nurtured the unconscious notion that psychotherapy could cure HIV. This unconscious notion resulted in driven behavior that was generally destructive to them and of no help to their patients. This unconscious conviction may, at least in part, be an internalization of the psychoanalytic conception of "cure."

Psychoanalytic thought is founded upon the notion that "cure" is possible for a wide range of difficulties and symptoms. To fail to achieve less than "cure" is often perceived as failure in toto. However, to achieve what is possible in psychotherapy with the gay man living with HIV, the therapist must give up the idea that she or he holds the

potential to eradicate his patient's HIV difficulties. Rather, the therapist must accept the idea that psychotherapy can help the patient
adapt to traumatic and changing life circumstances and that this
adaptation can include joy, satisfaction, and fulfillment, but not
"cure." A more complete discussion of countertransference issues will
be undertaken below. To be as helpful as possible to a patient, the
therapist must enter the psychotherapy relationship devoid of the
fantasy that she or he can effect a "cure."

Creating an Ambiance for Psychotherapy

Generally, the diagnosis of HIV infection, no matter how delivered or
by whom, is heard as a death sentence. Coupled with this is the
terrible notion that it is both a sentence with almost immediate
consequences and without appeal. Further, having received the diagnosis is something that cannot be discussed with others. This is a
forerunner of the later conflict regarding who can be told and whom
the secret must be kept from forever (Greif and Porembski 1989).
Many patients, as they think about telling others, immediately antic-
ipate the question of how they were exposed to the virus. For those gay
men who are not open regarding their sexuality, this is an aspect of
talking about the diagnosis that relegates it to secrecy. Shame and
guilt are obviously a part of this initial reaction.

   This dynamic should be at the forefront of the therapist's mind
as the patient reveals his HIV status. This revelation is almost a gift of
trust that the therapist will have but one opportunity to acknowledge.
The patient will be searching the therapist for any sign of rejection,
fear, or withdrawal. Although there is obviously no set way for the
therapist to respond, whatever response is made must cherish the
patient's trust. Such a response will move the patient a great deal
toward seeing his diagnosis without the blinding overlay of shame.

   Often, dynamically oriented therapists treat shame, however, as
an entirely internally motivated reaction. While our contention is that
many gay men are thoroughly tutored in shame, it is crucial for the

therapist to remember that ours is a very shaming culture. Put simply, the patient's concerns regarding being ostracized and rejected after revealing his diagnosis may have more than a slight potential for coming to pass. As well as being accepting of the diagnosis, the therapist must be aware that others may not be accepting (i.e., that the patient's concerns are not paranoid projections, etc.). The therapist's unwillingness to acknowledge this does violence to the patient's sense of reality and a disservice to his self-esteem. Acknowledging that the therapist understands that discrimination and rejection are realistic concerns furthers trust in the relationship. Initially, interpretations concerning the patient's guilt and/or shame are best left unsaid. The not-so-simple task of listening is a more helpful response.

It is at this point that the therapist, too, must give up the idea of "therapeutic neutrality" as it has been traditionally considered. The patient has opened dialogue about a matter of life and death—his life and death; there is no neutrality in this matter. The therapist must be willing to be firmly, unshakeably on the side of the patient and, further, be willing to show this. The blank screen interpreter must be replaced by a human being obviously and deeply concerned about his patient's welfare and one who avoids conceptualizing the patient's reactions as solely the products of internal conflict. This is not to suggest that an analytic attitude be dismissed, only that an austere environment that focuses exclusively on the displacement and projection of intrapsychic conflicts is not appropriate to clinical work with gay men who are living with HIV.

The diagnosis of HIV infection is almost invariably an overwhelming trauma for the patient. It is impossible to consciously integrate this trauma until he begins to talk about it. Some patients respond to this trauma with denial. These patients often attempt to integrate the trauma through action, particularly suicidal ideation and behavior, when words are unavailable. For example, Peter felt next to nothing when he received his diagnosis. He later reported that he thought this sense of numbness was expected. He did begin to question his lack of emotional responsiveness when it lasted for over two weeks and he found himself preoccupied with suicidal thoughts.

During an initial contact with the patient it is important to ask what he heard when told of his diagnosis. Some patients will have no memory, whereas others will be able to quote the conversation relating their diagnosis verbatim. It is important to inquire about this experience because it offers information to the therapist and patient regarding the level of denial being used to deal with the trauma. This also offers the therapist an opening to explore actions that are destructively maintaining the denial.

The initial contact sets the tone for the remainder of the therapy. If the therapist is sensitive, empathic, and ready to hear the patient's concerns, then the therapy moves into an exploration of the patient's guilt and grieving.

GUILT, GRIEF, AND GRIEVING

In our society, HIV has an inherent capacity to twice harm those it afflicts. First, the disease ravages the body; as this is happening, the person with HIV also has to struggle with feelings of guilt regarding the fact that he has the disease. The disease is biological, whereas the guilt is an artifact of our culture.

Sex and sexuality continue to be difficult for many people to accept as a healthy part of life. For all else that has changed since Freud practiced in Vienna, that fact has not. When venereal disease is added to this already complicated equation it is difficult, sometimes even for therapists, to avoid moralizing (Nichols, Mattison, and Shattls 1989). Many who are not therapists do not even try. The result of this is that most gay men living with HIV face open, and often virulent, condemnation. Rather than focusing on the fact that someone has HIV or AIDS, our society often focuses on *how* he was infected. No other life-threatening disease (e.g., cancer, heart disease) has the cultural stigma that is attached to AIDS. The fact that AIDS is often sexually transmitted is an integral part of this stigma.

Many gay men living with HIV mirror society in their ambivalence and conflicts about the morality of sex in general. However, in addition to this, most have faced societal condemnation and rejection for most of their lives for their homosexuality. This adds a second component to the guilt felt about acquiring HIV. It is not at all uncommon to hear a gay man with HIV moralizing about his sexual behavior and linking the HIV with some grotesque type of punishment for that behavior. This moralizing can take the form of direct invectives leveled against the self, or, more subtly, self-loathing humor.

Jake, a 38-year-old gay man, related in an initial interview that he was not "surprised" by having acquired HIV because "I was such a whore. I would spend all weekend having sex with men at the baths." Jake related this with laughter and seemed to be attempting to engage the therapist in the "humor" of his situation. Beneath the joviality, however, seemed an attempt to engage the therapist in a collusion to condemn him.

As the patient moves out of the initial phase of revealing his HIV status and moves into the phase of attempting to understand his life in juxtaposition to it, the therapist's first task is to illuminate the guilt that often remains tucked below the surface of the patient's conscious world.

The therapist must address the patient's guilt or it will block the completion of his grieving his HIV status and adaptation to the HIV. The first step in the process of addressing the patient's guilt involves helping the patient develop an awareness that he and HIV are not a single entity. A patient's restructuring of his identity around HIV, such that he views himself as a disease process rather than as a person, is not uncommon. Because a gay man is defined in our culture by his sexuality, it is difficult to separate his identity from HIV, especially if he acquired the infection through sexual contact. This is clear in men who refer to themselves as "infested," "disease-ridden," or "sick," as if these words describe their entire being. The therapist must continually relate to the patient as a person separate from HIV. In so doing, she or he brings to the patient's awareness the tendency to define himself as inseparable from HIV and thus challenges this definition.

On a broader basis, this unwillingness to define an individual's identity as inseparable from HIV infection can be seen in the movement away from the label "AIDS patient" to "Person With AIDS" or "Person Living With HIV."

The second step in the process of addressing the patient's guilt involves developing the patient's awareness of other manifestations of guilt and shame. These manifestations include treating the self unempathically, judging the self, and self-deprecation. Development of this awareness forms the basis for helping the patient work through guilt by tracing it comprehensively through his development.

There are a number of areas to grieve when a diagnosis of HIV infection is given. The effective resolution of guilt allows these to surface. First, the patient must come to terms with the fact that life is limited and he is mortal. Although an HIV diagnosis is not necessarily a death sentence, it is a stark confrontation to the patient's fantasy of himself as immortal. Second, men often have much of their identities invested in their careers. HIV, with the potential it brings for physical disability, threatens this identity. To add further to the injury is the fact that gay men who receive an HIV diagnosis are often young men in the prime of their careers who see years of hard work as wasted. They grieve that they will "never get to the top."

Gay men are often in their thirties when they receive a diagnosis of HIV infection. In Erikson's (1963) psychosocial conception of development, men in this age range are emerging from the conflict involving intimacy versus isolation. For many gay men this is the age at which they have chosen a lover with whom to share their lives. They have left a decade of higher interest in physical/sexual relationships (i.e., their twenties) and entered a time of increased interest in romantic/emotional relationships. Patients often report feeling that they finally had found one person to whom they could give love and from whom they could receive love. The specter of AIDS that hovers over an HIV diagnosis, or AIDS itself, robs the patient of a life with this person, and the grieving associated with this loss is of dramatic importance.

A corollary area of grieving involves those men who have

searched for long periods for a suitable lover and have not found one (Stein, McKillop, and Davis 1989). An HIV or AIDS diagnosis robs them of the hope that there is still time available to find a reciprocal, loving relationship. This can be underestimated by therapists who correctly assume that romance and love are not necessarily over for a person living with HIV. The underestimation, however, usually involves the therapist not being aware of the patient's sense of unworthiness to be in a relationship. The patient must be allowed to grieve the loss of his ability to offer himself to another as complete, whole, and undamaged. This perception of the self can be heard in statements such as "Who would want me?" or "Who is going to start a relationship with someone who's dying?" Obviously, this perception is related to shame about having HIV, but it is also a part of the grieving process. Anytime our bodies are damaged there is a mourning process that must take place. HIV is no exception.

There are three primary ways in which the therapist helps the patient progress through his grief. The first, discussed above, is working through the guilt which can block grieving; guilt, by its very nature, blocks anger and its expression. Feeling and expressing anger must be a part of adaptive mourning. A second way in which the therapist facilitates the patient moving through his grief is through the ability to resonate empathically to the range of feelings associated with mourning, which include anger, sadness, resentment, envy, and acceptance. The therapist must be willing to hear the patient as he attempts the bargaining inherent in mourning (Kübler-Ross 1969). She or he must be able to support the patient as he searches for treatments and listen as he describes joy and hope for those that help and rage and disappointment for those that do not. The therapist's capacity to function as an empathic selfobject provides the safe environment necessary for moving through mourning to acceptance.

The therapist's capacity to serve as an empathic selfobject contributes to the third area of work in mourning. This area involves understanding and working through the transference relationship that develops between patient and therapist. The transference relationship is particularly charged because of the seriousness of what the patient brings as the focus of work. The profound magnitude of the patient's dilemma, that it concerns life itself, electrifies this relationship.

The patient generally brings the expectation to psychotherapy that the primary relational patterns of his life will be repeated (Strupp and Binder 1984). Because, for the gay man, these often involve condemnation, rejection, and devaluation, he expects similar treatment from the therapist. The involvement of HIV adds a related but distinct dynamic as well. The patient expects to be found flawed in his humanity as a result of his physical condition (Castelnuovo-Tedesco 1991b). The initial transference relationship that develops will generally be characterized by the patient's fear, but simultaneous expectation, of rejection.

Obviously, an undercurrent to this transference is the patient's projections of his own lack of self-acceptance. He externalizes not only his self-representation, based on the characteristic ways others have treated him, but his self-loathing for having contracted HIV. Many gay men bring to psychotherapy a history characterized by acceptance based only on performance. They expect the therapist to similarly demand performance for acceptance; however, they also fear that their HIV status will disqualify any performance from pleasing the therapist.

As the therapist becomes a part of the patient's world, she or he and the patient must explore this complex transference. If this is done successfully, it enables the patient to mourn because it clarifies those areas of self-rejection that the patient ascribes to the therapist. Successful working through of the transference challenges the patient to differentiate internal from external. The capacity to understand much of his fear, anger, resentment, and disappointment as emanating from the self toward the self is a precursor to successful mourning (Freud 1917).

As a patient progresses through guilt and grieving, he begins a search for meaning in his life. Guilt and grief must be resolved, however, before this search can meet with success. Basically defined, this search is a spiritual journey in which the patient defines himself against the context of his beliefs regarding mortality, what follows death, and whether or not his fate is part of a larger design (Cornett 1992). This spiritual realm is one of the more difficult areas for a dynamically oriented psychotherapist to experience with his patient, without significant countertransference distortion.

Freud's writings (1913, 1939) disparage religion itself in favor of a psychological understanding of the need for and functions of religion. This is itself a spiritual, perhaps even religious, perspective (Cornett 1992). It is a perspective that pervades much dynamic clinical theory and practice. Fine (1979) proposes that: "No prominent analyst today could be said to believe that religion has any real value for mankind" (p. 449).

What often becomes problematic in this conception is the equation of religion with spirituality. While the former may inhibit self-expression, the latter is a basic form of self-expression. A therapist who equates these two very different phenomena can have severe difficulties responding empathically to the patient's search for a spiritual identity.

The opposite countertransference difficulty can also affect the course of psychotherapy. Especially among psychotherapists with a theological background, there can be a push to have the patient accept certain spiritual tenets for "his own comfort."

Patients must be allowed to define their own spiritual identity. As they come to understand that identity, it can offer enormous strength and soothing. In this process, the role of the therapist can best be described as responding empathically to the patient through the steps of this journey and preventing her or his own countertransference from bringing it to a premature conclusion.

Throughout the psychotherapy, the task of the patient is to review his life, look to what the future holds, understand and resolve his guilt, and mourn the changes in his life. The therapist's task is to maintain an empathic focus on the needs of the patient and his world. This is by no means an easy task when one works with people living with HIV. Indeed, there are a number of countertransference dilemmas to which the therapist must pay close attention.

COUNTERTRANSFERENCE

There are two broad areas of countertransference to which the therapist must be carefully attuned. The first of these areas involves the therapist's own grief and rage at the death of patients, perhaps superimposed upon the deaths of friends. The second area involves the defensive use of boundaries.

The inability to halt the progress of HIV in a patient can be powerfully evocative of narcissistic rage in the therapist. She or he must come to terms with a disease that is not amenable to psychotherapy. Psychotherapy may heighten the quality of the patient's life, and may, in this way, even prolong it. However, psychotherapy will not erase HIV as a constant in the patient's life, nor will it remove the threat of physical illness and death. The therapist who entertains fantasies (whether conscious or unconscious) to the contrary is vulnerable to massive narcissistic injury and resultant rage.

Even those therapists who are fully aware of the limitations of the care they can offer a person living with HIV are prone to periods of depression, frustration, and rage at their sheer helplessness to save the patients they have grown to care about. If the therapist's practice deals extensively with people who are HIV positive, then the therapist may have witnessed the loss of hundreds of people with gifts that enriched the world. The sheer magnitude of the loss of so many can be overwhelming and devastating.

Often the therapist has experienced losses in her or his personal life as a result of AIDS as well. The therapist must know of an environment to which she or he can retreat to resolve her or his own mourning. To effectively cope with all the grief she or he must face in working with people with HIV, the therapist should optimally have her or his own psychotherapist, a peer support group, and supervision that addresses the therapist's welfare. Such supervision should be sophisticated in its understanding of the many forms that mourning can take and should also be knowledgeable regarding the trauma of multiple losses and the manifestations of unresolved mourning in clinical work.

The primary manifestation of traumatic grief is a defensive use of boundaries. This may take two paradoxical paths. A therapist may retreat behind boundaries to fend off the consequences of further loss or may divest her- or himself of boundaries to minimize the impact of loss by minimizing her or his identity.

In the former type of countertransference the therapist stops utilizing boundaries to enhance clinical effectiveness with patients and begins using them to shield her- or himself from patients. The boundaries that the therapist sets take on an angry and arbitrary feel. The flexible use of boundaries is replaced by rigid enforcement of arbitrary boundaries. This type of countertransference utilizes boundaries in a manner that is not only unempathic, but devaluing in and of itself.

Jay, a psychotherapist at an AIDS social service agency, was asked by a patient to write a letter to help obtain disability benefits based on his very real psychological difficulties in adjusting to his HIV status. Jay procrastinated about completing the letter, saying, "He can wait"; he intimated that the request for the letter might have been manipulative. When finally confronted about his procrastination in the matter, Jay expressed anger about his lack of control over his patient's illness. He was, however, in control of *when* he acknowledged the extent of the illness.

In the second type of countertransference, the therapist discards all boundaries. Boundaries are not arbitrary; they are nonexistent. The therapist attempts to respond to all requests from the patient, no matter what the motivation. Through such actions the therapist exudes a sense of guilt. While therapists overly utilizing boundaries seem tightly in control, those underutilizing them seem completely out of control. Often, they seem harried in attempting to meet all of their patients' needs. Just as countertransference, which defensively sets too many arbitrary boundaries, can be devaluing, the therapist's divestiture of boundaries communicates to the patient a sense of danger; the safety of the therapeutic relationship can be lost in a panicked scramble to meet all of a patient's needs. This form of countertransference has aspects of atonement to it, but primarily it is an attempt to merge with the patient to offer some control to the therapist.

Barry, another psychotherapist with an AIDS service center,

would become overly concerned with the daily needs of his patients. If one was unhappy where he was living Barry would attempt to find him new housing. He would become anxious if he discovered that a patient did not have an appetizing meal. If he believed that the patient's medical care was imperfect he would contact the patient's primary care physician to confront this. Barry generally appeared anxious and overwhelmed.

The first type of countertransference is more easily confronted than the second. In the second, the therapist often rationalizes that she or he is simply being a caring human being. It often takes great effort to make her or him aware of the fact that attempting to meet all of a patient's needs is in itself harmful to the patient's sense of independence and adult mastery.

SPECIAL CONSIDERATIONS IN TECHNIQUE

The psychotherapist who works with gay men living with HIV must be flexible in her or his approach to management of the therapeutic setting. Psychotherapy with people with HIV necessitates that the therapist be able to tolerate a less than classical frame. It also requires an acute ability to differentiate expressions of acting out or resistance from real interferences imposed upon the therapy by the patient's physical health that are beyond the control of either participant in the process. This differentiation is not as easy as it may appear at first blush. One of the factors that contributes to making it a difficult task can be the therapist's perspective.

Eissler (1953) introduced the concept of parameters in a discussion of deviations from classical psychoanalytic technique. He proposed that, at some points, therapy may be endangered if the analyst does not temporarily step outside the classical, interpretive analytic frame. Although this notion of a pure therapeutic frame is hypothetical, and was originally applicable only to psychoanalysis, it has found its way increasingly into the realm of psychotherapy (Langs 1982). There is a danger in applying this view to psychotherapy with gay men who have HIV because, at some points (often of long duration), psychotherapy with this population can be a psychotherapy of parameters.

There are several areas of central importance to the psychotherapeutic frame that must be carefully reviewed by a psychotherapist working with an HIV-positive patient. The first of these is finances. Therapists have maintained that the patient must pay something for psychotherapy to feel that he is receiving a service of value. In some respects this is true, and we support the idea that a patient invest something other than his time in therapy. However, patients with HIV often have overwhelming medical bills, and another fee would be far more anxiety-provoking than a patient can tolerate. It does not necessarily mean that a patient will devalue a therapy experience if it is offered at greatly reduced cost or is free. Someone who is struggling with large medical bills in a life-threatening situation may value a therapist's help, and the reduced fee or lack of fee will not necessarily contribute to any form of acting out.

Obviously, Medicaid and/or other third-party reimbursement fall in a similar category. The introduction of a third party, especially in a reimbursement capacity, offers the potential for a number of dynamics to which the therapist must be attuned. However, the fact that the patient is receiving third-party assistance does not necessarily introduce problematic dynamics.

Missed appointments and/or extra hour contacts are another area of concern. A man with HIV whose health is deteriorating will often miss scheduled appointments. This *can* mean that he is avoiding something in the therapy, but it does not mean that he *has* to be avoiding something. A patient's health may deteriorate rapidly, necessitating sudden hospitalization. Under these circumstances a therapist may wish to visit the patient in the hospital, but find her- or himself ambivalent about doing so. It is our position that such an act of human connectedness seldom, if ever, does harm to the psychotherapy. Indeed, such interest by the therapist can go a great distance in militating against an oft-held view of the world as narcissistically preoccupied and interested only in that which is self-promoting.

Another area of concern for dynamic psychotherapists involves educative interventions. Despite attempts at safer sex education in some areas, and because of a lack of such attempts in others, a patient may not really understand the principles of HIV transmission and how to reduce its risks. A therapist can nonjudgmentally offer this information to the benefit of his patient (and perhaps to the benefit of his patient's sex partners). A therapist must realize that while there are psychological factors that inhibit the practice of safer sex (e.g., shame, guilt, masochism, etc.), there are also practical knowledge deficits. A therapist does his patient no great service by not offering this knowledge in order to avoid educative interventions.

Privacy can be an important issue for a patient who suffers from an HIV-related dementia. There may be times when it is necessary for the therapist to contact the patient's lover, a family member, or the patient's primary care physician when dementia hampers the patient's functioning. A therapist must guard the integrity of psychotherapy, and privacy is one of the foundational aspects of this integrity. However, a deterioration in the patient's sensorium with its concomitant threat to his daily well-being may be a development that necessitates the involvement of others in the patient's care.

In this brief discussion we have outlined only a very few of the areas that may require a deviation from standard dynamic technique. There are others too numerous to mention. The point of the discussion is not that a clinician should discard a perspective that considers the frame of therapy a potential context for expression of a number of dynamic issues. HIV, however, introduces an entirely new variable to be considered from this perspective. The therapist must be sophisticated in her or his application of this perspective and, to be as helpful as possible to the patient, must avoid application of doctrinaire or formulaic conceptions to understanding the wide range of extraordinary events and developments that can characterize psychotherapy with a person living with HIV.

Over the next several pages we will attempt to give life to the clinical issues outlined through a case study of a gay man living with HIV. Like most case studies, this one does not capture all the nuances of psychotherapy, but it is our hope that it will at least illustrate the complexity of clinical work with gay men with HIV, demanding creativity and thought on the part of the therapist.

PHILLIP

Phillip, a 38-year-old divorced, gay white male, sought psychotherapy just after being tested for antibodies to HIV but before he received the results. He presented reporting a desire to resolve "hidden issues."

Phillip had been married for ten years and was the father of two young children. He related a poor relationship with his ex-wife and a sense of alienation from his children. Following an "ugly" divorce two years previously, he had met a man he cared for deeply. He reported a very close relationship with this man, now his lover. Seth was 31.

Phillip was a seventh-grade teacher in an urban school. Although he enjoyed his job, he was concerned about the security of his position and believed that if his homosexuality was discovered he would lose his job. He cited examples of other gay teachers who had been terminated on "moral" grounds.

Phillip's homosexuality was a closely guarded secret. He had not discussed it with any of his family, asserting that they would neither believe it nor accept it. Seth was always presented as "just a roommate who helps out with expenses." It was clear from the first hour with Phillip that he was deeply ashamed of his homosexuality.

After relating his recent history and current life situation, Phillip discussed the difficulties that had brought him to the therapist's office. In addition to wanting to finally talk about his homosexuality, he was also concerned about a history of anonymous sex. Although he had been involved with Seth for nearly two years, he was haunted by the possibility that he had contracted HIV through these sexual activities, which had ceased with the inception of their relationship. He had had "a premonition" that he would test positive for HIV, and this had prompted the call to the therapist.

The premonition that Phillip reported can be seen as one manifestation of his shame. After meeting Seth he became increasingly convinced that he had contracted HIV. This conviction became a way to punish himself for the love and satisfaction that he found with Seth. He was also convinced that he had given HIV to Seth, adding to his misery (even though Seth had not been tested previously). HIV was the perfect weapon in Phillip's punitive stance toward himself.

After his first hour with the therapist, he telephoned to report, almost buoyantly, that his test had, in fact, come back positive. He stated that he had phoned because he did not believe that the therapist would want to see him now. He expected rejection and was surprised that the therapist was interested in scheduling another appointment. Noteworthy was the fact that the therapist had attempted to communicate very clearly to Phillip in their first hour his willingness to work with him, no matter how the test results came out.

In his second hour, Phillip reported a concern as to whether or not he should tell Seth that he had been tested or what the' result of the test was. He was accustomed to and adept at keeping secrets. He also related that he and Seth had regularly been having unprotected sex throughout their relationship. Even though he had been tested partly for Seth's benefit, he was now terrified that Seth would leave him. At this point he seemed to show no real cognitive understanding of what the positive test result meant other than that it represented a possibility for rejection. In this hour the therapist followed two themes in Phillip's communications. The first theme was his sense of unacceptability based on his HIV status, which was grounded in a deeper sense of shame and alienation. The second theme concerned attempting to help Phillip integrate an understanding of his diagnosis into cognitive awareness.

After his second hour, Phillip told Seth about his test result. Seth was supportive and reassuring. He vowed to stay with Phillip. Together, they decided that Seth should also be tested. Within two weeks Seth as well had a positive test result. In his therapy hours over the next few weeks Phillip talked about the enormous guilt he felt because he believed that he had exposed Seth to the virus. This seemed a part of a larger pattern of guilt that plagued Phillip.

Phillip and the therapist explored this pattern as it originated in his relationship with his rigid fundamentalist Christian parents. Their world-view was such that they believed everything untoward that happened to someone was the result of that person's "sins." The larger the sin, the larger the calamity. Phillip had internalized this mindset, which included a great deal of splitting and moralization. It was unthinkable to him that he might have caught this disease through no fault of his own. Faultlessness ran against the cosmic grain. There were no diseases that attacked the virtuous, no accidents that befell the righteous. He was convinced that HIV was God's terrible punishment being inflicted upon him for the unforgivable sin of being homosexual. The first six months of Phillip's therapy concerned his almost unshakeable perception that not only had he brought this terrible disease upon himself, but he had also introduced it to one of the few men whom he truly loved and who truly loved him.

During this period the therapist aided Phillip in reviewing his life, especially in light of his family's primitive world-view and the vicissitudes of this world-view in his current life. Toward the end of this six-month period Phillip began to relinquish his guilt and began to grieve.

Particularly difficult was his acknowledgment that his mortality would separate him from Seth and the warmth and affection he derived from this relationship. He was also angry about the impending loss of his children. He wanted to be their father and felt that to do so he would need to compact the lessons and gifts he could offer them as a father. He was keenly aware that there might ultimately be another man in their lives. He finally decided that he would tell his children about his HIV status. They were confused about what this revelation meant. They were also very angry and felt the same press to get as much from their father as they could before he died.

Phillip's children had a number of questions: When would their father die? What would it be like? What would happen to them and to him? These were, of course, powerfully provocative questions. Phillip talked many of them over with his therapist in searching for answers to what he knew to be the crucial concerns of his children. As he searched with the therapist for answers to offer his children, he worked through a great deal of his own mourning. He realized that the time of his death, while uncertain, would not necessarily be immediate.

In the eighth month of his therapy Phillip was hospitalized with a mild opportunistic infection. The therapist went to visit him in the hospital. During that visit the therapist's countertransference became painfully obvious. He found himself enraged and sad. He, too, felt the press of time and found himself thinking sadly about how much Phillip was having to leave behind. He fantasized that a timer had now been set that offered only a finite period of time for him to help Phillip work through all of the unfinished business of his life. He also felt angry at the doctors, nurses, and almost everyone else for not putting enough of a premium on Phillip's life to find a means of stopping this terrible disease.

The hospitalization helped Phillip put much into perspective. By the time he was discharged he had moved beyond much of his guilt and was moving through his grieving as well. The therapist had facilitated this through a focus on empathically understanding Phillip's world and helping him clarify the shame to which his family had made him heir. Phillip now began to plan for the future. He read about ways to take care of himself through nutrition and exercise, and he began to implement these in his life. Seth (who had also started psychotherapy) took part in these activities as well. Both men offered support and affirmation to each other.

The major impediment at this point to Phillip's completion of grieving was the therapist's countertransference. This was now beginning to cloud his ability to respond empathically to Phillip. He found himself questioning Phillip's acceptance and demanding to know why he was not angry about a number of issues. He was also beginning to interpret Phillip's acceptance as denial or some form of resistance. Through work with both his supervisor and therapist, however, he was able to subordinate his anger and sadness to a position that allowed him to once again immerse himself in Phillip's world.

As Phillip and his therapist reentered a phase of being able to work together, Phillip began to explore his spiritual beliefs. His shame briefly became a focus once again as he expressed an only mildly held concern that he might go to "Hell." He fairly easily dispensed with this concern, however. He ultimately arrived at a spiritual position that held that his development after death would be through his children. He would have an afterlife through the parts of him that they carried inside of them. Although the therapist was somewhat tempted to view this as a way of avoiding the reality of death, he quickly realized that this perspective was part of his own spiritual system, which did not need expression in Phillip's life.

Phillip's health steadily deteriorated and he had to resign his job. He became increasingly bound to his home. One area of his shame that remained active was his belief that he could not tell his parents the truth about his illness. He developed a complex lie to account for his deteriorating health, which they may have only partially believed but which comforted Phillip. He did not experience the need to mask the nature of his illness in any other area of his life but believed that his parents would simply not be able to cope with the truth.

In the closing hours of his therapy, which alternated between his home and the therapist's office, Phillip related that his life had come to completion through his work with the therapist. He felt whole and remained hopeful. Life became precious, and he savored the moments both of love and of sadness. He grew to look on death as a journey that could be adventurous as well as frightening. He stated, however, that the most important thing that therapy had offered him was the knowledge that he was not beyond human understanding and compassion; he was not alone and no longer lonely with his own company. Phillip's therapy ended after approximately thirteen months.

CONCLUSION

HIV has taken America's health care system by surprise. We have been unprepared for the extraordinary difficulties that this virus can create, both for those who live intimately with it on a daily basis and those trying to help them. Psychotherapists have not been exempt from facing the dilemmas of this disease.

Dynamic psychotherapists face particular challenges in attempting to help gay men living with HIV. First, they must move beyond traditional notions of homosexuality, which include moralistic overtones. These overtones often suggest HIV as a consequence (i.e., punishment) for "perverse" sexual behavior. The therapist must move beyond this frame of reference in order to empathically connect with the patient. Second, the therapist must reconcile her- or himself to the fact that she or he can assist a patient to adapt to his HIV infection and attendant concerns, but cannot "cure" him. Third, the therapist must be able to tolerate an extremely ambiguous treatment frame. Traditional conceptions of acting out and resistance are at best only partially applicable as the patient's health deteriorates. Finally, the therapist must have enough of her or his own supports to be able to tolerate the losses and other narcissistic injuries inherent in work with gay men with HIV without her or his countertransference overwhelming the therapy. HIV has offered us all terrible burdens. It has robbed us of lovers, friends, patients, and colleagues. The toll it has taken on mental health providers working with those who are surviving it has been dramatic. It has demanded that we, as therapists, look at our own vulnerabilities in practicing our craft. It has demonstrated that dynamic psychotherapy must continually be adapted and expanded to meet the needs of a changing environment. That burden, however, may also be an opportunity to assist our patients more effectively and to enhance our own growth.

REFERENCES

Bosnak, R. (1989). *Dreaming with an AIDS Patient*. Boston: Shambhala.

Cabaj, R. (1988). Homosexuality and neurosis: considerations for psychotherapy. *Journal of Homosexuality* 15:13–23.

Castelnuovo-Tedesco, P. (1991a). Psychological consequences of physical defects: a psychoanalytic perspective. In *Dynamic Psychiatry: Explorations in Psychotherapy, Psychoanalysis, and Psychosomatic Medicine*, pp. 207–223. New York: International Universities Press.

_____ (1991b). On "small" physical defects and the sense of being defective. In *Dynamic Psychiatry: Explorations in Psychotherapy, Psychoanalysis, and Psychosomatic Medicine*, pp. 225–242. New York: International Universities Press.

Cornett, C. (1992). Toward a more comprehensive personology: integrating a spiritual perspective into social work practice. *Social Work* 37:101–102.

Eissler, K. (1953). The effect of the structure of the ego on psychoanalytic technique. *Journal of the American Psychoanalytic Association* 1:104–143.

Erikson, E. (1963). *Childhood and Society*. 2nd ed. New York: W. W. Norton.

Fine, R. (1979). *A History of Psychoanalysis*. New York: Columbia University Press.

Freud, S. (1913). Totem and taboo. *Standard Edition* 13:1–161.

_____ (1917). Mourning and melancholia. *Standard Edition* 14:243–258.

_____ (1939). Moses and monotheism. *Standard Edition* 23:7–137.

Gochros, H. (1992). The sexuality of gay men with HIV infection. *Social Work* 37:105–109.

Greif, G., and Porembski, E. (1989). Implications for therapy with significant others of persons with AIDS. *Journal of Gay and Lesbian Psychotherapy* 1:79–86.

Kübler-Ross, E. (1969). *On Death and Dying*. New York: Macmillan.

Langs, R. (1982). *Psychotherapy: A Basic Text*. New York: Jason Aronson.

Nichols, S., Mattison, A., and Shattls, W. (1989). Gay male tests positive for HIV, but claims he is unable to stop potentially unsafe sexual practices. *Journal of Gay and Lesbian Psychotherapy* 1:11–15.

Shernoff, M. (1990). Why every social worker should be challenged by AIDS. *Social Work* 35:5–8.

Stein, T., McKillop, D., and Davis, L. (1989). Gay male client, 40 years old, complains of unbearable loneliness and isolation. Fear of AIDS complicates his situation. *Journal of Gay and Lesbian Psychotherapy* 1:3–10.

Strupp, H., and Binder, J. (1984). *Psychotherapy in a New Key: A Guide to Time-Limited Dynamic Psychotherapy*. New York: Basic Books.

8

The Homosexual Analyst: Clinical Considerations

RICHARD A. ISAY, M.D.

As a psychoanalyst who has become increasingly identified over the past years as a gay man, I have seen many gay men who specifically come to work with me because I am homosexual. Most of these patients are self-referred and are themselves mental health professionals. Some are referred by other gay psychiatrists who may be their friends or lovers. They seek analysis or therapy from a gay man because of their concern that the prejudices of a heterosexual therapist could interfere with their being treated with appropriate neutrality. For even when the heterosexual therapist is relatively unconflicted about his patient's homosexuality and attempts to be nonjudgmental, his adherence to the theory that the only normal developmental pathway leads to oedipal conflict and a heterosexual resolution of this conflict may make a neutral therapy difficult (Isay 1985, 1989).

Gay men and lesbians generally feel that there are specific developmental and social issues confronting them that most analysts and dynamically oriented therapists have little knowledge of. Because psychoanalytic developmental theory is based upon the development of heterosexual men and women, there is appropriate concern among knowledgeable homosexual patients that the lack of clinical or personal familiarity with their developmental issues may lead to incorrect or biased assumptions, interpretations, and formulations. For example, the special nature of the early erotic attachment of the male child to his father and the ways in which the repression of this attachment may influence adult gay relationships (Isay 1987), the nature of the process of coming out to oneself and to others, the effect of social and peer stigmatization, the particular nature of gay relationships and their difference from conventional heterosexual relationships are a few important aspects of development that most analysts are not knowledgeable about. Better informed gay men, particularly those who are themselves in the mental health field, are increasingly discriminating about the level of knowledge and expertise of the analyst or therapist from whom they seek assistance.

Those gay men who want therapy from a psychoanalyst or an analytically oriented therapist do so because they believe that a dynamic therapy will be most helpful for the neurotic or character problems that are affecting the quality of their relationships or their productivity in work-related endeavors. They are usually not seeking to alter their sexual orientation and most do not view their homosexuality as a problem. But many analysts will argue that an attitude on the part of the patient that excludes the sexual orientation per se as a focus for investigation and change precludes a successful treatment and indicates that this patient is not analyzable (e.g., Bieber et al. 1962, Kolb and Johnson 1955, Socarides 1978). I have presented a very different view based upon my clinical experience (Isay 1985, 1989). If a gay man wishes to change his sexual orientation, it is usually because early self-esteem injury and the internalization of social bias have resulted in an inability to consolidate and integrate his sexual orientation during adolescence and early adulthood, causing the instability of his homosexual identity.

THE ANALYST'S DISCLOSURE OF HIS HOMOSEXUALITY

A., who had been in an analytically oriented therapy intermittently for many years with a highly regarded psychoanalyst, left that treatment because he felt his therapist had always depreciated his attempts to express his homosexuality. This patient had nearly exclusive homoerotic fantasies for as long as he could remember. He had periodic gay experiences in high school but dated several women because he wanted to please and be accepted by his peers and was frightened of alienating his emotionally distant mother and very demanding, critical father. Mainly because of his longing for his father's love and acceptance and fearing his complete rejection if he became openly gay, A. continued to date women, then married, and became a father. While he was married, he continued to have sex at bathhouses and pick up men at gay bars. It was the anxiety caused by this double life and his increasing depression and unhappiness that led him to divorce his wife and then to seek treatment from his first therapist.

Over a period of time he gained considerable understanding of his continuing masochistic attachment to both of his parents. He also learned to understand the many ways he had of sabotaging his own happiness and success. However, in his therapy he began to conceal his homosexual desire and experiences because he believed that his analyst was subtly, and at times overtly, critical of them. He felt totally alone with the passion he felt for men, believing that his analyst had little understanding or empathy with this aspect of his life. He felt he should have an analyst who was more accepting and who was also more empathic and knowledgeable.

Although believing that I was homosexual, he made no direct inquiry about my sexual orientation. When he did, several months after beginning treatment, it was due to the increasing distress caused by his guilt and self-condemnation. Believing that not responding directly to his question at this time would serve no further useful function, and after exploring his thoughts and fantasies, I did confirm his belief that I was gay. Initially he expressed considerable relief, stating that at last he could express himself and would be understood. He felt that he had never had gay role models and that to him being homosexual had simply meant having sex with another man. He felt astonished that with me he could experience the beginning of an emotional connection with another man who, like him, was also gay.

In subsequent hours A. became quite anxious because of his longings for closeness evoked by the confirmation that I was homosexual. He wondered if he was making a mistake seeing me, and he began to express more openly his anger, including his contempt. By and large, however, he felt gratitude for my directness and great relief at being in treatment, but continued to be extremely frightened by the surge of positive feelings for me. He recognized rapidly that any intimacy with another man evoked both great longing and the conviction that he would be criticized and eventually rejected, as he felt he had been by his father. It was this conviction that had disrupted all past relationships and was beginning to threaten the stability of his relationship with his current lover.

It is possible that a heterosexual therapist, who was appropriately free of bias, could have provided the environment in which such a patient would be able to separate transference feelings and projections of internalized homophobia from reality. But this man needed a therapist who could also provide the necessary empathy and sensitivity to the issues of his past and current life that would help him make the transition to a life with a lover, including knowledge of and a nonjudgmental attitude toward the varieties of forms of intimacy in gay relationships.

Most important, working with a gay psychotherapist gave this patient the opportunity to have the positive model that he felt he had always lacked. The absence of identifiable models in the life of most gay men, particularly during their adolescence and young adulthood, makes the positive model of the analyst or therapist a valuable part of their therapy. But it is particularly valuable for those mental health workers who believe that being comfortable with their gay identity is important for their professional life as well as for their emotional maturation and well-being.

Most patients entering therapy assume that the analyst or therapist is heterosexual. Patients make this assumption in part because of the bias that gay men and lesbians would not be in a position of authority and prestige. There is also a commonly held belief, despite contrary evidence, that homosexuals are more emotionally disturbed than heterosexuals. Most patients, because they are predisposed to idealize the health of their caregivers, are for this reason as well likely to see the therapist as heterosexual. Furthermore, relatively few gay and lesbian therapists have identified themselves as such. The lack of visibility also reinforces the assumption of heterosexuality.

This heterosexual assumption is most commonly made by heterosexual patients. But it is also made by many gay men and lesbians who internalize society's prejudice (Isay 1989), leading some to believe that they are defective or sick and therefore that anyone from whom they are seeking assistance must be heterosexual.

Identification with aspects of the therapist's analyzing functions, including his reflectiveness and psychological curiosity, is important for any patient, heterosexual or homosexual, in order to do the difficult work of analyzing during treatment itself and self-analysis after termination. Essential to establishing and maintaining this identification are the perception and conviction of the analyst's integrity, not only concerning issues of his persevering psychological curiosity, but also in those aspects of his character and life that are unfailingly revealed in the intimacy of the therapeutic relationship. When a homosexual analyst chooses not to acknowledge to his patients that he is homosexual because of shame or fear of exposure, he is failing to provide the model of personal integrity that is essential for the difficult self-scrutiny of any successful therapy. For "we must not forget that the analytic relationship is based on a love of truth . . . and that it precludes any kind of sham or deceit" (Freud 1937, p. 248).

I am not, of course, suggesting that the usual uncovering and interpretive work of any dynamic therapy is not of major importance in treating gay men. I am not advocating a precipitous acquiescence to any patient's request for information without eliciting fantasies and associations over an appropriate period of time. Nor am I suggesting that any therapist or analyst, heterosexual or homosexual, give unnecessary information to his patients about his personal life. I do believe, however, that the gay analyst or therapist who hides or disguises his sexual orientation by refusing to acknowledge it implies that he is heterosexual and may further damage the self-esteem of his patients by conveying his shame, self-depreciation, or fear of disclosure. Equally important, he fails to provide a corrective for his patients' injured self-esteem that derives from internalized social attitudes and parental and peer rejection. Self-revelation through confrontation or confirmation at some appropriate point is, I feel, necessary and important to an effective therapeutic effort for a gay man in treatment with a gay therapist.

B., for example, was an experienced therapist who sought consultation primarily because of problems in his relationship of many years as well as because of conflict concerning his homosexuality in general. Early in our work he spoke of difficulties that had been arising in his professional work with gay patients. He found that he was having more difficulty working with some of the clinical problems that his patients confronted him with, because it necessitated his revealing that he was familiar with aspects of gay life and that his patients would infer that he was homosexual. On one occasion he felt obliged to hide from a patient his familiarity with sexual terms that showed that he had knowledge about gay sex, and on several occasions he made an effort to conceal his familiarity with the gay bars his patient mentioned. He believed that self-revelation or the discovery by the patient of his homosexuality would interfere with the neutrality of his work and with the transference. His anxiety, however, had caused him to become more and more reluctant to accept gay referrals and to be increasingly uncomfortable working with the gay patients he already had.

This man felt that he had been in a successful analysis that was completed three years before he saw me. He had heard rumors during his analysis of his first analyst's homosexuality and had even been told by a colleague that he had seen his analyst in a gay bar while at a meeting in another city. When B. confronted his analyst with these rumors, he had remained either silent or asked questions about his patient's fantasies.

In our work together over a period of about one year, B. was able to talk about how deceived he felt by his analyst, while also acknowledging how in so many other ways he appeared to be knowledgeable, forthright, and helpful. It became clear that the discomfort his analyst had with his own homosexuality had reinforced B.'s self-depreciatory views and attitudes, which were contributing to the difficulty he was experiencing working with gay men. And when B. did accept a gay patient, he found himself adopting his analyst's refusal to answer questions directly about his own sexual orientation. The result was that some patients failed to stay with him, and his work was anxiety ridden and not as gratifying as it might otherwise have been.

One might wonder if the revelation of sexual orientation is not a rationalized, self-indulgent manifestation of a countertransference need to please or be seductive. Reflection on my own work and knowledge of the work of supervisees indicate that the therapist's self-revelation is not overly gratifying to the patient; it does not lead to most patients having unrealistic expectations of the capacity or willingness of the analyst to satisfy needs and longings. In my experience it is not perceived as seductive. Most frequently it facilitates the analysis by confronting denial and a need to idealize the therapist when interpretation alone is insufficient.

A 45-year-old married man, C., with two children had been in analytically oriented therapy for several years before consulting me after the sudden death of his therapist. Neither C. nor the referring analyst knew at that time that I was homosexual.

He last had sex with a man two years after finishing college and shortly before marrying. He felt extremely guilty about his former homosexual activity as well as about his current exclusively homoerotic fantasies and his attraction to other men. He believed his homosexuality made him "bad."

His relationship with his wife was poor. He had not had sex for sixteen years, following the birth of the younger child. Projecting a good deal of his anger and guilt onto her, he spent a lot of time at job-related activities, attempting to avoid her criticism. He saw me throughout the first four years of our work as an idealized parent. I could make no mistakes, no incorrect or inadequate interpretations, no errors of judgment; he was oblivious of me as a person with human attributes. It seemed clear that he dared not risk seeing me in a less idealized way out of fear that any perception of a defect would so infuriate him that it would destroy the relationship. Interpretation of this aspect of the transference was met only with his denial and rationalization.

On occasions over the years he had wondered whether I was gay. He mentioned this when he would see other obviously gay patients in my waiting room. Once he saw me with my lover outside of the office and said "hello," but the next day he could not recall that I had been with someone.

During the fifth year of therapy, after the publication of my book, he hesitantly but directly asked me whether I was gay, and I responded equally directly to his question. Over several hours he told me of his scorn, particularly because I could not be "macho." He hated homosexuality because it was a sign of femininity in men. Some sessions later, for the first time, he mentioned that he believed his father, who preferred an older sibling, hated him for not being more masculine.

Over the next many months he became more accepting of his homosexuality. Although he chose not to have homosexual sex, he became much less critical of himself and stopped thinking of himself as "bad" because of it. He began to deal in an effective and, at times, moving way with the perceived rejection by both his parents. The relationship with his wife, although remaining asexual, did improve considerably. Concurrently an aspect of parental transference, of my being critical of him, began to emerge clearly for the first time.

For this man, confronting his denial and idealization by my self-revelation was beneficial in part because it made it possible for him to articulate his anger without the feared disruption of the important relationship with me. He commented that he saw me as a gay man he regarded highly, and therefore he could no longer see himself so readily as being altogether bad. In becoming more accepting of his homosexuality, he lost this displaced focus of his rage and was then able to confront more effectively the early roots of his self-loathing.

It may be important for ongoing work with some heterosexual patients, as well as with gay patients, to reveal or confront them at some point with the analyst's homosexual orientation.

One man, a heterosexual, had for several months been quite curious about my office, books, furniture, and especially about a second room where he had occasion to use the telephone to call his own office. He appeared often to be like a detective looking for clues. When I articulated this observation, he acknowledged that he was inquisitive about me, but he was uncertain what he was so curious about.

After the publication of my book on homosexuality in 1989, he asked me whether I was homosexual, and mentioned that my well-known interest in gay men must have some important roots in my own life. I attempted to elicit his thoughts about this, but he was unable to say much, and during the following several weeks our work came to a virtual standstill. Finally, I wondered if his concern about my being homosexual made it difficult for him to talk. He said that he feared it did, and wanted to know why I was avoiding answering his question. He commented that it made him feel I was hiding something that I was ashamed of revealing. I interpreted to him that he might be ashamed of and afraid of revealing aspects of his own sexuality. This was clearly correct but not helpful.

After several more weeks of unproductive sessions I did answer his question. There were a few perfunctory questions about my life and then a sigh of considerable relief. His subsequent hours took a dramatic turn. He spoke for the first time of sadomasochistic hetero-sexual fantasies that he had found troublesome throughout his life. He saw them as "perverse." In general he became more comfortable and less constricted in expressing his feelings and thoughts. When I inquired several months later about the change in the quality of our work, he commented that he had always felt I was too "good," too "conventional" to be able to understand his own "bad" sexual feelings. This belief, of course, had important transference implications and, to some extent, it derived from his projected self-criticism and shame. My failure to be initially responsive to his questions led to a stalemated treatment because it reinforced his sense of shame and a lack of trust in my veracity. The acknowledgment of my homosexual orientation, which he had long suspected, enabled him to accept and then gain understanding of fantasies he perceived as forbidden, making it possible for him to be less inhibited and have increased pleasure in sexual activity with his wife.

Another heterosexual patient, who had been in analysis for six years, saw me as being disinterested, distant, cold, and uncaring, like his self-involved father. He also knew of my work and had heard that I was homosexual, but did not want to know with certainty. He said, "If you were gay, I'd like you better. I told Roger [a gay friend] that I didn't know for certain. If you were, I wouldn't invest you with so much; I couldn't feel you were so cold and uninterested. I couldn't feel you were always telling me what I should do, how I should behave. I wouldn't have to be such a schmuck here."

Over time he became less frightened of and angry about his affectionate, loving, erotic wishes and longings for his father and, in the transference, for me. Then he was able to ask me to confirm his belief that I was gay. To him being gay, he said, meant being capable, unlike his father, of tolerating his desire for closeness. I believe that if I had not been responsive to his question at this point, it only would have served to reinforce his defensive need to experience me as depriving.

Not all heterosexual patients will use the knowledge or suspicion of my homosexuality to benefit their therapy. D., familiar with my patient population and with my writing, wondered for some time if I was gay. He had a very "correct," moralistic attitude about his own life and consequently about others. Not too long after the publication of my book, he announced that he wanted to stop therapy. There had been no suggestion of this heretofore, and our work, spanning many years, had been successful in most respects. He wanted to stop, he said, because he felt that I was critical of him, especially of his need for upward mobility and for social and professional acceptance.

He had spoken during the course of his long therapy of his disgust at homosexual behavior and of his phobic concerns that he or a member of his family could get AIDS from associating with gay men. Several times he wondered whether I was gay, but stated that he did not want to know. He was afraid that he would perceive me as diminished, insignificant, and disgusting if he found out that I was.

Displacement of rage stemming from the frustrated desire for closeness to his emotionally distant, frequently absent father manifested itself as criticism of men that he perceived as being in positions of authority. He was contemptuous of his desire for affection from and closeness to them and me, and this contempt was often expressed in the transference as homophobia. In many ways his therapy was successful, and he did gain some understanding of the extent of his anger at and longing for his father. However, because of the intensity of his anxiety over the conflicted, positive erotized transference, these feelings were incompletely worked through and contributed to his termination of treatment.

I can also confirm from my clinical experience that feelings about the homosexuality of the analyst may be a source of resistance and anxiety for some gay men. My understanding of and interest in the developmental issues of gay men and my expressed concern for their therapeutic well-being have been important reasons for some to seek treatment with me. Years of feeling alienated or rejected, however, causing many to be secretive about their sexuality, may encourage some to greet the possibility of seeing another gay man who is sympathetic, empathic, and "like them" with frightening and conflicted feelings that may cause intense anxiety. This manifestation of transference, when it occurs, is most frequently caused by the abrupt awakening of repressed longings for the father and/or by their projected self-contempt. If anxiety is evoked by working with a gay therapist, it must be interpreted early, for when the anxiety is severe and occurs before the development of a therapeutic alliance, it may lead to an abrupt termination. I have done several consultations with gay men where I believe this to have been a factor in their not wanting to return for treatment.

For some patients who are in analysis or therapy, the anxiety evoked by my being homosexual has led to resistance and stalemated treatment. One man knew that the psychiatrist who referred him to me believed that he should be treated by a gay therapist. He also was aware of the predominantly gay nature of my practice and had been told by another patient that I was gay. Nevertheless, he steadfastly maintained that I must be heterosexual. When confronted with his denial, he expressed his fear that if I was gay, his derision and contempt would cause him to leave therapy. The intensity of his anxiety was determined by a number of factors, including the contempt he felt for his demeaned father, the need to distance himself from affectionate and erotic longings for his father, and projections of his own self-contempt. But the intensity of the transference did not lead to the disruption of treatment, and his feelings about me and my homosexuality were a significant and productive part of the work of his analysis.

Another man, E., was 32 when he entered analysis. He had felt hurt and angry when a supervisor had spoken of homosexuals in a deprecatory manner. Although he lived openly with his lover, he generally kept his homosexuality secret at work. He experienced his sexual orientation as being normal for him, but he nevertheless held to a pathological model of homosexuality and believed his analytic supervisors who taught that homosexuality was a perversion and a symptom that was a result of developmental fixation.

He had wondered whether I was gay from being familiar with my papers and from what he had heard from others, but because I was a psychoanalyst and married at the time, he believed that I must be "straight." Like the previous man, he needed to believe that I was heterosexual in order to control his hostile feelings and the fear that his anger could destroy his relationship with me. Unlike the previous patient, however, E. was aware of his concern that I would not be able to tolerate his rage and contempt.

Treatment was stalemated for several months because of his need to deny my homosexuality. Interpretation, intended to point out the fear of his own rage, was also greeted with denial. At some point during this period, when he asked me directly, I did confirm that I was homosexual. He was startled and furious. Initially his anger was expressed as derision and contempt.

The work that followed suggested that the confrontation had provided a needed breakthrough in his treatment. He began to talk with more affect about his early relationship with his depressed mother, whose withdrawal, self-involvement, and lack of interest made him feel that he was bad and defective. It became clear that feelings of being defective had been displaced onto his sexuality and to some extent accounted for his hatred of his own homosexuality and his homophobia. He began to be more comfortable in bringing his hostility and aggression into the hour after he understood their relationship to his mother's neglect and the frustration of early needs. His difficulty in expressing his own anger did not cease, however, since his fear that he would harm me was also related to fantasies about an erotic attachment to his erratically impulsive, occasionally abusive father, and this factor was not understood until later in treatment.

TRANSFERENCE ELABORATION

There is a relatively recent but scant literature on the effects of cross-gender analysis on the development of transference. Some have questioned the ability of male patients to form a paternal transference with a female analyst (Karme 1979), but most work now suggests that male patients can form a variety of transferences with their female analyst (Goldberger and Evans 1985). These transferences include the transient passive "homosexual" fantasies that may express the negative oedipal component of the paternal transference (Chertoff 1989).

It has generally been believed a priori that to disclose sexual orientation would interfere with the development and elaboration of the transference. In my experience with gay men who are aware of my sexual orientation, the same can be said, as has been said, about men working with female analysts or women working with male analysts: "All transference paradigms will eventually be established" (Meyers 1986, p. 263). Throughout the analysis, distortions related to transference wishes and feelings continue to be elaborated relatively unabated and unaffected by knowledge of the analyst's sexual orientation.

An analysand who knew I was homosexual had heard from a colleague that I had gone to a professional meeting with my lover. After hearing this, he became preoccupied with how busy I was professionally, how complicated my life was, and how little energy I must have for my patients. He had a difficult time talking, and he was noticeably tense and emotionally withdrawn during the hour. In sessions during the subsequent weeks he had more difficulty articulating feelings, and he was very detached. After several weeks he began to recall, with affect, something he had mentioned in his early hours but had not brought up again: during his childhood his mother and father had left him each weekend with his grandmother. He had felt abandoned, jealous, and deprived. At this stage in his analysis his transference was maternal. He experienced me as cold and depriving like his depressed, preoccupied, withdrawn mother. He felt that like her I was secretive and ungiving. At other times in his analysis he perceived me as his abusive, uncaring father, who was often absent and emotionally unavailable, in part because of his frequent affairs.

I do not believe his knowing that I was gay altered the nature of the transference. If I were heterosexual, the same distortions would have occurred, because of the pressure of the transference for expression. This illustration of the persistence of transference distortion, which would be taken for granted in the work of a heterosexual analyst whose patients heard about or had a chance encounter with a spouse or child, is used to remind the reader that it also occurs when the analyst is known to be homosexual.

Another patient, who had learned of my sexual orientation from a colleague early in his analysis, illustrated further the tenacity of the transference. After consideration of his fantasies and other thoughts, I responded during his second year of analysis to a direct question about my sexual orientation, feeling that failure to do so would be harmful to him and our work in the ways discussed before.

During much of his analysis he had been preoccupied with longing for the love of his father, who favored a more troubled, more masculine older sibling. During one period in his third year of analysis he had been in the throes of feeling very angry and negative toward me for depriving him, as he felt his father had, by favoring other patients. He came to one hour with his fly unzipped. His associations early in the hour, when he was seemingly unaware of his unzipped fly, were to his father's loving women. My patient knew that his father had had a few affairs during his childhood. He himself would like to be a woman, he said, "like one of those women who took my father away from me." When I called his attention to his open fly, he said it felt like a dress unzipped up the side.

"I'd like to be a girl and have all these hot guys attracted to me," he said. This aspect of his transference was an expression of his early desire for his father and his childhood wishes of wanting to be like the women who had his father's attention, and it persevered despite his knowing I was gay.

Knowledge of the therapist's sexual orientation, like knowledge that any patient acquires of his analyst or therapist, will not disrupt the treatment process if it is used by the analyst in the service of the collaborative work, and if the well-being of the patient and the therapy remain in the forefront of the mind of the therapist. The cooperation of the patient in making use of such information depends upon his or her feeling that he or she is in a comfortable, safe, and trusting relationship with someone of personal integrity. When the primary motive for the analyst or therapist in revealing a significant part of his life is for his own and not his patient's well-being, or when a fact is inadvertently discovered and the analyst responds defensively or shuns acknowledging the truth of the patient's perception or knowledge, then the transference, I believe, will be significantly impaired. The analyst will then usually be perceived as the parent who made the patient feel helpless by distorting reality or by making the child feel that he cannot trust his own perceptions. Similarly, when information is offered excessively or gratuitously in order to appease the patient, to ward off anger, or to be seductive, the analyst will be seen as being manipulative and dishonest, and anxiety and anger may thwart the progress of treatment, including the development of the transference.

COUNTERTRANSFERENCE

To be a gay man in the profession of psychoanalysis today, and to a lesser extent in psychiatry, may be isolating. There is therefore the always present countertransference need to use one's gay patients to counter the sense of professional isolation. Revealing sexual orientation may at times be in the service of establishing a sense of social alliance through one's patients. Every gay therapist should be aware that such needs may influence his decision to reveal his sexual orientation. Obviously, such gratification should not be the primary motive for self-revelation. But, on the other hand, it should not inhibit the analyst from self-revelation of sexual orientation when it is in the patient's interest to do so.

Countertransference issues also arise when patients respond to the discovery of the analyst's homosexuality with homophobic attitudes. At times, one has to deal with the internalized homophobia of gay patients that may be expressed in demeaning or denigrating perceptions of the analyst. Such attitudes and perceptions may evoke intense feelings in the analyst. I told F. that I was homosexual after he had made several inquiries and after what I believed to have been a thorough investigation of his fantasies over an appropriate period of time. He subsequently became anxious, resentful, and contemptuous, and took every opportunity to attempt to humiliate me. The intensity of his feelings was related to his conviction that only a gay man, who himself was defective like he felt he was, would be interested in spending time with him. F. had a special interest in pointing out to me repeatedly that an eminent heterosexual analyst, whom he had seen in consultation before he saw me, had been too busy to work with him. This meant to him that the other analyst was or must be better than I, which he needed to assert repeatedly in order to deny both his sense of feeling rejected by him and his growing sense of attachment to me.

I grew increasingly irritated, not only by his continuing denigration, but also by his inability to deal with his positive feelings for me. My attempts to help him work with the intensity of the transference by interpretation of the humiliation that he felt from his father's rejection was not particularly helpful. I was little aware of how irritated I was until I confused this man with G., who had sought treatment with me specifically because I was gay. I asked him why he seemed to be avoiding any mention of the hour when he had been so angry and distressed because of my sexual orientation. Even though G. had previously acknowledged his own ambivalent feelings about my sexuality, he said that he believed I was confusing him with someone else. It was only during another hour later that week that I understood that I was avoiding my growing anger at F. by confusing him with a man who had been more accepting of both me and my sexual orientation.

The countertransference response that was most disruptive of treatment occurred with the heterosexual patient mentioned before, who knew of my publications and of my patient population and frequently wondered aloud, but would not ask, whether I was homosexual. He had expressed homophobic attitudes in the way he spoke of the role of gay men in the AIDS epidemic. He had commented that he would prefer not to live in the same apartment building as gay men because their "promiscuous life-style" would hurt the "family" atmosphere and lower the property value. Although we understood that his anxiety about proximity to gays was related by and large to his own fears about his "femininity" and to repressed longings for his father, his homophobia remained an apparently unanalyzable symptom. For a long period of time my anger made me unable to confront this important transference issue by asking him directly how his hatred of gay men related to his thoughts about me. It should also have been apparent that a comment I might have made to this man that could have moved our work along would have been a statement making my sexual orientation specific and clarifying his sadistic need to taunt me because I was homosexual. But my unconscious anger toward this man with whom I had worked so hard for many years was so great that I was unable to do this. He terminated treatment prematurely, I believe, in part because of this countertransference difficulty.

COUNTERTRANSFERENCE WITH AIDS AND HIV-POSITIVE PATIENTS

No discussion of countertransference issues of a gay analyst working today with gay men is complete without mentioning work with patients who are HIV-positive, have ARC (AIDS-related complex), or have AIDS in any of its manifestations. Two of my six patients with AIDS over the past seven years have been in analysis. Both have died. Although it is not germane to the general topic of this chapter to detail the nature of the treatment of these patients, it is relevant to mention how vulnerable to countertransference the gay therapist is in this epidemic.

Most of the gay patients with the spectrum of HIV-related diseases, who are being seen for emotional distress, are treated by gay mental health workers. I believe this to be appropriate, not only because this is usually the desire of most gay men, but because the empathy, understanding, and sacrifices required of the therapist demand that he have intimate knowledge of the pain, suffering, and emotional and physical devastation caused by the disease.

H. had been in analysis for four years before becoming symptomatic. He had severe narcissistic character pathology with masochistic symptoms that led him to place himself in self-destructive and, at times, dangerous situations in many aspects of his life, including in the seeking of sexual partners. In 1982, early in the epidemic, I pointed out to him that the sexual partners he sought out, usually 42nd Street hustlers, many of whom were intravenous drug abusers, might not only be a threat to his physical safety but to his health as well. Although he was also a physician, he denied any knowledge of the disease and would not stop behaving self-destructively. Although his behavior did begin to change in the following year, it was not until he noticed lymphadenopathy and was having occasional night sweats that H. stopped having unsafe sex. When he finally saw a physician and received a diagnosis of cytomegalovirus of the colon, he developed the calmness characteristic of those who have achieved a long-anticipated goal. For him, his disease was punishment for his rage and represented the long-sought destruction of his mother, whom he held responsible for his unhappiness.

During his second or third visit to his physician, who was an infectious disease specialist involved in AIDS research and treatment, H. was advised to try a drug that could possibly enhance his flagging immune system. He refused. The exploration of his refusal revealed even more about his ambivalence about getting better. His illness protected him from fear of his mother's rage by having inflicted on himself what he feared she would eventually do to him. The offer of his physician to place him on a new protocol evoked a recurrent nightmare of a lurking woman with a knife who was going to kill him in his bathtub. He also had a fantasy, which I had not heard since early in his treatment, of being pushed underwater by a mysterious person, probably a woman.

In one hour I expressed my frustration because of his unwillingness to accept help. By this time I had two more patients who had symptoms of AIDS, along with many others who sought help because of anxiety about possibly having the disease, one close friend who had died, and several acquaintances who were sick. I was aware that my angry response was partly a displacement of my general feelings of helplessness in the face of this epidemic that was affecting many people I knew. Fears of my own mortality, enhanced by an identification with H., also contributed to the intensity of my feelings.

Several months later, a few weeks before I was to go on my summer holiday, H. became sick with a cough, sweats, severe diarrhea, anorexia, and a precipitous weight loss. Against his wishes he was hospitalized and a diagnostic workup revealed that he had several opportunistic infections. It was unclear whether or not he would survive, and during this period when H. was unable to speak with me, I kept in touch with his nurses. About three weeks after entering the hospital he asked if I would come to see him.

Because I had planned to spend the early part of my holiday in the city, I was able to see him daily in the hospital. He was thin and very pale and had intravenous infusions in both arms. I attempted to hold his hand and to make him more comfortable in his bed. He rebuked me lightly, called the nurse, and asked her to move his bed from the wall to the middle of the floor and to position a chair behind his bed. He asked me to sit behind the bed and to continue his analysis. As best he could, H. attempted to free-associate, although his associations were punctuated by requests that I do one thing or another to make him more comfortable, which I was eager to do.

The idea of continuing an analysis with this dying man made me uncomfortable. I felt it was inappropriate. Although he continued to need psychological assistance, I believed that he would now benefit most from a treatment modified from traditional psychoanalysis in order to provide him with necessary support. During this first hour in the hospital, I asked him why he wanted me behind the couch and to maintain the analytic formality. His response was, "Don't you understand that if you change your role with me now, I'll know you think I'm going to die? I don't want to think about that yet!" The intense distress about seeing my first AIDS patient dying and my anxiety about the possibility that I might have or could acquire the virus made it impossible to empathize with his need to maintain his denial at that particular time in his illness.

After his release from the hospital, H. continued to come to my office for several weeks. He was able to permit me to be more supportive and active and physically helpful. I was able to help him talk about fears of dying and to make practical plans and decisions. In this phase of our work, exploratory analytic work did not cease, but

his increasing difficulty ambulating and his decreasing sight demanded supportive and physical interventions on my part when he
was in my office. Soon, because of his total loss of vision, he would
have to move to the suburbs to be cared for by his parents in their
home. In anticipation we cut down the frequency of sessions and set a
termination date.

Over the subsequent year I maintained contact with him by
telephone. At times he called me; often I called him. We had no
established appointments. I intentionally attempted to evolve the
analytic relationship into one of a supportive, warm, and comforting
friendship during the last year of his illness when he was totally blind.
He died in early 1989.

Most of us who deal with AIDS on a daily basis in our practice
and in our lives have noticed that it affects the way we see the
problems and difficulties of other patients, the uninfected, gay or
straight. This work can have the effect of decreasing empathy for
many of the painful day-to-day problems affecting those patients who
are not dying or in acute physical pain. There is the inclination to
conserve one's emotional strength by not investing as much in those
less in need in order to be able to give to the most needy.

An awareness of this tendency to be less invested in one's
patients generally and of the inclination to defend oneself against the
pain of these mortally ill patients has to be maintained if any therapist,
particularly one who is gay, is to continue to work effectively and with
maximum sensitivity and empathy in the context of the AIDS epidemic. If the therapist does remain emotionally responsive to the
anxiety of being confronted daily with his own mortality and the
distress of patients who have AIDS and those who love them, then it
is even possible to increase the capacity for empathy and for tolerance
of the emotional pain of all patients.

REFERENCES

Bieber, I., Dain, H., Dince, P., et al. (1962). *Homosexuality: A Psychoanalytic Study.* New York: Basic Books.

Chertoff, M. (1989). Negative oedipal transference of a male patient to his female analyst during the termination phase. *Journal of the American Psychoanalytic Association* 37:687–712.

Freud, S. (1937). Analysis terminable and interminable. *Standard Edition*, 23:216–253.

Goldberger, M., and Evans, D. (1985). On transference manifestations in male patients with female analysts. *International Journal of Psycho-Analysis* 66:295–309.

Isay, R. (1985). On the analytic therapy of homosexual men. *Psychoanalytic Study of the Child* 40:235–254. New Haven, CT: International Universities Press.

———— (1987). Fathers and their homosexually inclined sons in childhood. *Psychoanalytic Study of the Child* 42:275–294. New Haven, CT: International Universities Press.

———— (1989). *Being Homosexual*. New York: Farrar, Straus, & Giroux.

Karme, L. (1979). The analysis of a male patient by a female analyst. *International Journal of Psycho-Analysis* 60:253–261.

Kolb, L., and Johnson A. (1955). Etiology and therapy of overt homosexuality. *Psychoanalytic Quarterly* 24:506–516.

Meyers, H. (1986). How do women treat men? In *The Psychology of Men*, ed. G. Fogel, F. Lane, and R. Liebert, pp. 262–276. New York: Basic Books.

Socarides, C. (1978). *Homosexuality*. New York: Jason Aronson.

9

The Heterosexual Analyst
and the Gay Man

JAMES L. NASH, M.D.

DR. WALLACE

Dr. Wallace was born in the early 1940s, in an average small town in the segregated South. Franklin Delano Roosevelt was still President, and the United States had recently entered World War II, an event that awakened the citizens of the country to the existence of a world beyond its borders. At the time of Dr. Wallace's birth, one-third of the U.S. population still used outdoor toilet facilities, and only one household in seven had a telephone. The rudimentary nature of information transmission and the slow and difficult nature of transportation led to a narrow vision of the world. Nevertheless, only three years after the United States celebrated its coronation as the leader and standard setter of the world, Alfred E. Kinsey and his research team at Indiana University (1948) published their volume on male sexuality and shook the foundation of middle-class morality forever.

Dr. Wallace was, of course, far too young to know about the publication of the Kinsey Report. He would know about it later, hearing it quoted as gospel and attacked as propaganda (Reisman and Eichel 1990), but he would never quite know what to think about it. Could it be true that 10 percent of the U.S. population was homosexual? Was bisexuality really more the norm than heterosexuality? His parents certainly heard about the Kinsey Report. Not that they talked about it; whispered was more like it, for one did not talk openly about such matters. To do so would be unseemly. After all, Indiana seemed far away, and research centers and academic institutions seemed disconnected from real life. It was easy to believe that it was simply not true, and even if it were true in Indiana or some other far away place, there were no "queers" around these parts. And even if there were, the problem would be handled—in the same way that the "Negro problem," the "Jew problem" (if there were any Jews), and any other "problem" (which meant anything that was different and therefore un-American) were handled. The democracy that the United States had fought so fiercely to defend was indeed a fragile concept.

The young Dr. Wallace was a bright kid, and his parents meant well. They really meant no one any harm. They loved each other (for the most part), slept in the same bed, went to church on Sunday, worked hard, and were proud to be Americans. They voted for Truman ("Give 'em Hell, Harry!") and wanted the best they could afford for their son. They would gladly make sacrifices for him to live the American Dream, and they would do what was necessary to protect his piece of the dream from the communists as well as from just about any conceivable minority threat. They were proud of the public schools and worked hard in the PTA.

The school was the small white neighborhood variety where everyone knew everyone. To be sure, there were some children in the town who were different and existed outside the mainstream. There were passive boys who didn't say much, and there were girls who were stronger than most of the boys. These children were largely ignored and sometimes joked about. There were no blacks and very few non-Protestants. There was really not too much to worry about other than a girl "getting in trouble."

Sex? The unspoken understanding was that boys will be boys. As far as the girls were concerned, there were good girls who didn't, and bad girls who did, and if you got pregnant you left the state, and any good girl wore a girdle and didn't jiggle. But homosexuality? To be "queer" was clearly to be sick and weak and somehow a threat to all decency. Homosexual individuals were no more welcome in the locker room than they were in the military. The average citizen had no understanding of the mind set or behavior of a homosexual man. Images of predation prejudiced average minds, and occasional public disclosures amidst great disgrace were reminders of the threat to national security and the threat of personal blackmail.

For kids, the 1950s were not really any different from any other era. There were good times and bad times. Baseball and Saturday matinee westerns taught boys who their heroes were. Men smoked Lucky Strikes and got a new car every other year, and boys wanted to be men. Like other boys, Dr. Wallace ached when he looked at some of his female classmates. Sure he went behind the garage with another boy a couple of times, but they never really touched each other. They were just practicing for girls and both knew it wasn't for real. Sex was never preoccupying. Immediately it was off to the park to play football and smear somebody. The big heavy Schwinn with the springer fork, which rode like a cloud, was the nice boy's Harley, the symbol of phallic potency that directed him toward his goals. Dr. Wallace's role was clear to him. He was male, masculine, and heterosexual. He would know fear when threatened by a stronger male, but he clearly knew his view of the future and looked forward to maturing.

The 1950s were also a time of the beginning of reports calling for a loosening of the conceptualization of homosexuality as a disease. England's Wolfenden Report called for the decriminalization of homosexuality. Nevertheless, the archaic but evocative term "crime against nature" remained a shibboleth for the uninformed who clung desperately to the order of things.

Social disorder was, however, on the horizon and arrived in the 1960s. Things started out pretty quietly, though. Dr. Wallace went to a good university. He studied most of the time, and there wasn't a whole lot other than grades to worry about. Rock 'n' roll had been straining the bonds of social propriety for some time, and although his parents had not been more than snide about Elvis Presley, hearing the singer decried from multiple pulpits in the South had alerted him that a serious confrontation between old and new mores was in the air. Popular music had also introduced Dr. Wallace to outrageousness in the form of acts like "Little Richard" Penneman. This good-natured display of androgyny and social change was about to be followed by a harder edge.

Traditional sexuality was not the only societal institution subject to change, of course. Dr. Wallace had noticed that there were girls in the college Pre-Med Society. He had been taught that girls were supposed to be doctors' *wives*. When he went to medical school, there were women in his class. It seemed clear that something was about to happen. John F. Kennedy had sent advisors to Vietnam, Cuban cigars weren't available, and federal troops were in the South. Then one day he was in pathology lecture and the professor interrupted it to say that Kennedy had been shot in Dallas. Everyone's world was changed forever.

There was nothing surprising about the fact that Kennedy's assassination changed Dr. Wallace. Everyone and everything was changed by this event. Dr. Wallace did not *want* to be changed, however, and he was quite practiced in the ability to suppress things that threatened to deflect him from his path. He was on a mission of a highly personal sort, and although he was motivated by forces that at the time he understood only dimly, he believed very strongly in the rightness of what he was about. In fact it was this sense of rightness that was central to his character. He was conservative, a straight arrow, a solid-citizen type with a strong sense of the way things should be. He was intrigued by what he saw as deviant behavior, but he took a clinical perspective on such things. He had not been a great fan of Kennedy and was not impressed with Camelot. There were too many things about Kennedy that were unfamiliar; how could you trust or love someone who was so different? Not only that, Kennedy had sent federal troops into his beloved South.

But the fact was, Dr. Wallace didn't understand the Deep South any more than he did the Catholic East. He had gone on a tour of the South a year earlier by hitchhiking his way down to New Orleans. Outside of one of those small towns some threatening guys in a pickup had asked him if he was a Freedom Rider. He easily convinced them that he wasn't, but he had known a different sort of fear, the fear of generations of black people. Why couldn't people just leave each other alone? Don't mess with me and I won't mess with you. It was dawning on him that this simple formula was not sufficient. You can't turn your back on social injustice just because it isn't affecting you directly.

Murder, even under the euphemistic name assassination, isn't the answer either. You don't kill someone because he believes something you don't believe. Kennedy's death taught Dr. Wallace that if you take a position on something and someone doesn't like it, you may get hurt. He knew that this wasn't acceptable and realized he could no longer ignore the enormous hypocrisy woven into the American Way, the foundations of what he had been taught.

So many things happened in the 1960s that terrified Dr. Wallace: the Civil Rights Movement, *The Feminine Mystique* (Friedan 1963), and women's liberation. Also the exploration of space and the Vietnam War. The tumult of this social period swirled about him as he followed his chosen path. He believed that he was much too busy to even consider sitting in, marching, getting high, or getting laid. In fact, the social disorder frightened him. To his way of thinking, young people seemed irresponsibly out of control. He married in the 1960s, but children were postponed. He worried about the war in Vietnam because he had a medical deferral and knew he would have to serve. Although he was politically conservative and no great fan of the Kennedys or Martin Luther King, their deaths struck him with great force. It was obvious that times were changing rapidly and that change would be asked of him, too.

He worked with gay male patients during residency as he learned the rudiments of psychotherapy. These patients, usually young men, were typically ineffectual and filled with shame and fear. He was sensitive to their social disadvantage (Freud 1935) and tried to understand it. It seemed apparent to him that they needed to change their sexual orientation, and he understood from supervisors and the literature that this was happening (Bieber et al. 1962). He questioned whether a heterosexual man could change his sexual orientation and become homosexual; this seemed absurd to him. The answer given, of course, that homosexuality was the result of neurotic conflict and that resolution of the conflict changed the orientation, was taken on faith. Nevertheless in his clinical work he observed only despair and dropping out. He gradually shied away from gay patients, viewing them as difficult and untreatable.

The NIMH (National Institute of Mental Health) Task Force on Homosexuality was created while he was in residency. The time was certainly right for such a thing, but to his mind that was a large part of the problem—how do you separate science from politics in psychiatry (Socarides 1992)? Maybe you couldn't. Social policy was being changed in all directions, and taboos and myths needed mollification on many fronts. Clearly, homosexuality was not well tolerated in society, and clearly sexual behavior between consenting adults was being restricted by archaic laws that were laughable. The 1960s showed him, though, that social change seldom results from mild-mannered, reasonable persuasion. A lot of brave people put themselves on the line for a lot of causes. From a distance he marveled at people who let themselves be arrested, beaten, humiliated, and even killed to demonstrate the basic unfairnesses in our society.

The Stonewall riot in 1969 is generally credited as launching the Gay Rights Movement in the United States, but by then gays had been demonstrating on behalf of their life-styles for years. The Gay Rights Movement had found its time in history, though, aided by its companion movements. Women's liberation had suggested a new masculine standard, extolling the androgynous sensitive male, and the traditional notions of masculine and feminine were well under siege, as was the sexual conservatism of the American psychiatric profession. The Sexual Revolution was challenging America's sexual conservatism in ways from which there would be no return.

He served his military stint during the height of the Vietnam War, emerging with only minimal scars. He had seen a lot of unhappy young men, however, and was increasingly awakening to the reality of human suffering. Homosexual men were, of course, to the military an official problem to be gotten rid of. Although his youthful arrogance and misconceptions were taking a beating, he still felt that the military was manifestly correct about this. But he was also hearing about professional football players who were coming out, and yet, somehow, their teams seemed to be doing all right. This was confusing and mostly he didn't think about it.

The word *homophobia* was coined in 1972. This ironic term was introduced in the same year that Dr. Wallace, then a Vietnam veteran, attended his first American Psychiatric Association meeting. He saw picketing, disorder, and anger. He saw male psychiatrists dancing together at a ball. Like the assassinations of the 1960s, like the Civil Rights Movement, this Gay Rights Movement intrigued him and terrified him. He tried to understand everyone's point of view; he was beginning not to know what he believed himself. Political forces seemed unquenchable and intertwined with scientific debate until the two were inseparable. Homophobia seemed to be a statement that gays were in part their own political enemies. It seemed that oppression was emanating not just from the straight world, but from gays themselves, some of whom were unable to embrace the fact of their own sexual identity, albeit largely influenced by the heterosexual culture.

His psychoanalytic training, including his personal analysis, came at a good time for Dr. Wallace. It was the 1970s. He and his wife were having children and his preparation for life was behind him. He was excited about his chosen profession and thought he would be good at it, but he was torn between thinking, as he always had been, that he knew everything, and acknowledging a new truth, of which he really knew very little.

Dr. Wallace had become a member of the American Psychiatric Association by the time its Committee on Nomenclature, anticipating the landmark *DSM-III* (American Psychiatric Association 1980), met with the Gay Activist Alliance and the Mattachine Society to begin a discussion on the deletion of homosexuality from the diagnostic nomenclature. Dr. Wallace was a psychoanalytic candidate by the time (December 14, 1973) the APA Board of Trustees voted unanimously (two abstentions) in favor of the resolution.

Dr. Wallace did not know what to think about this decision. His newly cathected psychoanalytic organization was working hard to challenge this political-scientific position (Kirk and Kutchins 1992). He wished to be an analyst and wanted to think like an analyst. Ironically, it was in the process of acquiring this new identity that he began for the first time to feel himself a member of a minority that was the object of ambivalence and, at times, hatred.

Psychoanalysts were largely responsible for the APA General Membership referendum in April 1974, at which time the membership voted to uphold the Board of Trustees' decision. The psychoanalytic establishment seemed to him to be taking a harder line on homosexuality than Freud himself, but that was not unusual. The position seemed generally unpopular, but he had little experience with gays other than in the clinical or political activist settings, neither of which was conducive to the generation of a sympathetic posture from others. While he studied psychoanalytic theory and technique he learned again to shy away from homosexual patients; although they were supposed to be homosexual because of conflicted development, they were viewed as risky undertakings for a candidate.

If Dr. Wallace had been asked at this early point to undertake the treatment of a gay man, the treatment likely would have been marked by misconception, misunderstanding, and miscommunication. He followed the developments of the next fifteen years with interest, however, as a stream of biological and sociological studies of the homosexual phenomenon helped clear away the cloud of misinformation and prejudice. Nowhere was the biopsychosocial model (Engel 1977) more applicable, with new research into areas such as prenatal hormonal influences predisposing to homosexuality (Dorner et al. 1975, Gladue et al. 1984, Money et al. 1984), childhood gender identity disorders and twin studies (Green 1987, Imperato-McGinley et al. 1985, Stoller 1985), the role of genetic factors in the elaboration of erotic fantasy (Eckert et al. 1986, Pillard and Weinrich 1986), and

the study of social and cultural factors generating homophobic attitudes and secondary conflict states. Political scientists and interdisci-
plinary theorists examined historical perspectives and the effects of
stigmatization, laws, persecution, and discrimination. While ethnolo-
gists looked for animal models, anthropologists examined socially
sanctioned homosexuality and sociologists defined homosexual life-
styles. Gay studies programs were created at many universities, and
new journals were founded specializing in the publication of research
into phenomena specific to the gay situation. Writers concentrated on
such issues as coming out (Troiden 1979), gay identity and role (Isay
1987), interpersonal relationship issues, legal issues (couples, custody,
adoption), varieties of sexual behavior (Arndt 1991), and AIDS.
Professional organizations, including Dr. Wallace's own American
Psychoanalytic Association, were adopting an increasingly receptive
posture on the matter of admission of gay members, both in student
and leadership positions (American Psychoanalytic Association
1991). Although by the late 1980s and early 1990s there were still
many battles to be fought, it appeared that both professional organizations and society at large were coming to a more measured and
accepting position on the matter of the homosexual life-style. Dr.
Wallace was now feeling comfortable with the idea of taking on the
treatment of gay men.

JACK

Jack was born in the midwest just as World War II was becoming a
reality for the average citizen in the United States. Both of his parents
were intelligent, educated, and professional, although Jack's father
had been orphaned at an early age and was raised in a series of foster
homes and institutions. Jack could not remember his father ever
talking about his boyhood and had no sense of a cross-generational
heritage on his father's side.

The separate careers of Jack's parents were getting underway when he was born. Jack's father was studying out of town and was frequently absent during his early years. His mother pieced together a 1940s' version of day care, so Jack's memories of life alone with mother were very sparse. He felt that he was probably the apple of her eye because he was her only child and her husband was away much of the time. In retrospect he believed that he probably was even more important than he thought, as he came to understand the conflictual nature of his parents' relationship and his mother's use of him as a selfobject (Kohut 1971).

Jack's memories of his preschool years were mostly creations of old photographs: sidewalks, cars, fedora hats, backyard outings, all fairly standard stuff of the period. He fretted, though, about certain photographs. One had him sitting on a potty, which he felt very embarrassed about. The most troublesome one showed him from behind, bending at the waist with his pants pulled down, exposing his buttocks, as he looked back at the camera smiling. His embarrassment over this photograph was of a deeper sort than that felt by most people when viewing reminders of childhood. He was profoundly troubled by this shot, humiliated and yet somehow aware of a wish to show the photograph to others. He felt chagrin over the realization that his facial expression in the photograph was coyly seductive. He could barely bring himself to look at it.

Jack's childhood memories increased in number as he recalled his school years. They were, for the most part, unpleasant. He never remembered feeling good about himself or about any of his relationships, either with his parents or with friends. He wasn't exactly a "sissy" and, in fact, tried to emulate a Tom Sawyer image, in fantasy at least. He was not, however, interested in rough-and-tumble play (Saghir and Robins 1973) and was not good at sports. He felt awkward and uncoordinated and generally preferred solitary activities such as reading adventure stories and science fiction or listening to radio programs. His relationships with friends were marred by his tendency toward easily hurt feelings. He didn't feel comfortable with either boys or girls his own age. He was more comfortable with adults, especially when they fussed over him under the orchestration of his mother, who loved to display him and brag about his accomplishments. Just what it was about him that she was so proud of escaped him, however. He was good at the piano and was verbal and charming with adults, but he was gradually developing a sort of round and soft appearance that troubled him. He needed glasses early, and his "nerdy" appearance filled him with a mixture of shame and defiance.

Jack felt different from the other children, unmasculine although not feminine. His mother fussed over him, groomed him, and dressed him, while his father sang to him and patted him when he went to sleep. For the most part, however, he recalled being alone. He fondly recalled riding in the car with his father but had very few memories of doing anything specific with his parents. He made good grades, clearly a source of pride for his parents. They strongly encouraged his academic achievements but seemingly nothing else. He thought that they simply were too interested in their own careers to have much time for him.

Jack couldn't remember when he first began to think about sex or how he learned about it. There were memories of early encounters with other children in the neighborhood, such as playing doctor. These games had involved some looking and touching. He was aware of a great curiosity about the other children's bodies, especially the boys'. He recalled that by the time he was 8 or 9 he was thinking "a lot" about sexual matters while feeling very isolated and lonely. He used the word "chum" to refer to the type of relationship for which he yearned. This seemed to be just what Sullivan (1953) meant by the word, but he was blocked from the collaborative element inherent in chumship by the hypertrophy of his lustful wish to "make" other boys. He attempted to befriend the boys whom he envied. They were lithe, masculine types who were close to the Tom Sawyer ideal that he could only dream of being. He would become "worked up" over another boy and would "set my sights on him," pursuing him vigorously and attempting to seduce him into a sexualization of the relationship. He handled these encounters in ingenue style, however, and was quick to claim a misunderstanding when he sensed impending rejection.

He became increasingly troubled as preadolescence turned into

adolescence. He became preoccupied with sexual fantasy and mastur-
bated frequently, although his exclusive interest in boys troubled him
greatly. Many of the boys for whom he was "on the make" were
disdainful of his approaches. He also felt shut off from his parents, and
his father had become something troubling in his own right. Increasingly remote and sulking, his father seemed pouty and participated less
in decisions concerning the household. Jack fantasized that he had
achieved more influence with his mother than his father had, although he did not kid himself; Mother did things her way. A powerful
image of his father encapsulated for Jack the transformation that had
occurred: his father standing in the kitchen holding a beer, crying.
Jack's mother was drinking a lot too, he recalled, although she would
never admit it. In fact, no one ever talked about much of anything, as
he remembered. Later, he came to reflect on the distinction between
privacy and secrecy. He felt the latter played a prominent role in
family dynamics.

In high school Jack tried to create a heterosexual role (Lewes
1988). He had by then occasionally been called homosexual by male
peers. He tried to convince himself that it wasn't true and even tried to
convince himself that he didn't know what the word meant, but he
knew full well that it was true. He desperately yearned for things to be
otherwise. He tried smoking cigarettes and engaging in mildly antiso-
cial acts such as skipping school and sneaking out at night in order to
actualize his "barefoot boy with cheek" fantasy. He dated girls, kissing
them and trying to fondle them and hoping they would notice that he
had an erection. He did not tell them, of course, that he was using
homosexual fantasy to become excited.

That Jack went far away to college was both a tribute to his
ability to develop some self-confidence and autonomous function and
testimony to his mother's need to have him go to the "right" school.
Things did not, however, go well for Jack as a college freshman. He
was able to do the academic work, but he found it took a great deal
more effort than he had expended in high school and was accompanied by significant anxiety. Socially he felt "like a basket case." He felt
different from everyone, had no interests beyond school work, devel-

oped no friends, and had no sexual encounters. Finally he entered counseling at the student mental health service.

Late in the year Jack's mother called him on the phone; his father had been arrested for making sexual advances to juvenile boys under his tutelage in a local scouting group. This was a galvanizing moment around which Jack's world was forever altered. His parents' marriage rapidly fell apart, and Jack saw his father only occasionally after that. He hated his father from that point on but not so much because of what he had done, because Jack had suspected for some time that his father had a secret life. Jack hated his father for the secrecy, the duplicity, and the lack of courage to proclaim the truth about himself. At the same time, however, he sadly knew that he would never be able to reveal his own personal truth.

As Jack's mother's health began to deteriorate, Jack became conflicted about whether to cleave to her or follow his own life trajectory. He completed college in desultory fashion and found work, but remained dependent on his mother's approval for professional direction. In his early twenties he developed a homosexual interest that became rather stable, but simultaneously he began to feel a powerful need to be married and have children. He did not understand this internal push; he knew it was not about sex. He had learned to perform sexually with women in a somewhat fumbling fashion, especially if he got considerable encouragement. He knew, however, that female bodies did not attract him, and he believed women could sense this. He feared that women would be disdainful of him and see him as a trivial pest. He knew nevertheless that he wanted to live with someone and he could not go public with his homosexuality. He therefore was persistent with women, and his proposal of marriage was turned down by two women before a third accepted it. By then he was in his late twenties and still actively involved in his by now long-standing (but continued secret) homosexual relationship. As had been true in his parents' marriage, he had discovered that secrecy and denial conspire nicely to avoid embarrassing disclosures.

There was little sexual activity in his marriage. Jack's wife did not seem to mind that they had intercourse very infrequently. She was busy with the children, who came quickly, and was happy to be a part of a seemingly conventional family structure. Jack as well was relatively happy during this period. His tender side was allowed considerable expression with the children. He continued to fear and despise his homosexuality and found that he was able to suppress it while he had youngsters to love and career goals to attain. He was good at his profession, and his work provided him with a great deal of narcissistic satisfaction.

Jack drifted away from his male lover and instead masturbated regularly, daily or more, while thinking about sex "any time I wasn't thinking about something else." His fantasy life involved mostly narcissistic themes that were sexualized. He strove in his work attainments and material acquisitions to be admirable, even enviable, at the fantasy level. He exercised ritualistically in hopes of having a body that other men would want, not in a sexual sense but to covet for themselves. It was threatening to him to think that another man would be attracted to him sexually, for that would mean to him that he was not masculine. He had no interest in a homosexual life-style, fearing social ostracism, but he nevertheless found certain males very exciting. These were younger men who were less privileged than he. He yearned to be looked up to by them, to be admired by them and have them wish for him to mentor them. His most enjoyable sexual fantasy involved his aiding another male to experience the joy of sex for the first time. This introduction to sex would in his fantasy result in the other man being eternally grateful and bonded to him out of gratitude.

Jack's carefully constructed narcissistic supports broke down when he became middle-aged. He was unable to deny the effects of advancing age on his body. Male pattern baldness and presbyopia dismayed him. It became more difficult to hold his weight steady, and vigorous workouts became increasingly painful. His children were grown and gone, and his wife began increasingly to look to him for love and companionship, a turn of events that confused and frightened him. He did not want to be sexual with her but did not know how to avoid raising suspicions about his thoughts, feelings, or activities.

He became less sure of himself at work, because he had reached the top of his ladder and no longer had specific new attainments within his grasp. He became dissatisfied with the gratification achieved by his fantasies and began to yearn for more specific, more tangible mirroring. He began anonymous cruising, which he had never done before. He didn't think of himself as homosexual; he simply couldn't. Neither did he think of the other man as homosexual. He enjoyed the fantasy that he, a powerful heterosexual "stud" with a powerful sexual organ, was irresistible to another man who wanted to worship at his altar, in effect, in order to discover the secret of his great power. Once his power was acknowledged, he would happily do anything the other man wanted, as an act of largesse. He knew that he was engaged in a risky activity. He knew that his city was cracking down on prostitution and was running stings, but prostitution was anonymous and therefore better for him than gay bars or other meeting places. It occurred to him regularly that he had much to lose if arrested, but he felt strangely compelled. When he was finally arrested, his life as he had known it was over. Psychiatric evaluation and treatment were court-mandated, and although he was dismayed at what had happened to him, he manifested a quiet calmness that was concordant with a feeling that finally, perhaps, he would come to grips with his own identity.

THE TREATMENT

It was suggested by a professional colleague that Jack consult Dr. Wallace, with whom Jack had had a passing prior acquaintance. Jack knew Dr. Wallace's reputation as a competent psychoanalyst, and he knew that, like himself, Dr. Wallace had a wife and family. He assumed that Dr. Wallace was heterosexual but, in fact, never inquired directly and Dr. Wallace never volunteered this information. Jack explained that Dr. Wallace's presumed heterosexuality was something of a prerequisite in his mind, as it marked the therapist as "normal." It struck Dr. Wallace from the beginning that Jack's transference to him would have two poles of ambivalence. On the one hand, Jack wished for his therapist to be the perfect man with whom he could identify and from whom he would obtain power. His therapist would be brilliant intellectually and highly potent sexually. He would be calm and utterly competent, never ruffled in any situation, never experiencing anxiety. Women would find him an object of admiration and he would move easily among them, satisfying them sexually with grace. On the other hand, Jack needed to be certain that Dr. Wallace would be unable to influence him in any direct way. Jack would have to reach insights before Dr. Wallace did or else face a sense of humiliation and internal criticism. Jack would have to be certain not to do anything that seemed to represent what Dr. Wallace wanted him to do. He referred to such presumed directions as "marching orders" and felt he must dig in his heels in opposition to any such inference.

Dr. Wallace and Jack had a fundamental difference regarding Jack's homosexuality, opposite to the stereotypical picture of the analytic treatment of the gay man. Jack had a profound, virulent antihomosexual bias. He grudgingly acknowledged that his predominant psychic erotic reactivity was homosexual and that his sexual dreams were virtually exclusively homosexual in content. He abhorred this about himself, however; he saw homosexuality as a weakness, as "sick," and he viewed homosexual men as objects of scorn. He had no homosexual friends, he laughed at gay-bashing jokes, he initiated snide remarks about effeminacy or sensitivity in males, and the thought of taking a political stand against discrimination of gays was laughable to him. He denied the existence of any effeminacy in himself. (He expressed some concern over the appearance of a shoulder bag he carried, but he felt it necessary for his work. He considered his reputation for being identifiable by a cologne-produced aroma as a tribute to his uniqueness.) He wished to purge himself of his homosexuality; in his fantasy he would become a subtle version of the swaggering macho male who yells crude remarks at women and swills beer. This image, totally unlike him and undesirable in his reality, nevertheless in split-off fashion represented the ultimate in masculine potency and desirability.

Dr. Wallace had by now acquired a neutrality about homosexuality that was deeply held and determined by a number of forces. Primarily and in contrast to Jack, he was not inclined to see homosexuality as the problem, but rather as a side issue to more problematic character structures (Kernberg 1984), in this instance narcissism. To Dr. Wallace the homosexuality was essentially incidental. Jack's homophobia on the other hand was seen as very much a problem: Jack had a vague wish that somehow he would one day "wake up" and be changed. Dr. Wallace saw no reason for Jack to try to be something he wasn't and, for his part, genuinely didn't care what Jack's sexual orientation was. Jack's expressed wish to be changed was never stated as a goal that he was setting for the therapy, nor did Dr. Wallace hear it as such. For Jack, the wish was a manifestation of a yearning that a number of things he knew to be true about him be otherwise. He would apply a rueful "Oh, I wish it weren't so" lament to characteristics about himself that were considered to fall short of a vision of perfection that existed as a powerfully self-described ideal within him. Homosexuality was on a list that included short stature, male pattern baldness, myopia, and lack of vertical leap (!). He wistfully fantasized how nice it would be if some combination of sorcery and plastic surgery could correct all the "flaws" in his character and body, including his sexual orientation, but he had known since adolescence that he was not stimulated erotically by women and never would be.

Dr. Wallace assumed that Jack's antihomosexual bias derived from multiple sources, interpersonal and cultural. In fact Jack could not recall ever being the object of scorn or derision when he had revealed his sexual interest directly to others. Rather than his homophobia deriving from personal experience, it seemed to derive from negative identification with his despised father and envy of the objects of his father's affection, boys and young men who he understood to be highly appealing to his father but in his fantasy were nevertheless exclusively heterosexual. Jack saw his father as a fraud, an impostor who was without a redeeming feature. In Jack's eyes his father pretended to be heterosexual and admirable while secretly preferring the sexual attentions of males. At the same time, Jack yearned to be loved by his father but felt he could not compete with his father's "catamites," whom he saw as perfect and unapproachable. Jack's mother, on the other hand, used denial to cope both with her husband's behavior and with her own alcoholism, in support of an idealized image of herself as a sort of queen bee surrounded by admirers and sycophants.

Jack was felt to have a narcissistic personality disorder of the "hypervigilant" type (Gabbard 1991, p. 573). As is characteristic of this type of individual, his internal self-esteem regulation was seriously flawed, and he was dependent on a steady flow of external success and environmental reassurance that he was "all right." He constantly attempted to manipulate others into mirroring his grandiose fantasies, and when his selfobjects failed him, he would fragment into anxious hypochondriasis, with special emphasis on his sexual function. While masturbation at such times would reassure him of his bodily intactness, a sexual liaison orchestrated by him soothed his tattered self in a more fundamental way.

Jack was seen to manifest a number of issues frequently found both in the gay male patient and in the more specific situation of the gay male patient of the heterosexual male therapist. Jack demonstrated:

1. A preponderant homosexual psychic erotic reactivity but bisexual behavior, the heterosexual behavior (marriage) defending against a homosexual identity and social role.
2. Marked homophobia (antihomosexual bias), both experienced internally as self-loathing and expressed externally in gay-bashing jokes and remarks.
3. Sexual issues embedded in a problematic character structure with a tendency to sexualize nonsexual aspects of his life, including his

therapy. Although the process of sexualization has interpersonal ramifications, it is primarily an intrapsychic phenomenon. Sexualization of thought is a more precise designation. Like other "primitive" mental mechanisms, it is inherently ego-weakening and adversely affects the individual's reality testing. In order for one to know the difference between a private matter and a secret, one must be able to assess relevance and to distinguish between thought and deed.

4. A secret life; the patient comes to therapy when he has been "caught," revealed to have a homosexual or perhaps paraphilic facet to his life. A secret is defined by the need of the other person to know, a private matter by the possible wish of the other to know but wherein the information serves no legitimate utilitarian purpose. The keeping of secrets or the living of a secret life may be understood as sociopathic and manipulative if the individual's object relations are based on power. If, however, as with hypervigilant narcissists, object relations are mirroring devices, the keeping of secrets is not in the interest of exploitation. Secrets are fundamental building blocks for fictions that must not be just believed, but actually true.

Jack did not distinguish sexual thought from sexual deed, and he was ashamed of his homosexual thoughts. Whether he acted on the thoughts was irrelevant to him. Nevertheless he believed that others could know what he was thinking, were vitally interested in his thoughts, and were "prepared to go for the jugular," to humiliate him whenever possible. He did not discriminate another person's need (or lack thereof) to know about him. To Jack, secrets were necessary to protect him from humiliation, and he found so many of his thoughts unacceptably imperfect that his only recourse was a reactive "dog and pony show" that was lacking in any inherent genuineness.

Economic circumstances enabled Jack to have the treatment that he wanted, which Dr. Wallace felt he needed. An agreement to an open-ended, multitimes weekly psychoanalytic therapy was reached. Although Jack had unreasonable hopes to pin on the treatment, he was able to agree with Dr. Wallace about most of the goals for the treatment, generally expressed as improved functioning through increased stabilization of the self, with less need to rely on archaic selfobjects. Jack remained somewhat skeptical of Dr. Wallace's vision of the role of Jack's homosexuality in the treatment picture. It was not that he either disagreed or wanted to disagree with Dr. Wallace about the centrality of his homosexuality; it was more that he dared not agree, for he might be hugely disappointed. Jack compromised on the matter; he maintained that he was not sure what his sexuality was, but "whatever it turned out to be" he wanted to be comfortable with it. Dr. Wallace felt that Jack was predominantly homosexual and wanted Jack to be comfortable with this fundamental aspect of his character, whether he lived a homosexual life-style or not. Dr. Wallace felt that an empathic exploration of Jack's self-structure, both within the here-and-now of the transference and within the context of his present-day relationships, and illuminated by an in-depth exploration of his early object relations, would eventually improve the stability of Jack's sense of self, rendering Jack less vulnerable to humiliation and states of fragmentation.

The treatment was predictably protracted but ultimately satisfying to both Jack and Dr. Wallace. The psychoanalytic treatment of disordered narcissism requires that the therapist make no value judgments on the patient's verbal productions; psychological structures must be taken at face value and as understandable (in light of the patient's interactions with primary figures) and necessary supports for a fragile sense of self unable to perform basic stabilization functions on its own. The threats of profound fragmentation, hypochondriacal decompensation, and premature and traumatic treatment interruption hang over such a treatment and demand that the inevitable failures of the therapist to function effectively as a mirroring object be carefully titrated. Over time, through the process of transmuting internalization, the effects of chronic parental empathic failure can be modified in the patient. The patient is enabled to choose more mature selfobjects, to soothe the self more effectively, and to emerge relieved from the slavish dependence on external mirroring for internal coherence. As the patient experiences the therapist as one who will indeed take him at face value, who will make no demands on him, and will only attempt to understand him, and who will accept him without the requirement that he be perfect, the patient will become freed up to allow his authentic self to emerge.

Homosexuality in the male seems at this point in our understanding to be best conceptualized as a biological and psychological fact about a man that is embedded in whatever is otherwise the man's character structure. Quoting Friedman (1988):

> Common sense and clinical experience suggest that the causes of most pathological sexual behavior are integrally related to the causes of disordered ego and superego functioning and disordered object relations. To understand sexual pathology, then, one must understand character pathology. There is no homosexual or heterosexual character type. In fact, it would appear that homosexuality, bisexuality, and heterosexuality are distributed across the entire range of character types and character structure. [p. 81]

Like heterosexuality, homosexuality in the male is subject to intrapsychic conflict that will also be colored by social forces. In addition, other intrapsychic conflicts may exist in the individual that will impact on his sexual life but which may have nothing to do with the shaping of his fundamental proclivities. Jack's conflicted and fear-driven feelings toward certain women, including his wife, exemplified such a situation. As in Jack's case, the gay man may fear certain types of women who trigger affect states originally generated by untoward aspects of primary relationships, although these fear-driven states are neither causative nor explanatory of the man's homosexuality. In such a situation the therapist errs if he strays from basic psychic erotic reactivity as the bedrock-defining principle in determining the nature of his patient's real sexuality.

Homophobia in the male homosexual is a particularly troublesome phenomenon that is multiply determined but which ultimately represents the result of disordered narcissism impacting on a fact of the person's life that is clearly not an advantage. The man's homosexuality per se is no more a problem than the color of his skin or his ethnic background. It becomes a problem when it conflicts with the individual's internal vision of the ideal. The individual then is unable to integrate his sexuality into his vision of himself-in-world. He may even be unable to integrate it into his internal reality but rather splits it off for representation in a segment of his life that is denied and kept at bay by primitive defenses. The patient may then, as Jack did, exist in a fictionalized world in which no commitments are publicly held and homosexual behavior is limited to fleeting, anonymous, and rationalized encounters that are unstable, unsatisfying, and potentially dangerous.

Jack's homophobia was modified in parallel with the modification of his pathological narcissism. In this regard, the goals of the treatment were satisfactorily, if (as always) incompletely, realized. Jack's goals for his life would indeed be a lifetime pursuit. The treatment enabled Jack:

1. To acknowledge that his predominant psychic erotic reactivity was homosexual; he now accepted this as a fact of his life, of which he was neither proud nor ashamed. He feared the disadvantages of a homosexual social role, but his fears were assuaged by his growing acquaintance with, respect for, and acceptance by the larger homosexual community.

2. To recognize that the pursuit of perfection was a futile curse flowing from his parents' disordered narcissism. He began to acquire wisdom and perspective consistent with his age but previously lacking and was moved by his own past inadvertent contributions to prejudice and discrimination.

3. To understand the difference between privacy and secrecy, and how to distinguish a sexual situation from a nonsexual one. He became more at ease in his relationships and in his concerns about dress, appearance, and previously driven behavior. Others found him easier to be with.

4. To appreciate the gratifications, the limitations, and the responsi-

bilities that flow from sexual relationships. Sex was no longer seen as an end unto itself, used to soothe transient states of fragmentation. He now looked forward to a relationship in which sex was an integrated and shared pleasure.

Jack's treatment ended on an optimistic note. He no longer desperately feared criticism as potential humiliation with devastating effects. He had openly acknowledged his homosexuality to his wife, and they had mutually agreed to dissolve their fiction of a marriage. This major step had not been without pain. His wife had sought therapy herself at this juncture and had used it not only as support for her position but also as a moderating voice to soothe her rage. Both Jack and his wife were looking to the future with a mixture of optimism and trepidation. Both believed that better days were ahead and that mutuality and sexual fulfillment were possible. Both feared, however, leaving the security of their improbable marriage.

Of course, Jack was not at all sure of the future shape of his life structure. He had attained the ability to refrain from ill-advised sexual encounters and believed that he could live a happy and productive life without a sexual relationship if he were unable to locate a suitable partner. He was, however, much more optimistic about the location of one, mainly because he no longer despised homosexual men, including himself. The idea of an admirable homosexual man, once an oxymoron, was now a viable concept.

REFLECTIONS

A patient's selection of a psychotherapist is a choice determined by many forces, only a few of which are rational or scientific. Transference considerations are a predominant determining force in the selection process, manifesting themselves well before the therapist is actually consulted. Once the decision to seek therapy has been made, a patient will choose a particular therapist because (a) he thinks a given person will by dint of specific training or personal characteristics understand him; (b) he thinks a given person will not challenge a treasured belief or value system, and will therefore make a comfortable fit; (c) he admires a given therapist and wishes to emulate him or her; (d) he is reacting against some other group and wishes to choose by exclusion; or (e) he idealizes a given therapist's training and anticipates that he or she has special powers and secret knowledge that he will somehow be able to obtain for himself.

In the current social and political climate, patients tend not to stray very far from their own self-image in selecting a therapist. This is especially true when the patient's clinical situation presents social and political overtones. The gay man who has come out and has integrated his sexuality within his overall personality may at the present time be less likely to seek therapy from a heterosexual male therapist, especially a psychoanalyst who may still be anticipated to harbor traditional views of homosexuality that are anathema to him. This potential patient may view the heterosexual male analyst as unlikely to be sympathetic to his sexual preference, incapable of understanding it, and feeling that the only recourse is to change it. In other words, the overt gay male may expect the heterosexual analyst to apply the disease model to his sexuality and either be unable to help him resolve any conflictual aspects of his sexuality or misperceive the centrality of importance of the sexuality in the clinical presentation. The closeted, homophobic gay male potential patient may, on the other hand, expect that the heterosexual analyst will possess the secrets to relieving him of his hated sexual preference and will agree with him that his sexual "perversion" is indeed the problem, whatever else may be the nature of the clinical presentation. It is therefore likely that heterosexual male therapists/analysts will be consulted by certain gay male patients, and that in the process both realistic and specifically unrealistic goals for the therapy will be brought to the therapy situation. The heterosexual male therapist may find it helpful to consider the following as fundamental underlying principles of therapy for a gay male:

1. The sexual orientation of the therapist (both that which is presumed by the patient and that which is in actuality an internal truth for the therapist) makes a difference in the form and content of the therapy but neither is, must be, nor should be a factor limiting the success of the treatment or determining its direction.
2. Transferences characteristic of the particular patient or character type will inevitably and inexorably manifest themselves. These transferences will be colored by the actual, perceived, or assumed characteristics of the therapist (i.e., male/female, heterosexual/homosexual, white/black, old/young, etc.), but the fundamental transferences that the patient needs to create, work through, and ultimately resolve will be established with any therapist who allows them to occur.
3. The therapist must be neutral on the matter of the patient's sexuality. The therapist must be free of antihomosexual bias, but must as well be free of any desire or need (conscious or unconscious) for the patient to adopt any particular life-style (legal restrictions notwithstanding). The achievement of therapeutic neutrality is a complex process. Its central core involves personal comfort with one's own sexuality, including partially conscious or unconscious homosexual or paraphilic components. Empathy rests in the balance. Although the patient may not understand (and the therapist should be careful with his language) that the therapist does not care what the patient's sexuality is, it is this neutral position that must be felt, protected, and maintained. Friedman (1988) states:

. . . patients are not usually helped by simple reassurance about the normalcy of "sexual preference." The clinician's expressed conviction that homosexuality is a disease or disorder will generally not be greeted with enthusiasm either. If the clinician is observant of the interactions between the four major dimensions of sexual orientation (erotic fantasy, erotic experience with others, sense of identity, and social role) and the personality organization of the patient, sound treatment plans may be formulated. . . . [p. 142]

4. When the therapist is heterosexual, he will likely be faced with powerful resistance enemies in the form of homophobic attitudes in the patient. In order for the patient to experience improved function and liberation from conflict, the sources of his homophobia must be uncovered and a cognitive restructuring achieved. Working through the sources and effects of these resistances will be time-consuming and difficult work. Contributing to the difficulty will be reactions in the therapist, who has achieved a liberal position on the matter, to the expressions of rigid, prejudiced, stereotyped, and at times viciously punitive attitudes that the patient directs at himself but that are felt by the therapist to be aimed at him personally.

5. The homosexual patient may manifest significant envy of the heterosexual therapist, who is perceived as in possession of all those traits that the patient feels are desirable but which he personally lacks. Masculinity, potency, self-assurance, wealth, and strength will all be credited to the therapist and will be the source of prolonged negative therapeutic reactions. Any demonstration by the therapist of effectiveness, insight, or wisdom of perspective may be experienced by the patient as a put-down, a humiliation. The patient may not allow himself to be helped by the therapist, for to do so would be to confirm his powerfully negative self-perception.

6. Successful and effective work with the homosexual male patient does not require that the heterosexual therapist engage the scientific and political debate over whether homosexuality is a disease, an aberrancy, a perversion, or an alternate life-style, preferred or otherwise. Neutrality and empathy as integral to proper psychoanalytic technique inform both flexible and attainable goals for a therapy. A knowledge of regional cultural forces and of recent advances in the understanding of the homosexual condition, including causative forces of a biological and psychological nature, developmental principles including that of gender identity, homosexual life-style issues, the effects of discrimination, and the chronic effect of emotional abuse are all, however, a necessary prerequisite to the management of the therapy of a gay patient.

7. The homosexual male patient may place a much greater emphasis on the importance of sexuality than will the heterosexual therapist. Although the patient may be intensely conflicted about his sexuality and his sexual behavior, he may give a great deal more emphasis to it in the therapy than the therapist feels is warranted. A difference in viewpoint may develop over the process of sexualization. At various times during the patient's associations or reporting of events the therapist may muse, "What does sex have to do with this? Why is he making sex a part of this or that relationship?" The therapist must understand that the patient does see many things through the sexual lens, and although the patient will ultimately be much relieved to achieve an altered context, the process of change must be conducted in an atmosphere that avoids humiliation of the patient. The homophobic gay man will come to understand that any new man he meets in the course of his daily life is not measuring their respective sexualities and finding his lacking. It will be comforting to disconnect sexuality from inherently nonsexual situations, but the process of confrontation will be felt as shame-inducing. The gradual, step-by-step establishment of a new frame of reference for the gay man's sexuality will allow the gay man to place sex in a context consistent with his age, situation, and phase of life.

FINAL THOUGHTS

As is true in all psychotherapeutic encounters, Jack and Dr. Wallace came together at a unique and specific point in each man's personal journey. When two life paths intersect, both life courses are affected by the intersection. And while it is also true that our shared humanity makes it impossible for patient and therapist not to have things in common, therapeutic intersections can have profound impacts on the personal development of the two individuals when the coming-together occurs at a critical phase of life development for each man.

Jack's needs were, of course, the raison d'être for the encounter, and Dr. Wallace understood the importance of not allowing the therapist's needs to be the patient's concern. Both men were nevertheless inevitably struggling with midlife developmental tasks, and the resolution of these various tasks would largely determine the color and texture of their late years. Jack, who had spent most of his life living in a fictional house of cards, pursuing unattainable goals and terrified of real personal expression, had needed help. The intersection of the two men's lives allowed Jack to take a giant step toward personal authenticity, toward the "acceptance of one's one and only life cycle as something that had to be" (Erikson 1985, p. 268). For Jack it was potential psychological death that had to lose its sting before he could achieve an integrity of ego that would allow him any hope of viewing his life as a real success story. The intersection of lives led to this, and for this both men were glad.

Dr. Wallace had had a long journey as well, and he needed a period of time to rest a bit and take stock. Like Jack and all other young people, he had had youthful dreams, and he, too, was facing the harsh reality that some of them would not be realized. In addition, he was reflecting on how hard he had worked, both to acquire his professional skills and to throw off the restricting prejudices of his background. He needed confirmation that his path had been the right one and that the sacrifices had been justified. He emerged refreshed from his work with Jack, with a renewed zest for the "impossible profession" (Malcolm 1981) and his next twenty years. Although Jack did not specifically know these things about Dr. Wallace, he could feel the human truth that was part of the touching of their lives. Both men were glad for that, too.

REFERENCES

American Psychiatric Association. (1980). *Diagnostic and Statistical Manual of Mental Disorders*, 3rd edition. Washington, DC: American Psychiatric Press.
American Psychoanalytic Association (1991). Resolution on homo-

sexuality. Proceedings of the American Psychoanalytic Association meeting, May 9. Published in *Journal of the American Psychoanalytic Association* 39:1109–1110.

Arndt, W. (1991). *Gender Disorders and the Paraphilias.* Madison, CT: International Universities Press.

Bieber, I., Dain, H., Dince, P., et al. (1962). *Homosexuality: A Psychoanalytic Study.* New York: Basic Books .

Dorner, G., Rohde, W., Stahl, F., et al. (1975). A neuroendocrine predisposition for homosexuality in men. *Archives of Sexual Behavior* 4:1–8 .

Eckert, E., Bouchard, J., Bohler, J., and Heston, L. (1986). Homosexuality in monozygotic twins raised apart. *British Journal of Psychiatry* 148:421–425.

Engel, G. (1977). The need for a new medical model: a challenge for biomedicine. *Science* 196:129–136.

Erikson, E. (1985). *Childhood and Society.* New York: W. W. Norton.

Freud, S. (1935). Letter to an American mother. Reprinted in *Homosexuality and American Psychiatry: The Politics of Diagnosis,* by R. Bayer, p. 27. New York: Basic Books, 1981.

Friedan, B. (1963). *The Feminine Mystique.* New York: Dell.

Friedman, R. (1988). *Male Homosexuality: A Contemporary Psychoanalytic Perspective.* New Haven, CT: Yale University Press.

Gabbard, G. (1991). *Psychodynamic Psychiatry in Clinical Practice.* Washington, DC: American Psychiatric Press.

Gladue, B., Green, R., and Hellman, R. (1984). Neuroendocrine response to estrogen and sexual orientation. *Science* 225: 1496–1499.

Green, R. (1987). *The "Sissy Boy Syndrome" and the Development of Homosexuality.* New Haven, CT: Yale University Press.

Imperato-McGinley, J., Peterson, R., Gautier, T., and Sturla, E. (1985). The impact of androgens on the evolution of male gender identity. In *Sexuality: New Perspectives,* ed. Z. Defries, R. Friedman, and R. Corn, pp. 125–140. Westport, CT: Greenwood.

Isay, R. (1987). The development of sexual identity in homosexual men. *Psychoanalytic Study of the Child* 41:467–489. New Haven, CT: International Universities Press.

Kernberg, O. (1984). *Severe Personality Disorders.* New Haven, CT: Yale University Press.

Kinsey, A., Pomeroy, W., and Martin, C. (1948). *Sexual Behavior in the Human Male*. Philadelphia: Saunders.

Kirk, S., and Kutchins, H. (1992). *The Selling of DSM: The Rhetoric of Science in Psychiatry*. New York: Aldine.

Kohut, H. (1971). *The Analysis of the Self*. New York: International Universities Press.

Lewes, K. (1988). *The Psychoanalytic Theory of Male Homosexuality*. New York: Simon and Schuster.

Malcolm, J. (1981). *Psychoanalysis: The Impossible Profession*. New York: Knopf.

Money, J., Schwartz, M., and Lewis, V. (1984). Adult erotosexual status and fetal hormonal masculinization and demasculinization: 46 XX congenital virilizing adrenal hyperplasia and 46 XY androgen-insensitivity syndrome compared. *Psychoneuroendocrinology* 9:405–415.

Pillard, R., and Weinrich, J. (1986). Evidence of familial nature of male homosexuality. *Archives of General Psychiatry* 43:808–812.

Reisman, J., and Eichel, E. (1990). *Kinsey, Sex and Fraud: The Indoctrination of a People*. Ed. J. Muir and J. Court. Lafayette, LA: Lochinvar.

Saghir, M., and Robins, E. (1973). *Male and Female Homosexuality: A Comprehensive Investigation*. Baltimore: Williams & Wilkins.

Socarides, C. (1992). Sexual politics and scientific logic: the issue of homosexuality. *Journal of Psychohistory* 10:307–329.

Stoller, R. (1985). Gender identity disorders in children and adults. In *Comprehensive Textbook of Psychiatry*, vol. 1, ed. H. Kaplan and B. Sadock, 4th ed., pp. 1034–1041. Baltimore: Williams & Wilkins.

Sullivan, H. (1953). *The Interpersonal Theory of Psychiatry*. New York: W. W. Norton.

Troiden, R. (1979). Becoming homosexual. *Psychiatry* 42:362–373.

Index

AIDS
  and denigration and devaluation
    of gay men, 53, 152
  and therapist's revulsion to
    description of gay sex, 103
Alexander, F.
  on emotional relationship with
    therapist, 86
American Psychoanalytic
    Association
  on homosexuality, 51
  and receptive posture on
    admission of gay members,
    207
Analytic neutrality, 28
Androgyny, 19
Anxiety, 14
Arlow, J.
  report on ego defects in
    homosexuals, 23
Arndt, W.
  on varieties of sexual behavior,
    207
Autistic phase, 10
Autoerotic sex, 16

Bacal, H.
  and Winnicott's conception of
    transitional phenomena, 62
Bandura, A.
  on modeling, 86
Batcheler, E.
  on homosexual acts as sickness
    and evil, 42
Bayer, R.
  on battle over homosexuality and
    psychiatric nomenclature,
    147
  on Menninger's reaction to
    Wolfenden Report, 27
  report on fight against AMA's
    decision to delete homo-
    sexuality from *DSM-III*, 27
Beach, F.
  on nonpathology of
    homosexuality, 26
Bean, J.
  and androgyny, 19
Begelman, D.
  and sexual orientation is not
    "healthy" or "sick," 146

Clinical material
  analysts' conduct during therapy,
    29–40
  life-study of Gerard, 127–145
  Micah and self psychology,
    63–72
  Phillip and HIV infection,
    169–174
  various derivations and uses of
    homosexuality, 13–18
Coleman, E.
  on treatment of homosexuality,
    5
Cooper, A.
  on etiology of homosexuality, 13
Cornett, C., i-xvii
  on gay men living with HIV,
    151–176
  on homosexuality and therapist,
    101
  on religion, 162–163
  on "resistance" to therapy,
    93–115
  on self psychology, 45–76
Countertransference, 19, 62

Davis, L.
  and HIV diagnosis and search for
    suitable lover, 161
Davison, G.
  on behavioral intervention with
    homosexuals, 7
  on therapy with gay men, 58
De Cecco, J.
  and components of sexual
    identity, 11–12
Denial, 14
Depression, 14–15, 17, 36, 38, 117
  caused by attempts to change
    sexual orientation, 29

Diagnostic and Statistical Manual,
    (DSM- I), (DSM-II), (DSM-III),
  on Borderline Personality
    Disorder, (DSM-III), 121
  exclusion of homosexuality as a
    mental disorder, (DSM-III),
    24, 27, 154
  Identity Disorder, (DSM-III), 126
  listing of homosexuality, 4, 24
Dorner, G.
  and predisposition to
    homosexuality, 206
Dulaney, D.
  and therapy with gay men, 58

Eckert, E.
  on genetic factors in erotic
    fantasy, 206–207
Ego
  defects, 23
  defenses, 124
  ego-syntonic pathology, 4, 8
  epigenesis, 89
  internalized homophobic content
    as component of, 78–81
  psychology, 10, 58
Eichel, E.
  on Kinsey, 200
Eissler, K.
  on deviations from classical
    psychoanalytic technique,
    166
Engel, G.
  and biopsychosocial model, 206
Erikson, E.
  on acceptance of life cycle, 226
  on identity formation, 79, 88
  on model of ego epigenesis, 89
  on psychosocial conception of
    development, 160

Erotic fantasy, 206–207
Evans, D.
  on male patient and female
    analyst, 189

Faderman, L.
  and gender identity, 122
  and "homosexual" relations (late
    1800s), 123
Fantasy, juvenile, 29
Fear, 15, 97
Ferenczi, S.
  on emotional relationship with
    therapist, 86
  on resistance to treatment, 96
Ferguson, M.
  and self psychology and gay men,
    47
Fine, B.
  and definition of interpreter, 57,
    59
  on origin of homosexuality, 51
Fine, R.
  on Freud's self-analysis and
    resistance, 95
  on religion, 163
Flexner, E.
  on women's liberation
    movement, 124
Ford, C.
  on nonpathology of
    homosexuality, 26
  on setting for psychotherapy, 55
French, T.
  on emotional relationship with
    therapist, 86
Freud, A.
  on modifying ground rules in
    treating some homosexual
    patients, 48

Freud, S.
  on accepting homosexual
    applicants for
    psychoanalytic training,
    41
  on anaclitic depression, 117
  on analytic relationship based on
    truth, 181
  on changing homosexuality to
    heterosexuality, 24–25
  and homosexuality, 4
  and interpretation, 59
  and mourning, 162
  and narcissism, 46, 47
  on religion, 163
  and society and gay patients, 42,
    158, 203
  and his theories, x
  on transference and resistance in
    psychoanalysis, 95–97
Freund, K.
  on sexual orientation, 3
Friedan, B., 203
Friedman, R.
  on detection of gender
    nonconformity with high
    probability of abuse, 52
  on homosexuality as
    constitutional in origin, 51,
    219, 223
  on juvenile fantasy, 29

Gabbard, G.
  on narcissistic personality
    disorder, 216
Gay, V.
  on fear of change as fear of
    death, 97
Gay-affirmative psychotherapy
  description of, 81–82

Hooker, E.
  study on projective psychological
    tests and homosexual men,
    26–27
Horner, A.
  and object relations theory, 10
Hudson, R.
  on gay men living with HIV,
    151–176
  on homosexuality and therapist,
    101

Identity, 19, 122, 206
Imber, R.
  and self psychology, 50
Imperato-McGinley, J.
  on gender identity disorders, 206
Inderbitzin, L.
  on analyst as interpreter, 57–58
Interpretation, 59
Intrapsychic forces, 7
Isay, R. A.
  on alienation from selfobjects as
    part of homosexual boy's
    world, 51–52
  on analytic therapy of
    homosexual men, 23–44
  on gay identity and role, 207
  on homosexual analyst: clinical
    considerations, 177–198
  on homosexuality as
    constitutional in origin, 51

Jacobson, E.
  and self psychology, 50
Johnson, A.
  on analytic neutrality, 28
  on no desire to change on part of
    homosexual, 178

Kaplan, A.
  and androgyny, 19
Karasu, T.
  and influence of values and
    attitudes on psychotherapy,
    83
Karme, L.
  on female analyst and male
    patient, 189
Katz, J.
  and gay liberation movement,
    124
Kelly, J.
  and therapy with gay men, 58
Kernberg, O.
  on Borderline Personality
    Disorder, 118–120, 141
  and object relations theory and
    narcissism, 50
  on severe personality disorder,
    215
Kiernan, J.
  on homosexual couples (1884),
    123
Kinsey, A.
  research on normal and
    abnormal male sexuality,
    123, 125, 199–200
  statistics to support
    nonpathological view of
    homosexuality, 25–26
Kinter, T.
  on psychoanalysis and
    homosexual clients, 1–22
Klein, G.
  on revisions of psychoanalytic
    thinking, 19
Kohut, H.
  and Borderline Personality
    Disorder, 117, 118
  on resistance to therapy, 98–99